Moving Viewers

Moving Viewers

American Film and the Spectator's Experience

CARL PLANTINGA

University of California Press

BERKELEY   LOS ANGELES   LONDON

University of California Press, one of the most distinguished university presses in the United States, enriches lives around the world by advancing scholarship in the humanities, social sciences, and natural sciences. Its activities are supported by the UC Press Foundation and by philanthropic contributions from individuals and institutions. For more information, visit www.ucpress.edu.

University of California Press
Berkeley and Los Angeles, California

University of California Press, Ltd.
London, England

Library of Congress Cataloging-in-Publication Data

Plantinga, Carl R.
  Moving viewers : American film and the spectator's experience / Carl Plantinga.
      p.   cm.
  Includes bibliographical references and index.
  ISBN 978-0-520-25695-8 (cloth : alk. paper)
  ISBN 978-0-520-25696-5 (pbk. : alk. paper)
  1. Motion picture audiences—Psychology.
2. Motion pictures—United States.   I. Title.
PN1995.9.A8P53   2009
302.23'43—dc22   2008035578

18   17   16   15   14   13   12   11   10   09
10   9   8   7   6   5   4   3   2   1

For my parents

Contents

Illustrations

Acknowledgments

My sincere thanks extend to all of those whose encouragement and help aided in the writing of this project. Calvin College granted me a sabbatical leave, research fellowships, and various travel grants that were instrumental in allowing me to finish this book. I thank Janel Curry, dean for Research and Scholarship, and the Office of the Provost for their support. Richard Allen, Cynthia Freeland, and Paisley Livingston carefully read the entire manuscript and offered many helpful suggestions for revision. In each case, their efforts went beyond the call of duty. My colleagues at Calvin College, Roy Anker and Christopher Smit, read and commented on various chapters. Other colleagues, including Bill Romanowski, Peggy Goetz, Randy Bytwerk, and Helen Sterk, contributed their consistent interest, support, and good cheer. During my recent semester as a visiting scholar at Lingnan University, I learned a great deal from many conversations with Paisley Livingston; thanks to him and Mette Hjort for inviting me. My father, Alvin Plantinga, was always willing to discuss any issue—philosophical, practical, irrelevant, or nonsensical. Conversations or other interactions with Joseph Anderson, David Bordwell, Noël Carroll, Amy Coplan, Lisa Fehsenfeld, Jonathan Frome, Torben Grodal, Toni Perrine, Stephen Prince, Robert C. Roberts, Greg M. Smith, Murray Smith, and Ed Tan all were important in helping to develop my ideas. I would also like to thank my students at Calvin College for their lively questions and interesting conversations. I have almost certainly left out the names of persons important in the writing of this book, and I apologize for doing so.

Portions of Chapter 7, "The Rhetoric of Emotion: Disgust and Beyond," were taken from "Disgusted at the Movies," *Film Studies: An International Review* 8 (Summer 2006): 81–92. Thanks to Mathew Frost and the University of Manchester Press for permission to reprint. Portions of Chapter 1, "Pleasures, Desires, Fantasies," were published in quite different form in "Movie Pleasures and the Spectator's Experience: Toward a Cognitive Approach," *Film and Philosophy* 2, no. 2 (1995): 3–19. Thanks to editor Daniel Shaw for his permission to reprint.

This book also benefited from audience responses to public lectures during which I tried out many of the ideas present in this book. In this regard, I'd like to thank Tom Wartenberg at Mount Holyoke College; Angela Curran and Carol Donelan at Carleton College; Leger Grindon at Middlebury College; David Bordwell at the University of Wisconsin, Madison; Neven Sesardic, Zheng Yujian, and James Rice at Lingnan University; Xiaohong Zhu (whom I know as "Rachel") at Fudan University; and Shen Liang ("Daniel") at the Shanghai Theater Academy. Thanks also to Anne Bartsch, Jens Eder, and Kathrin Fahlenbrach for organizing the symposium "Audiovisual Emotions," held in Hamburg, Germany, in 2005, at which I could present some of these ideas.

Thanks are also due to my editor, Mary Francis, for her careful reading of the book at various stages and her faith in its potential. Any faults or errors in this book are mine alone. Finally, my deepest gratitude goes to my wife, Cynthia Kok, for her consistent support for me, and for wise counsel in helping to develop the ideas presented.

Introduction

Affect and the Movies

> [The] cinema . . . makes it possible to experience without danger all the excitement, passion and desirousness which must be repressed in a humanitarian ordering of life.
>
> ROGER MANVELL[1]

I experienced movie fright early in my childhood. At the ripe age of seven I was taken to a drive-in to see Alfred Hitchcock's *The Birds* (1963), and I spent a good portion of those two hours cowering beneath the dashboard of the car. Despite all that cowering, I was thrilled. To this day I love that film and wonder how that initial childhood experience figures into the attraction. Years later, I saw how movie terror can affect an audience at a screening of Ridley Scott's *Alien* (1979). The show was nearly sold out. My companion and I arrived late, and our only option was to sit in the front row; behind us an audience was about to scream and shriek in ways we had never heard before. The crowd was clearly enthralled with *Alien* from the beginning. The usual chewing and slurping sounds (courtesy of the concession stand) were soon drowned out by anxious murmurs and nervous laughter. I remember well the moment when the film transformed our experience from merely somewhat frightening to flat-out terrifying: it was when the carnivorous alien baby unexpectedly and gruesomely bursts from the crewman's stomach, its high-pitched scream doubling the terror and sending much of the audience into an extended fit of shrieking from shock, fear, and revulsion. From that moment on, we all understood that for the length of the film we could never rest easy, for we might get the hell scared out of us again at any moment.

Some may dismiss these moments, however powerful, as of negligible interest or as the kind of idiosyncratic, subjective information that belongs in someone's diary, hardly important to the understanding of the workings and significance of movie spectatorship. In this book, I take a different position. The images and sounds of *The Birds* and *Alien* have been seared into the memories of generations of moviegoers, becoming cultural icons. And it is the ability of those films to strongly move audiences that make the films memorable to many viewers. Strong emotions have a tendency to make a mark, leaving lasting impressions that transform our psyches and imprint our memories. For that reason alone, the means by which the movies elicit emotion are worth taking seriously.

But let us consider other sorts of affective experiences inspired by the movies, experiences that are more difficult to analyze than a fear response. A viewer watching a melodrama may simultaneously weep and feel ashamed of weeping. At the end of *The Royal Tenenbaums* (2001), when Royal finally learns how to care for his family, audience members may find themselves inexplicably teary-eyed. *Titanic* (1997) has become one of the highest-grossing films of all time, yet it recounts a horrifying tragedy with stark realism and features the agonizing death of one of its protagonists. Viewing some of the films of Alfred Hitchcock may elicit responses remarkably similar to guilt and shame. But how can a movie possibly cause an audience to experience the self-directed emotions of guilt or shame? After all, what does an audience, as a mass entity, have to be guilty for or ashamed of? Why would audiences put themselves through the experience of such negative emotions? Aristotle found the elicitation of emotion to be one of the key strategies of persuasive discourse. How are emotions at the movies used for rhetorical or persuasive ends?

My early experiences with movies sparked my interest in these questions and initiated the research and thought that has culminated in this book. During my graduate studies, it seemed to me that many scholars either failed to grasp the importance of film-elicited emotion or (like me) had no idea how to research the issue. In all of the academic talk about film interpretations, meanings, negotiated readings, comprehension, and so on, what is often forgotten is that for the vast majority of film spectators, movie viewing is first and foremost a pleasurable experience, suffused with affect. Audiences are willing to pay for this experience with money, time, and effort, and in exchange they expect to be fascinated, shocked, titillated, made suspenseful and curious, invited to laugh and cry, and in the end, given pleasure. On this foundation of pleasurable affect rests the multibillion-dollar international media industries.

Film and media scholars sometimes use the tired literary metaphor of "a reading" to describe the viewer's encounter with a film. Not only does this terminology deny the essential differences between viewing images and reading words, it implies that film viewing is a cool, intellectual experience. Perhaps for some audiences, and in relation to some films, the experience *is* cool and intellectual. A "reading" is what some academics do in the classroom, days after the screening. Audiences at the movies, however, are often thrilled, excited, or exhilarated; moved to tears, laughter, scorn, or disgust; made fearful, expectant, curious, or suspenseful; absorbed and focused; outraged, angered, placated, or satisfied; given elevated heartbeats, sweaty brows, and galvanic skin responses; made to scream, yell, and excoriate the bad guys; and usually, relieved and calmed at the film's end. Are all of these affective elements of film spectatorship mere epiphenomena, the throwaway detritus of what is worthwhile about the film viewing experience? Can these aspects of viewing movies be safely ignored in favor of what is often thought to be the heart of the matter—the abstract themes or symptomatic revelations in a film teased out in a "reading"?

In the analysis of films and literature, traditional interpretation searches for hidden meaning, as though each work of fiction embodies abstract propositions in the form of messages or themes. It is the job of the critic and the viewer or reader to ferret out these messages, lift them from their context within the work, reorient them into some kind of brief philosophical treatise, and take the implication of that treatise as the purpose of the film, or at least as the locus of its true worth. But this way of thinking about film diminishes the art form by reducing it to a bare bones propositional message. It ignores the spectator's experience in viewing the film, places ultimate value on the propositional content that is later distilled from that viewing, and misunderstands the function of the viewing experience in developing the film's themes and ideas. Such a mistake is commonly called the "heresy of paraphrase."

As film critic and scholar V. F. Perkins writes, "Too great a concentration on what a film 'has to say' implies that the significance of a movie is reducible to the verbal concepts which its action suggests." Instead, Perkins suggests, "the movie's claim to significance lies in its embodiment of tensions, complexities and ambiguities. It has a built-in tendency to favour the communication of vision and experience as against programme."[2] I would put Perkins's suggestion slightly differently. Any abstract meaning that a film might have is ancillary to the experience in which that meaning is embodied, an experience that elicits emotions that are dependent on the formation of desires in the audience with respect to various narrative outcomes. Experience creates its own meaning, and in some cases the meaning to be taken from the experience of the film may contradict the abstract meaning an interpreter might glean from film dialogue, for example. Affective experience and meaning are neither parallel nor separable, but firmly intertwined. The viewer's affective experience in part determines meaning, and a lack of attention to, or an inability to understand, affective experience could well lead one to misunderstand and mischaracterize the thematic workings of a film, and perhaps even to misunderstand the story itself.

THE SIGNIFICANCE OF AFFECT

Why have affect and emotion in film viewing received relatively little attention in film studies? The reasons for this neglect are several. A strong strain of Western thought has considered emotion to be antithetical to reason and an obstacle to logical and/or critical thinking. Recent developments in cognitive psychology and philosophy, however, have challenged this idea. It is now commonly believed that emotions may be either rational or irrational, but that to consider emotion to be *prima facie* irrational is simply confused. Bertolt Brecht, the influential Marxist theorist of the theater, seemingly embraced this distrust of emotional response as antithetical to critical thinking, and argued that the politically useful play should not arouse the emotions so much as estrange and alienate the spectator to keep him or her cognitively sharp and somewhat skeptical. The neo-Brechtian screen theory that dominated film studies at the end of the twentieth century evinced an implicit disdain for the "soft," bourgeois—or at any rate, somewhat embarrassing—emotions of the audience.

Other reasons could be given for the neglect of the emotions. The reliance of screen theory on psychoanalysis moved attention away from emotions and toward drives and instincts. One suspects that an implicit (and simple-minded) sexism may also have been at work in film studies and in the broader culture, devaluing emotions as feminine; we see this in the special disdain some have for the "sentimental" emotions, while the ostensibly masculine anger and vengefulness, which would seem to be much more potentially harmful, rarely receive such contemptuous treatment. Indeed, when one hears the emotions denigrated, it is usually the sentimental or sympathetic emotions that bear the brunt of the criticism. Yet another reason the emotions have been neglected is that they have been thought to be subjective and private, and thus not the proper object for academic study. Perhaps people may write about their emotions in diaries, discuss them with their friends over a coffee or a whiskey, or better yet, visit a therapist. But why study emotion or the means by which films elicit emotion? Academic film studies has been focused almost entirely on ideological studies of film, such that the means by which films generate an audience experience colored with emotion and affect is unimportant, unless it can be clearly shown to relate to ideology. To my mind, such a view not only devalues the experience of movie viewing (as important only in relation to class, gender, race, etc.) and fails to see the centrality of emotion in the ideological work of movies, but also mischaracterizes emotional experience as necessarily subjective and idiosyncratic, as though emotions were not subject to causality.

As the course of this book will make clear, I reject all of these perspectives. I argue that the expression and elicitation of emotion in film is a central element of the film experience, an experience that is worthy of study in its own right. Moreover, emotion and affect are fundamental to what makes films artistically successful, rhetorically powerful, and culturally influential. Hugo Munsterberg wrote in his fascinating 1916 book, *The Film: A Psychological Study*, that to "picture emotions must be the central aim of the photoplay."[3] Munsterberg is surely correct that a narrative film must centrally represent or "picture" the emotions. But my focus in this book with be not on how emotions are represented, but how they are elicited and how emotion and affect figure into the experience of the movie spectator. Any satisfactory account of film reception and its implications for ideology, rhetoric, ethics, or aesthetics had better be able to take film-elicited affect and emotion into account.

The following are several ways in which emotions and affects function in films:

1. The experience of emotion is one of the principle motivations for the viewing of movies. The sources of this pleasure and/or value viewers take from filmic emotions are both intrinsic (emotions that are enjoyable in themselves) and extrinsic (emotions that lead to pleasing meta-emotions, social communication, or some other use value).[4]

2. Emotions provide narrative information that is necessary for audiences to follow the narrative. In extra-filmic life, our emotions focus our attention on salient details of the environment; the emotions elicited in a film function similarly, often drawing our attention to those elements that the film constructs as essential to understanding the narrative. Emotions, moreover, assist the film's narration in the creation of sympathies and antipathies for characters. Emotions also provide a direction for audience desires for one narrative outcome over another. Storytellers both elicit and depend on narrative emotions such as anticipation, suspense, and curiosity. In sum, the spectator's emotions assist in the comprehension and interpretation of the narrative.

3. Emotions and affects color the viewer's perception of a narrative, making it vibrant, enchanting, exciting, disgusting, suspenseful, fascinating, sad, happy, and so on. Emotions and affects may involve bodily responses, such as an accelerated heartbeat, tensing up and squirming in the seat, tears, laughter, or moaning. The viewing of a narrative film is not merely an intellectual or cognitive exercise, but one colored by affect and emotion. Emotions enable entertainment and enjoyment. The aesthetic excellence of a film, I would claim, is partly determined by its ability to elicit emotion and affect appropriate to its narrative focus and concerns.

4. Emotions are intimately tied to our cognition, inferences, evaluations, and all of the other mental activities that accompany the viewing experience. Emotions and affects have implications for ideas. Since emotions and affects make ideas and images salient and memorable, they play a role in the creation of both cultural and individual memory.

5. Emotions can also be used for rhetorical purposes. People routinely turn to their feelings for guidance when making judgments and decisions. It would not be too bold to say that the movies influence human feeling. In the short term, the function of emotion and affect is to make film viewing powerful, rather than merely an intellectual exercise. In the long term, such experiences may burn themselves into the memories of audiences and may become templates for thinking and behavior.

This book offers a theory of affect elicitation in mainstream American narrative fiction films—what some call Hollywood movies. Hollywood offers movies as packaged experiences, commodities designed to engage audiences affectively and emotively, providing a pleasurable and/or thrilling experience. Although this book is in part a general theory of affect elicitation in film, I concentrate on Hollywood movies for four reasons. First, the film medium embodies works of such diversity that a theory of emotion-elicitation risks becoming unfocused were it to deal with the medium as a whole. In confining my study to what has been termed "classical Hollywood cinema" and to less mainstream films that draw from that tradition, I hope to be able to shed light on one particular sort of filmmaking and its mechanisms for eliciting affect. Needless to say, I would hope that the concepts developed here would also be of use in the study of affect in experimental, documentary, and other modes of narrative filmmaking throughout the world.

Second, I concentrate on Hollywood film because it is a particularly emotional cinema. Mainstream American films rarely offer the kind of distanced, intellectual stance characteristic of some independent films (the work of Jim Jarmusch comes to mind) or various works of the European or international art cinema (such as the cinema of Michelangelo Antonioni, Andrei Tarkovsky, or Wong Kar-wai). Hollywood films tend to be either (1) robustly sympathetic, eliciting the congruent emotions that accompany strong sympathies with favored characters; (2) action films that ply in excitement, thrills, and spectacle; or (3) humorously ironic, making up for a distanced perspective with a tendency toward broad and ironic humor. In any case, mainstream films avoid audience boredom at all costs and attempt to elicit strong, clear (if also sometimes mixed) emotions throughout the viewing process.

Third, Hollywood filmmaking is important because it extends its influence around the world. It intrigues me not so much for its aesthetic excellence (although I do think that some Hollywood films are artistically excellent) but for its rhetorical and ideological power. Fourth, since emotion is to some extent culturally constructed, confining this study to the American context reduces, but does not eliminate, the possibility of a kind of cultural myopia. As an American, my understanding of the assumptions of American filmmakers in constructing films for maximum emotional power, and of the cultural assumptions American audiences bring to films, is more accurate than it would be for filmmakers and audiences in Japan, India, or Brazil, for example. I would add that in confining my study to American film, I do not mean to imply that mainstream American filmmaking is superior to any other cinema.

This being said, however, the theory of affect elicitation developed here has clear applications to much of popular narrative cinema. Thus, many of the processes of emotion elicitation described in the following pages can also illuminate the appeal of Chinese popular films such as Zhang Yimou's *Hero* (*Ying xiong*, 2002) and *House of Flying Daggers* (*Shi mian mai fu*, 2004), the Bollywood spectaculars produced in India, or European popular films such as Sergio Leone's spaghetti Westerns or various James Bond movies.

To speculate about how individual films elicit emotion is clearly an interpretive activity firmly rooted in the arts and humanities—or at least, this is how I see it. Nonetheless, I draw on scientific and philosophical theories of human emotion and affect and attempt to locate the most persuasive current theories of emotion and affect from the broader academic and scientific arenas. In this book, I appeal primarily to research in film and media studies, psychology, and philosophy. I call my theory "cognitive-perceptual," in part to draw attention to its recognition not only of conscious cognitive processes in affective experience, but also to preconscious cognition and automatic, "cognitively impenetrable" processes. Affect arises from many sources, and a good theory of affect in the movies will be eclectic and open rather than rigidly myopic. Some film scholars reject cognitive approaches because they are thought to be rationalistic, seeming to assume a purely logical, conscious spectator. And it is sometimes thought that if we reject psychoanalysis, we no longer have a way to talk about the unconscious. A cognitive-perceptual theory, however, preserves room for unconscious and nonconscious spectator responses and for responses that, while not necessarily illogical or irrational, bypass the conscious inference-making that is mistakenly thought to underlie all cognitive film theory.

A THEORY OF AFFECT AT THE MOVIES

Some will be surprised to see that I discuss psychoanalytic theories of affect quite extensively, especially in Chapter 1. It is true that psychoanalytic film theory, often called screen theory, does not occupy the central position in film and media studies that it once did. Yet it is still a force in film theory and criticism, holding an undeniable attraction for many film and media scholars. Screen theory introduced several concepts that many believe to be central to the study of cinema reception—concepts such as pleasure, desire, and fantasy. It makes sense to write of the "circulation of desire" in a film or to see a movie as, in some sense, a fantasy. Screen theory also found a way to account for the unconscious mental activities of the spectator.

Unfortunately, screen theory failed to provide adequate models of how such mental phenomena operate. Serious criticisms of the theory have been leveled elsewhere and need not be repeated here.[5] Many psychoanalytic interpretations of film not only tend to be counterintuitive to our experience of film texts but also test the limits of plausibility. To the outsider or the skeptic, the applications of psychoanalytic theories to film criticism can seem fantastical and absurd. Given this, Chapter 1, "Pleasures, Desires, Fantasies," argues that we can preserve the concepts "pleasure," "desire," and "fantasy" by displacing them from their technical moorings, as developed in screen theory. In part, my purpose is to advocate for a nontechnical use of these words, and to discuss and defend their use as common terms in folk psychology and in a cognitive-perceptual theory of film. My claim is that when these terms and the processes they describe are extricated from the conceptual thicket of screen theory, they can better be employed to reveal the richness and diversity of the film experience.

Chapters 2, 3, and 4 further develop the cognitive-perceptual theory of film affect and emotion. Chapter 2, "Movies and Emotions," proposes a grounding theory of the kinds of emotions elicited by films. In this chapter, I characterize emotions as "concern-based construals," that is, as judgments or perceptions by an agent of how a situation affects her or his concerns. Emotions are vastly complex entities, but in this book I concentrate on their relational properties, on emotions as ways that agents perceive and construe the world around them. I also discuss similarities and differences between those emotions that occur inside and outside of the movie-viewing context.

Chapter 3, "Stories and Sympathies," moves deeper into the elicitation of emotions in movies, drawing attention to the temporal and narrative character of emotion and demonstrating how the narrative scenarios of fiction films are designed to elicit a temporal sequence of particular emotional responses. The chapter also explores the structure of Hollywood storytelling and its conventional means of eliciting emotion. Character engagement is one of the most intriguing elements of the spectator's experience, figuring centrally in the viewer's emotional responses. The chapter also develops a theory of the spectator's interaction with film characters.

If we take emotions as one sort of psychological entity among a broader class of affects, then a theory of affect-elicitation cannot ignore affective experience that extends beyond emotions proper. Chapter 4, "The Sensual Medium," demonstrates how the direct, visceral nature of the film medium contributes to the affective experience films offer. In this chapter, I discuss bodily engagement, or how the nature of sound and image and movement interact with the body of the spectator, making possible a sensual experience unique to the medium. The chapter also shows how representations of the human body in film initiate responses such as mimicry and emotional contagion. Along the way I discuss psychological phenomena such as auditory entrainment and mirror neurons, the discovery of which promises to contribute significantly to our understanding of spectator response. The study of the direct, sensory, and perceptual nature of film viewing is in its infancy. The function of this chapter is to highlight some of the approaches that might be taken, as well as some of the most interesting existing research in this area.

Emotions (and other affective experiences) unfold in time; they are not like snapshots, but rather more like narratives. In Chapter 5, I argue that the spectator's emotional experience is largely directed by the film's narration, primarily in relation to narrative point of view, narrative structure, and character engagement. In this chapter, I argue against theories that in my opinion harness the spectator's responses too closely to the sympathetic protagonist. I argue that although the spectator's emotional response depends on and is related to the supposed emotional responses of a favored character, viewer response is most often independent of the protagonist to a significant degree and is most influenced by the narration at its highest levels. In this chapter, I also claim that the affective trajectory of a narrative film for a viewer can often be characterized as one of synesthetic affects, that is, as a host of orchestrated affects that together are designed to characterize a kind of emotional experience, not necessarily by eliciting the paradigmatic emotions associated with that experience, but by eliciting associated affects that characterize the feel or phenomenological qualities of having an emotion or emotions. To make this case, I analyze the evocation of synesthetic guilt and shame in some of Alfred Hitchcock's films.

Chapter 6 explores what I call the paradox of negative emotions. Why do mainstream movies elicit emotions that are typically thought to be unpleasant? Do audiences enjoy seeing representations of the horrific or tragic events that elicit negative emotions, or is audience displeasure in these cases the price spectators are willing to pay for deferred gratification of another sort? Using the popular blockbuster *Titanic* as an example, I investigate the psychology of negative emotions in popular film, describing how the negative emotions elicited in *Titanic* are first psychically managed and attenuated, then transformed into positive and pleasurable emotions. I also examine the concept of catharsis, ultimately rejecting it as a form of purgation in favor of the "conversion" or "transformation" of negative into positive emotions. I end the chapter with an examination of the cultural significance of such sympathetic narratives of transformation.

Whether one wishes to understand what V. F. Perkins calls "the naïve response of the film fan"[6] or to gauge the broader implications of the elicitation of emotion, one sees that questions of emotion elicitation quickly shade into ethical, ideological, and broader cultural concerns. The most fruitful way to explore the cultural significance of affect in film, at least in relation to textual dynamics, is to examine the rhetorical uses of affect. My contention is that before such an investigation can occur, however, the critic must have a good understanding of the types of emotions and affects at work in the film or films. Chapter 7 offers some general principles about analyzing the rhetoric of emotion in films. It also demonstrates how such an analysis might be undertaken with respect to a particular emotion, in this case, the emotion of disgust. This chapter is meant as an illustration of one way to approach the rhetoric of emotion in film, an area of inquiry that is certainly in its infancy.

Emotions are an enormously complex psychic phenomenon, and any theory of emotions is likely to pick out a segment of its causes, functions, and expressions at the expense of others. Marxists and sociologists emphasize the social determinants of emotion; physiologists and neurologists, the biological elements; many feminists emphasize gender and difference; those committed to psychoanalysis favor discussion of affect as filtered through particular theories of the unconscious. In this book, I explore the elicitation of emotion in mainstream American films. Similar analyses should be undertaken with regard to other traditions and types of filmmaking. Moreover, in this book I am interested in the evocation of what might be called "mass emotions." It would also be of interest to explore more personal and idiosyncratic responses to films.[7] It should be clear that this book is not meant to be a comprehensive study of film and emotion in all of their aspects. My chief goal is to contribute to the ongoing discussion of the important topic of film and affect, and if some of the treatments of particular issues are seen as suggestive and provocative rather than complete, I will not be much bothered by that.

Evan Cameron writes, in an essay on suspense in Hitchcock, that a "snag in writing about the way a film produces its effects is [that] finally one has to depend on a very subjective analysis of one's own feelings."[8] It is true that gauging actual affective response of viewers is interpretive and somewhat speculative, especially when the critic begins asking the more interesting questions. But Cameron seems to assume that emotions are purely idiosyncratic and subjective, with no determining patterns. My argument in this book is that elicited emotions and affects are characterized and differentiated by structural features, such that the film's intended affective focus can be reasonably well determined in many cases. One can substantiate these analyses by noting personal response in addition to the reactions of other critics and audiences. It is also true that an understanding of the objective causality of affect, rooted in philosophical and psychological research, makes one more confident in making claims about a film's affective work. Thus, I have strong sympathies with an approach to film criticism that is rooted in an appraisal of the moment-to-moment sympathies and reactions of a hypothetical spectator.[9] But I also hope to bolster such interpretation with an appeal to psychological theories and philosophical understandings of the nature of human affect in response to the movies.

IN DEFENSE OF FILMS

Before arguing for my theory, beginning in the next chapter, it is necessary to say a few words about the methodological assumptions and terminology at work in this book. Film and cultural critics became interested in spectator response early in cinema history, as soon as it became apparent that the medium had mass appeal. Yet film studies did not coalesce as a discipline until the 1970s. The screen theory that dominated the discipline in its early years—an amalgamation of Barthesian semiotics, Althusserian Marxism, and Lacanian psychoanalysis—took a rather deterministic view of the effects of classical Hollywood films, positing a uniform ideological and psychological effect not only for the films, but also for specific techniques such as classical continuity editing and narrative closure.

As the theoretical pendulum swung away from the reductionism and determinism of screen theory toward audience studies, theoretical postulations of the effects of texts on spectators have reached the other extreme. Many film and television scholars seem to hold that meaning and effect derive not from film texts, but from the historical specificity of viewing contexts. Psychoanalysis is increasingly seen as reductive and little able to deal with historical specificity. It is seen as making response universal, rendering the appeal to spectator difference difficult. Psychoanalysis may offer an explanation of affective response, but it not only fails to account for the means by which different social groups respond differently, it lacks a theoretical mechanism to understand human difference, with the exception of gender differences.

We might broadly consider these more recent approaches as historical or cultural reception studies. Their aim is the discovery of the ways that audiences have actually interpreted, been affected by, and/or used films within a sociohistorical context. Historical reception studies are often case studies of the reception of films that rely, as much as is possible, on historical evidence of actual spectator responses.[10] As Janet Staiger puts it, reception studies try to understand an event (the viewing experience) while textual studies examine an object (the film). And the viewing event is understood in concrete, materialist terms. Staiger rejects notions of an ideal viewer, and does not attempt to understand how viewers *might have* responded, or how an ideal viewer *would* understand a film. Staiger is interested in actual spectators' responses.[11] The reception scholar, then, denies that textual meaning adheres in the film, but holds that this meaning is more centrally a function of context. In addition, reception studies hope to move beyond the study of meaning to a broader conception of the historical effects or implications of a film on particular audiences, whether it be psychological, political, or otherwise.

Historical reception studies have been a favorable development for the discipline and a necessary corrective to the reductionist and deterministic theory that they have in part replaced. It is certainly true that meaning and effect cannot be deduced merely from the examination of a film in isolation, but must take into account the historical audience and context. Moreover, historical reception studies have made some progress toward the writing of a history of film and television reception.

That being said, however, the rhetoric of some reception theory, perhaps initially justified as it attempted to establish itself, underestimates the importance of the film text itself in influencing spectator response. The effects of a film and the responses it engenders are a complex matter; effects and meaning are not solely context-, text-, or audience-generated. Effects and meanings result from the interaction of all three. It is legitimate for scholars to concentrate on any one of these elements, so long as claims for what one has discovered remain circumspect and measured. Just as scholars may claim too much for the film, independent of context, so others may claim too much for the context, seemingly independent of the film itself.

Estimations of the *actual* historical reactions and interpretations of audiences will always be somewhat speculative, unless one limits oneself to self-reports, the empirical observations possible through viewing audience behavior or measuring physiological response, or the measurements of heart rates and facial expressions. The most interesting actual audience responses are quite often lost to history, and for the reception historian, the best means to recover what they might have been—through movie reviews, for example—are often as questionable and/or partial as film-based estimations. Take the movie review. A movie review might be thought to be unproblematic evidence of the response of one member of a film audience, the reviewer. First note, however, that one critic's written review is a very small sample of general audience response. In addition, such a review is a heavily mediated, institutionally constrained report of the public response of a professional reviewer who may or may not share much in common with other viewers.[12] The reviewer may report on general audience response, but such a report is limited to one or two screenings and to the subjective impressions of the particular reviewer.

I insist on the value of film analysis in the examination of audience response for several reasons. First, most films, much of the time, are constructed so as to generate intended or preferred responses.[13] Films are designed such that audiences, for example, will feel suspense during the battle between good and evil, pity as the protagonist grieves the loss of a loved one, anticipation as she approaches the hoped-for romantic rendez-vous, or mixed feelings of admiration and sadness when lovers must part for the greater good of the social group. The process of filmmaking is, in part, the estimation of the way various narrative turns and film tech-niques will influence the spectators' understanding and experience of the film text. Moreover, the very notions of negotiated (uneasy or conflicted) and oppositional responses to films presuppose the possibility of preferred or intended congruent responses. If negotiated and oppositional responses are possible, then so are preferred and congruent responses.

If one accepts the notion of a congruent or intended response as a pos-sibility, then one might discuss the prevalence of congruent responses in relation to the negotiated and oppositional. Staiger argues that spectators all are more or less "perverse" in that they "use" films for their own pur-poses. But such perverse responses are less frequent than many reception theorists would like to think.[14] It strikes me that the spectator's own pur-poses are often aligned with the intended functions of the text, and thus cannot legitimately be called "perverse." I would suggest that congruent, preferred, and/or partly negotiated responses are by far the most common types of responses. In the media-saturated environments of the West, at least, there exist a variety of choices about which film to view, and audi-ences often choose films on the basis of genre, stars, critical reviews, or, as I argue, on the basis of the kind of affective experience they believe such films will afford. Movies are less like blank slates than they are like an immersion into a virtual environment in which responses are largely manipulated by strong sensual cues. Resistance is hardly futile, but resis-tance isn't what draws audiences to the experience in the first place, and resistance takes a lot of effort. Although we need not accept the determin-ism of 1970s screen theory, neither is the spectator's experience of motion pictures undertaken under conditions of absolute psychic freedom. The motion picture industry is an institution that strongly encourages certain viewing practices and assumptions about how films are to be understood and responded to.

Moreover, it is essential to realize that the oppositional spectator—that is, the audience member who self-consciously rejects the ideology of a film during its viewing—may nonetheless enjoy many of the intended responses generated by the film. Jacqueline Bobo has rightly noted that congruent or "dominant" responses to some elements of a film are some-times coextensive with oppositional responses to other of its elements.

1. An audience is sometimes able to take a critical stance toward a film—in relation to what are taken to be racist stereotypes in *The Color Purple* (1985), for example—*and* simultaneously enjoy the affective pleasures the film offers.

It is not a case of either/or. Thus, she argues, African-American women can simultaneously recognize the racial problematics of *The Color Purple* (1985)—what some take to be its reinforcement of racist stereotypes—and nonetheless enjoy many of the affective pleasures the film offers.[15]

Audiences choose films for the experiences they offer, and they most often relish that experience, or at least wish that they could and blame the filmmakers for not having produced a product that offers them what they want. After having chosen a film, what sort of response might this spectator expect at the actual screening? Although other viewing practices certainly exist, the most common sort of theatrical experience—in the United States, at least—encourages the audience to give rapt attention to the screen. It is not necessary to rehearse the extensive means by which filmmakers and exhibitors endeavor to engage and maintain such attention, such as through the darkened theater, the gustatory comforts of food and beverages, the large screen, warnings not to talk during screenings, narratives constructed to maintain anticipation and curiosity, continuity editing, fascinating images, engaging stars, and so on. The theatrical experience, unlike the experience of viewing a film alone at home, is a group experience, subject to the psychological condition of emotional contagion that strongly pulls for common response (as I discuss more fully in Chapter 4).

My point is not that audiences will agree about the quality of the film or interpret a film in the same way. My claim is that congruent or primarily congruent responses—that is, affective responses aligned with the intended effects of the film—are very common for many films. Thus, when one considers the totality of factors that must enter into considerations of film effects on spectators, the film itself stands as one of the essential elements of the equation. This is true in part because the viewing context is designed to focus spectator attention to the film, to momentarily erase the audience's extra-filmic concerns, and to encourage a shared response to the film being projected.

In addition, it must be added that as objects of study, film texts are inherently more interesting than film reviews or fan magazines (or at least so it seems to this "perverse" spectator). Reviews and fan magazines are essential sources of film scholarship that can help shed light on films and spectatorship; it would be folly to deny this. Yet one can easily imagine being fascinated by a film independent of having read film reviews; it is less likely that we would be fascinated by film reviews without having first seen the film. This has little weight in deciding whether the film has significant influence on spectators, except to say that to make textual analysis peripheral in film and media studies would not only be somewhat bizarre on the face of it, but would also sap the discipline of much of its particular interest.

My argument, in brief, is this. Audience response is ultimately determined by a complex formula consisting at least of "conditioners" (context, audience characteristics) and "elicitors" (textual stimuli).[16] Ideally, film and media critics and scholars generate their estimations of audience response in relation to as many factors as possible. Yet it may be the best strategy at times to focus on one of these in isolation from the others. Or it may be the only strategy available when evidence of actual audience response is lacking. Thus, I find context-centered, audience-centered, and text-centered studies all to be of value, assuming that they maintain a certain humility of outlook. In this book, I concentrate on the specifically textual, filmic elements designed to elicit spectator response, but I occasionally make reference to the historical audience and context as well.

SPECTATORS AND ROLES:
A BRIEF NOTE ON TERMINOLOGY

One last note on terminology is in order. For decades, it has been the practice of film scholars to distinguish between a mysterious entity called "the spectator" and the empirical, flesh-and-blood viewer. The spectator is conceived of as a hypothetical entity, a "position," "role," or "space" constructed by the text.[17] Such talk of the spectator as a role or a position remains even in work that questions psychoanalytic theories, revealing vestiges of subject-as-position theory that still run in strong currents through film studies.[18] But more importantly, such a technical use of the term encourages confusion for both the theorists and the reader, and it is worth demonstrating this to justify the changes in terminology that I propose in this book.

Robert Stam, Robert Burgoyne, and Sandy Flitterman-Lewis, in their book about terminology in film semiotics, write that in psychoanalytic theory, the spectator or "the viewer" is "an artificial construct produced by the cinematic apparatus" and a "space" that the cinema "constructs." So far, this is unproblematic. Their next move, however, is to assign human characteristics to this constructed "space" or "position." In describing the psychoanalytic conception of this spectator, they write that in viewing a film, a "state of regression is produced" and "a situation of belief is constructed."[19] One wants to ask how a role or a position can regress or have beliefs. This ambivalent understanding of the spectator is symptomatic of the terminological confusion of screen theory, which at times argues that the spectator is not a flesh-and-blood person, but then describes the spectator in ways that apply to human beings and not to abstract entities. Theorists may claim that the spectator is a concept or a structural term, a construction of the text, but then write that the classical stylistic system leads to a change in text-spectator relationships, as though the spectator were an actual person separate from the text.

In his introduction to film theory, Robert Stam implicitly recognizes this problem when he awkwardly distinguishes between the "spectator" and the "actual spectator."[20] Were we to take up this terminology, we might then refer to the position or role established by a film as the spectator, and to the people sitting in the theater as "actual spectators." But why refer to a role or position as a spectator at all, given the confusions the terminology has generated? To avoid such ambiguities, I use the word "spectator" independent of the confusing technical meaning it has accrued in screen theory. I use the terms "spectator," "viewer," and "audience" interchangeably to refer to actual or hypothetical persons, depending on context.[21] Films *do* offer viewers a role or position (or multiple positions), which the viewers accept or reject, in whole or in part. I refer to such entities, unsurprisingly, as roles or positions.

1. Pleasures, Desires, Fantasies

> Don't take it as a matter of course, but as a remarkable fact,
> that pictures and fictitious narratives give us pleasure, occupy
> our minds.
>
> LUDWIG WITTGENSTEIN[1]

Film scholar V. F. Perkins claims that for most films, critical appreciation begins with a reconstruction of "the naïve response of the film-fan."[2] That response—perhaps not so naïve as is sometimes assumed—has significant implications beyond aesthetic appreciation for the relationship of film to psychology, culture, and ideology. The nature of the film spectator's response is key to many of the questions we want to ask about film.

Actual spectator responses are varied and complex, involving pleasures, desires, emotions, affects, and moods in relation to the diversity of spectator differences, viewing contexts, and historical periods. Any complete examination of the responses of actual spectators must take all of these into account. Nonetheless, as I argued in the Introduction, the rejection of text-based theories of affect would be a serious error. Such theories can provide a foundation for further studies by identifying the grounds of response, rooted in the relationship between the human psyche, textual characteristics, and viewing context.

My purpose in this chapter, in part, is to explore the nature of pleasures, desires, and fantasies in the viewing of movies. The viewer's motivations for viewing films, the pleasures films offer, and the desires a film elicits are central to the ability of a film to provide an experience colored with emotion and affect. Psychoanalytic film studies, however, have so circumscribed and appropriated the terms "pleasure," "desire," and "fantasy" that it is necessary to renew our sense of their complexity and diversity and free them from narrow technical usage. Throughout the chapter I give a good deal of attention to the psychoanalytic use of these three terms. My purpose is not so much to claim that psychoanalysis is misleading as a psychological theory (although I believe it to be misleading in some regards), but rather to propose less technical uses of these terms, and a concomitant widening of conceptions of the pleasures of film viewing and the function of desires and fantasies within narrative.

My proposal is that in each case, we revert to the common usage of "pleasure," "desire," and "fantasy" found in folk psychology. One might legitimately ask how this could possibly be an improvement on the technical uses of these terms as developed in various film theories. For one thing, as I shall argue below, the technical uses of these terms are dependent on psychoanalytic film theory that is, in many cases, problematic and at worst, vacuous. Moreover, folk psychology is often the best available psychological theory for understanding other minds. It must be considered in light of the most plausible psychological theories and supplemented by other academic constructions. But it will do in a pinch, and is frankly more plausible than some of the scientific-sounding but counterintuitive theories current in film and media studies. As Gregory Currie notes, we employ folk psychology "so often, with such facility and success, that it can be surprising to learn that one is using 'knowledge of other minds.' "[3] In a given day, we successfully gauge the intentions, motivations, thoughts, and desires of others using our own knowledge of folk psychology. Were it not so—were the psychologies of those around us utterly baffling and unpredictable—social life as we know it would cease to exist. This is not to say that other minds are wholly transparent to us, or that we cannot be fooled. It is only to make that claim that our folk psychological knowledge, in many contexts, is remarkably adept at gauging the psychology of others. This suggests that folk psychology is a powerful and useful tool, and in this context, I will assume that it is important for understanding spectator psychology.

MOVIE PLEASURES

Christian Metz suggested that the cinema is in part an institution that treats pleasure and desire as commodities, and this is certainly true when we speak of Hollywood. Most movie viewers expect a pleasurable experience, and it is pleasure (as opposed to some more utilitarian function) that motivates mainstream viewers most of the time. To put it another way, film viewing offers enjoyable sensations and emotions, myriad satisfactions, and various delights, all depending on the individual viewer, social and viewing context, mode, genre, film, and film scene. The commodification of spectator pleasure is especially characteristic of classical Hollywood cinema, which, as Richard Maltby claims, "deals in economies of pleasure."[4] This is in distinction from art cinema or avant-garde film, which are often thought to require more effort in the viewing, favor difficulty and intellectual austerity, and submerge spectator pleasure beneath the lofty concerns of "art," humanism, or a supposed realism.

What sorts of pleasures are offered by movies? In film studies, the most comprehensive attempt to explain spectator pleasure emerged from the psychoanalytic/Marxist theory that dominated film theory in the 1970s and 1980s.[5] Screen theory, as I call it, claimed to have uncovered the deep levels of spectator pleasure that were said to originate in repressed and unconscious desires. Psychoanalysis emphasizes the importance of childhood development in the formation of the mature adult psyche. Assuming this, Jean-Louis Baudry argued that mainstream films encourage a regression to primitive stages of human development, a return to a facsimile of infantile wholeness and homogeneity. Baudry and other apparatus theorists described classical cinema as a powerful, univocal fantasy machine (the "apparatus") with a specific purpose—to encourage pleasurable, yet regressive and infantile, psychological states that implement the subjection of the spectator to dominant ideology.

The major criticisms of screen theory are by now well known.[6] The attraction and at the same time weakness of the theory was its simplicity (sometimes clothed by obfuscatory jargon). Under the banner of a Lacanian/Althusserian meld of psychoanalytic and Marxist theory, it claimed to have found the essential psychological and ideological effect of mainstream film. Positing these monolithic effects allowed screen theory to take an unequivocal position on the allegedly harmful psychological and ideological consequences of viewing classical Hollywood films. The ideological function of classical Hollywood films was to mystify audiences, to lure them through pleasure into trancelike, passive psychological states that made the spectator prone to ideological subjugation.

The assumption of a uniform psychological effect and a wholesale subjugation as the norm for an ostensibly passive spectator, however, has been rejected by more recent scholarship.[7] The spectator's experience in viewing mainstream films is more complex and contradictory than screen theory allowed. Screen theory failed to account for the diversity of the pleasures of the cinema. It became reductionistic, or perhaps we could say it illustrated reductionism in its most robust form. No unified theory of movie pleasures is possible; the pleasures available to the spectator are simply too diverse. Hollywood films offer multiple avenues of access, not a single pleasure or a single kind of pleasure.[8] What I provide instead, then, is a phenomenological account of various types of film pleasures. I posit no essence to film pleasure, as screen theory did, but rather identify some of its chief sources.

A phenomenological account of spectator pleasures is a prerequisite to exploring the role of pleasure in spectator response because pleasures are motivators for the spectator. Audiences watch films, in part, for the pleasures that they offer. And one of the ways that the film narration directs attention and response is by promising, suggesting the possibility of, withholding, and/or granting various sorts of viewing pleasures. The promise of pleasure plays an important role in narrative because it elicits spectator desires for various narrative outcomes and ensures forward-looking mental activity on the spectator's part.

Five of the most essential sources of audience pleasure in mainstream films are (1) cognitive play, (2) visceral experience, (3) sympathy and para-social engagement, (4) satisfying emotional trajectories rooted in narrative scenarios, and (5) various reflexive and social activities associated with film viewing.[9] Though I present these pleasures as discrete, they are rarely experienced in isolation; the artificial separation I offer merely serves a heuristic function.

COGNITIVE PLAY

Since much of human action is motivated by the need for survival and adaptation to the environment, it is unsurprising that elements of spectator activity relate to human adaptive skills. People delight in exercising the cognitive skills required to survey, understand, and interact with their environment and its inhabitants. Humans are motivated not simply by physiological needs, but also by cognitive needs. We have a drive to know; we are curious. We also seek to mentally stimulate ourselves by playing games, solving challenging puzzles, telling or listening to stories, and engaging in various crafts and hobbies. Cognitive play has obvious adaptive benefits, since we must learn and practice skills enabling us to effectively relate to our environment. This is more than a human phenomenon. Research shows that monkeys, dogs, and even rats are aroused by situations of novelty and the need for mental stimulation. It may be that, with regard to our arts, amusements, and entertainments, drive induction—the arousal of drives or desires—is a stronger motivation than the drive reduction assumed by psychoanalysis.[10]

Cognitive film theory has not previously taken up the issue of spectator pleasure, but it has often implicitly assumed a spectator fundamentally motivated by the pleasures of cognitive play. David Bordwell and Edward Branigan, for example, write of the cognitive processes by which spectators comprehend film narratives; a desire for comprehension is itself implied to be the spectator's primary motivation.[11] Bordwell's analysis of *Rear Window* (1954) is a case in point. Bordwell gives an account of the types of spectator inferences cued by the film and of the means by which it plays on the spectator's desire to know by suggesting outcomes, teasing with alternative possibilities, and presenting surprises.[12] Branigan considers narrative primarily as a means of information processing, calling it "a perceptual activity that organizes data into a special pattern which represents and explains experience."[13] Similarly, Noël Carroll describes what he calls the erotetic narrative, in which succeeding scenes are related to preceding scenes as answers are related to questions.[14] The implied premise of much cognitive theory has been that spectators are motivated by curiosity, suspense, anticipation, and other narrative emotions; delight in discovery; and the pleasures of orienting themselves to the unfolding narrative events of a fictional world.

All narrative genres incorporate cognitive play of this sort, but none so thoroughly as the mystery. In this regard, it is noteworthy that Alfred Hitchcock promotes suspense above mystery. "In a whodunit," he says, "there is no suspense, but a sort of intellectual puzzle. The whodunit generates the kind of curiosity that is void of emotion, and emotion is an essential ingredient of suspense."[15] Where the mystery teases the spectator with an intellectual puzzle, the suspense film presents the spectator with the relevant information, then creates a kind of anxiety about whether a desired or a feared outcome will occur. In a good suspense sequence, suspense will increase until the threat of the feared outcome subsides, and the desired outcome is achieved. Nonetheless, although Hitchcock dismisses pure mystery, his films incorporate mystery throughout. The pleasures of *Rear Window* come not from suspense only, but also from spectator curiosity about the film's mysteries: whether Thorwald (Raymond Burr) murdered his wife, how he disposed of the body, and whether the hypotheses of Jefferies (James Stewart) about the murder are correct.

While the mystery story plays on the spectator's interest in the solution to a crime, other genres, such as the science fiction film, depend on the pleasures of orientation to and discovery of unusual environments and alien beings. Imaginary alien worlds, our world in the future, strange beings, or the dinosaurs of the Earth's past all engage the curiosity of the spectator. Yet cognitive play extends beyond environments to an interest in characters, for viewers orient themselves not simply to the physical environment, but also to the social world. For that reason it would be wrong to claim that family melodramas, for example, depend little on these cognitive pleasures. Various genres engage cognitive play in ways designed to take advantage of varied spectator interests. Viewers do not share identical interests, and their curiosity and fascination is elicited by different films and genres. Given this diversity of interests, Hollywood films are often designed to aim appeals at varied audiences simultaneously.

In a mystery, the murder (or other crime) elicits little compassionate concern for the victim or sympathy for the investigating sleuth, but depends on the pleasure of an intellectual puzzle gradually solved. That such pleasures are predominantly intellectual is mirrored in the superior intellect of the sleuth, for example, in the cases of Sherlock Holmes, Hercule Poirot, or Jessica Fletcher. In vicariously enjoying the character's intellectual prowess, the audience not only celebrates intelligence as an inherent value, but also gains a vicarious satisfaction in the solution to the mystery.

In part, the pleasures of cognitive play are narrative—but only in part. Spectators also enjoy looking and hearing, because images and sounds fascinate people (though only briefly) and because they are a primary means through which viewers orient themselves to the narrative world. *Rear Window* has become a touchstone for discussions of spectatorship in part because many claim that its narrative situation mirrors that of the film spectator. The protagonist, L. B. Jefferies, is himself a spectator and a voyeur, peering through his neighbors' windows and perhaps witnessing a murder. In fact, much psychoanalytic film theory assumes that pleasure in looking, or scopophilia, defined as essentially a voyeuristic and sexual pleasure, is central to spectatorship.

While voyeurism may be among the spectator's pleasures, it is characteristic neither of looking in general nor of the pleasure offered by most images and sounds. Although the allure of some films stems from the enticements of sexual pleasure in looking, to describe spectatorship as essentially voyeuristic in this sense oversimplifies the viewing situation. Voyeurism requires two features that confine it to specific situations in specific films: (1) the voyeur derives sexual gratification from observing others, and (2) the voyeur observes others while being unobserved, from a secret vantage point.

Erotic attraction certainly constitutes one of the dominant pleasures of movie spectatorship. The enjoyment of looking and hearing per se, however, is not necessarily sexual, but is as varied as the visual and aural world itself. For example, viewers derive pleasure in looking at beautiful objects, unfamiliar scenes, or odd characters. Spectators also enjoy using their senses as a means of orientation and discovery. The senses are a primary means by which people gather information about their environment, and again, to exercise those senses in the unfamiliar environments offered by films can be rewarding. The soundtrack in *Rear Window* is a case in point, as through its subtle mixture of ambient sound—traces of strangers' conversations and faint music wafting through the air—it orients the viewer to the film's world and creates an intriguing sense of setting.

Spectators also enjoy "discovering" visual and aural information. Think of the significance of the wedding ring in *Rear Window*. Jefferies resists the idea of marrying Lisa (Grace Kelly), though Lisa wants to marry him. When Lisa enters Thorwald's apartment, she finds the wedding ring of Thorwald's wife, reinforcing the suspicion that the woman has been murdered. Lisa slips the ring onto her finger, and waves her hand behind her back at Jefferies, who views the whole situation through his binoculars. The irony of the ring and what it signifies is subtly communicated through visual means. The pleasure here is not merely derived from recognizing the ring's thematic significance, but in the visual "discovery" of that significance.

Part of my intention in this chapter is to recover the folk-psychological use of terms such as *pleasure, desire,* and *fantasy* for film theory, and thus to escape the narrow and sometimes reductionist definitions of the terms in psychoanalytic film theory. We might do the same for *voyeurism.* Perhaps we can conceive of voyeurism not as an essentially sexual activity, but more broadly as the enjoyment of clandestine spying on others. In this sense, Jefferies is colloquially a voyeur because he takes pleasure in looking at his neighbors unobserved. Even this broader conception of voyeurism, however, fails to characterize film viewing in general. To identify film viewing as essentially voyeuristic, we would need to show that the spectator's situation mimics the secret vantage point of the voyeur. Some of the visual pleasures of *Rear Window* are undoubtedly voyeuristic in this sense, as Jefferies peers at unsuspecting neighbors and, through point-of-view editing, the spectator is given his vantage point. We can plausibly characterize viewers of *Rear Window* as vicarious voyeurs, however, only because the protagonist, with whom they are perceptually aligned, engages in voyeuristic activities.

Movie viewing is nothing like Jefferies's peeping, and it carries none of the implications of danger, social opprobrium, or secretiveness accompanying Jefferies in *Rear Window.* Unlike Jefferies's clandestine snooping, film viewing is a public and accepted activity. In *Rear Window* we

2. Unlike the voyeurism of Jefferies (James Stewart) in *Rear Window* (1954), film spectatorship is typically a public and socially sanctioned activity.

see from a voyeur's perspective, but in many films the protagonist looks openly and publicly. Were I spying on my neighbors as Jefferies does, I would not want to be discovered in this activity; at the very least, it would be embarrassing. Yet I would bear no embarrassment, shame, or guilt were I to be discovered watching the film *Rear Window*, nor would most spectators. It is wrong to see film viewing as inherently voyeuristic, in relation to either technical or colloquial definitions of voyeurism.[16]

VISCERAL EXPERIENCE

Films work directly on our senses of sight and hearing, as I detail in Chapter 4. Recent trends in home viewing call for the replication of aspects of the sensual experience of the movie theater, without the syrupy floors and annoying talkers. We now speak of "home theater," with large-screen monitors and digital multichannel sound. With better home viewing technologies, it is becoming possible to replicate the optimal viewing conditions of a quality movie theater.

Consider the following true story. Hearing that Stanley Kubrick's *2001: A Space Odyssey* (1968) was a film not to be missed, a small group of friends, all infrequent moviegoers, rented a heavily panned and scanned, well-used VHS copy of the film to view on their 19-inch television set located a good distance from the couches on the other side of the great room. The television set was outfitted with a single, monaural speaker through which the soundtrack played. By the film's midpoint, the friends were beginning to fall asleep; soon after, they had switched the film off entirely. *2001* seemed to them an interminable bore.

Originally filmed in Super Panavision for both 35mm and 70mm formats, *2001: A Space Odyssey* relies on the sensuousness of the theatrical setting and, as Kubrick himself said, is "essentially a non-verbal experience."[17] The film's narrative is loose and ambiguous, with long stretches carrying no dialogue. Not only does Kubrick rely heavily on the ability of the medium to evoke a sense of place and atmosphere through stark compositions (the vast expanses of space) and subtle sounds (think of the sound of the voice of Hal, the computer, for example), but musical compositions also play a major role in several of the scenes. Watching a panned-and-scanned video copy of *2001* on a 19-inch television with a poor mono speaker is like listening to a symphony orchestra through a tin can. You are guaranteed to wonder what all the fuss is about. (As a side note, *Star Trek: The Motion Picture* [1979] features scenes that alternate shots of what is meant to be an awe-inspiring alien structure of some sort and the amazed reactions of the various crew members. When seen on a small screen, the supposedly awesome alien structure becomes an incoherent and altogether unimpressive hodgepodge of lights and movement, more baffling than sublime.)

2001: A Space Odyssey is certainly not a typical movie, but it is different in degree, not in kind, in the way that it provides a sensual experience far different from reading a book or listening to a book being read. Watching movies is sensual in that it implicates sight and hearing in providing a full-blown visceral, physiological, bodily experience and relies in part for its effects on the same kinds of perceptual, cognitive, and affective processes that viewers bring to their interaction with the world outside the theater. For this reason, when I discuss spectatorship in this book, I am for the most part assuming a theatrical experience rather than one involving a small screen and monaural sound.[18] Yet most (but not all) of the processes I describe in the following pages also apply to viewing a film on a monitor, television, or computer screen, and certainly to a well-outfitted home theater system.

To admit its sensual nature isn't necessarily to claim great things for the medium of film; affective experiences dependent on sensory stimulation or simple pre-reflective responses are not always highly valued by the critical community. Chases and pursuits; jumping, fighting, and falling; high-speed travel; explosions; extreme violence; nudity and voyeurism; spectacle; representations of the disgusting and repulsive; shocks and surprises—this is the stuff of some of the most popular contemporary films. *Jurassic Park* (1993), one of the top five grossing films of all time, did well in part because viewers wanted not only to see a realistic portrayal of dinosaurs such as the *Tyrannosaurus rex* but to experience (something like) being chased by one. Film images and sounds are compelling in part because they are both imitative and transformative, relying on the real-world perceptual capacities of the spectator and simultaneously exaggerating and otherwise altering the visceral components of what is represented.[19] Neither television nor literature can equal the sensual experience *Jurassic Park* presents on the big screen.

But affective, visceral experiences can be presented subtly, and are not necessarily opposed to the pleasures of cognitive play and sympathy. In contrast to *Jurassic Park*, *Rear Window* is spare in its visceral effects. This isn't surprising, given the restricted space of the film: the action, such as it is, occurs either in Jefferies's apartment or in what he can see through its windows. Examples of the visceral power of the cinema in this film include Jefferies waking from a nap to find Lisa in his apartment, very close and about to kiss him. The scene is set in the early evening, the camera panning slowly across the courtyard behind Jefferies's apartment. We hear the ambient sounds of the neighborhood, including a soprano practicing her scales. The panning camera comes to rest on Jefferies asleep in his wheelchair. The shadow of a person rises up his chest as the person nears. We cut to our first view of Lisa, directly facing the camera in close-up and moving closer. The soprano's scales cease on the soundtrack, focusing the spectator's attention on the visual. The camera cuts to Jefferies as his eyes open. The shadow moves up his face, and he smiles. The camera cuts to Lisa again, this time with her face very close, in a tighter close-up. Then the camera cuts to a two-shot, as Lisa and Jefferies kiss. Through what seems to be either step-frames and/or slow motion (but what Hitchcock claims to be a shaking camera), the tempo of this shot has been manipulated for a stylized effect of subjective time, which together with soft focus (as well as the effect of Kelly's striking visage) conveys some of the visceral sense of the kiss.

The climactic point of any film is often its visceral peak. In *Rear Window*, this occurs after Thorwald discovers that Jefferies is spying on

3. Lisa (Grace Kelly) approaches the camera in extreme close-up, just before she kisses Jefferies in *Rear Window*.

him. When the murderer enters Jefferies's apartment, Jefferies delays him with a series of flashbulb bursts, and Thorwald responds angrily by dumping the incapacitated Jefferies out the window. In this scene, film technique also conveys affect and visceral experience, through lighting (the darkness of Jefferies's apartment that keeps Thorwald, initially, in the shadows), the bursting flashbulbs as Jefferies tries to blind the approaching Thorwald, the point-of-view shots Hitchcock uses to approximate Thorwald's temporary flash blindness, the facial expressions and visible bodily exertions of the struggle between the men, and the sounds—shouts, grunts, whimpers, the sound of a body falling on a hard surface—that accompany the struggle and its aftermath.

To some extent, the strength of spectator affective responses at these points depends on allegiance with Jefferies. However, affective response is at times independent of sympathy for characters. Hitchcock himself recognized that responses to situations are partly independent of character engagement. The director gives the example of an intruder who enters a stranger's room and rummages through his drawers. When the audience sees the room's occupant approaching the door, it feels suspense, and wants to warn the "snooper" that the other approaches. As Hitchcock says, "even if the snooper is not a likable character, the audience will still feel anxiety for him."[20]

In this book I distinguish between emotions—what I characterize in the next chapter as "concern-based construals"—and the broader category of affect, which I define as any state of feeling or sensation. Emotions are thus a kind of affect. Affects would include the "startle response" that occurs, for example, when your infant daughter unexpectedly screams in your ear. Simple reflex responses are affects. Your feeling of being hot or cold, that bad aftertaste, generalized anxiety or giddiness—all of these are affects. Affects, as I use the term, include desires, emotions, pleasures, moods, and all manner of feelings and sensations. The automatic shock and revulsion many viewers feel when the alien bursts from the crew member's stomach in *Alien* (1979) is an affective experience. Emotions, as I discuss in the subsequent chapter, result from someone's perception or construal of an event or situation in relation to her or his concerns, and thus have a stronger cognitive component. Affects, on the other hand, are often cognitively impenetrable, that is, their causal chain may be inaccessible to consciousness. But affective experience, although it may be itself "cognitively impenetrable," can certainly contribute to the cognitive complexity of a film. The affects elicited by a film need not be blunt and superficial to have import for the way a film embodies ideas and complex ways of experiencing a fictional world.

Film technique is essential in shaping visceral effects, whether perceptual or affective. Sergei Eisenstein wrote of the "montage of attractions" as a means of producing perceptual effects in the spectator. The "Odessa Steps" sequence of *Battleship Potemkin* (1925), for example, creates visceral effects through a montage of contrasting screen directions, movements, graphic compositions, and rhythms. Hitchcock insisted on the use of film technique to create and sustain the appropriate effect. In *The Birds* (1963), for example, he speaks of the "emotional truck" in the scene where the mother (Jessica Tandy) discovers the body of the dead farmer. As she flees the house, Hitchcock exaggerated the sound of her footsteps as she approaches her truck and the screech of the engine as she starts it up (to convey her anguish). The dirt road leading to the farmhouse had been watered down to film the truck's arrival to minimize the dust kicked up by the wheels. As she escapes the gruesome scene (filmed prior to the shot of her arrival), however, Hitchcock not only had the truck kick up clouds of dust, he also had artificial smoke billowing from the tailpipe.[21] As I will later argue, such film techniques elicit visceral effects that can increase or decrease the power of the viewer's emotional experience.

Filmmakers can use style for aggressive purposes, whereby the filmmaker causes shocks and otherwise aggressively "assaults" the spectator through formal means.[22] The nature of affect depends on the mental set of the spectator, on expectations and assumptions in part cued by the film itself. A clear example is the shower murder in *Psycho* (1960), in which Hitchcock does everything possible (within the bounds of the "allowable") to maximize the shocking nature of the scene. Marion Crane (Janet Leigh) has stolen a large sum of money, but after a conversation with Norman Bates (Anthony Perkins) at her motel, decides to return it the next morning. Just as she begins to enjoy the literal and figurative cleansing of the warm shower, and just as the audience begins to relax in the presumption that her decision will put things right, the brutal murder occurs without warning or intimation. Not only has the audience been set up cognitively for this shock, but Hitchcock's rapid editing and Bernard Herrmann's shrieking musical score add to the visceral mayhem.

All of this might lead some to dismiss film viewing as inclined toward mindless visceral experiences, something like riding in a roller coaster or walking through a carnival fun house. But one wonders about the denigration of all such experiences in film, as though only the cool distance of the intellect is of value in the appreciation of narrative art. Moreover, images and sounds, though sensual in nature, can be used to generate thought. And it must be remembered that film is a medium not simply of raw images and sounds, but also of language—of dialogue, intertitles, and voice-over narration. It is sometimes said that watching films short-circuits the imagination, since instead of imagining the look of characters or settings, as we do when we read literature, the perception of characters and settings in film seemingly requires little imagination. But we can easily turn the tables on literature here, and complain that whereas some literature explicitly tells readers what characters are thinking and feeling (leaving little to the imagination), in nearly all films, spectators must infer and imagine the character's thoughts and feelings. Literature and film invoke the imagination differently, and the fact that film is a more sensual medium does not preclude its also being a medium that elicits thought, inference, and imagination. Films can provide viewers with a complex meld of image, sound, music, and words, and the means by which films elicit response and thought, and provide pleasure, are the topic of this book.

SYMPATHY, ANTIPATHY, AND
PARASOCIAL ENGAGEMENT

We will examine sympathy, empathy, and antipathy fully in Chapter 3. Here I would merely point out that the viewer's engagement with characters is one of the primary pleasures of both fiction film and literature. It is relatively easy for filmmakers to engage the sympathies and antipathies of audiences, because viewers seem to take inherent pleasure in strongly desiring various outcomes for the central characters of a narrative. The fact that spectators are fascinated with fictional persons in scenarios of trouble or conflict can be partially explained from a Darwinian functionalist perspective. As social beings, humans gain adaptive benefit from the imaginative rehearsal of various human predicaments. This may account for the interest in predicaments, but it doesn't explain the strong psychic connection to characters that viewers often feel and the pleasure taken in observing their fortunes. Perhaps for now, with a few provisos, we can be content with Adam Smith's observation: "How selfish soever man may be supposed, there are evidently some principles in his nature, which interest him in the fortune of others, and render their happiness necessary to him, though he derives nothing from it except the pleasure of seeing it."[23] The provisos would be, first, that Smith's "fellow feeling" applies not just to actual persons, but also to fictional characters, and second, that it often takes the form of antipathy as well as sympathy, both of which may be sources of pleasure.

Above I mentioned Hitchcock's contention that audiences find certain narrative situations suspenseful, even when characters are unlikable. He adds, in reference to Lisa's trespassing in Thorwald's apartment in *Rear Window*, that "when the character is attractive, as for instance Grace Kelly in *Rear Window*, the public's emotion is greatly intensified."[24] We might add that familiarity can breed liking as well. Hence the star system. In this case, the viewing public may also have been familiar with Kelly's star persona due to her earlier appearances in *High Noon* (1952) and *Mogambo* (1953). Strong sympathy for characters is not a necessary element in the mix of audience pleasures; in fact, certain genres, such as horror and action/adventure, often minimize audience sympathy. Nonetheless, sympathy is one of the primary means through which many films engage emotional response. Sympathy provides a moral and ideological compass for the viewer, a means of appraising situations according to their implications for favored characters.

Just as powerful in many films, however, is a strong antipathy through which some take pleasure in negative reactions to oppositional characters or antagonists. Adam Smith may have been utopian in his emphasis on human sympathy. In film viewing, at least, a strong and interesting antagonist—someone who is appropriately loathed and otherwise hated—is necessary to provide the pleasures of antipathy that cannot be ignored. Strong antipathies often result in a desire for vengeance, harm, retribution, or punishment. It is a desire that fuels the pleasure taken in films such as Charles Bronson's *Death Wish* series (1974–1994), *Lethal Weapon* (1987) and its three sequels, or Western films centered on scenarios of revenge. But the pleasures of vicarious revenge are surprisingly common in many films, extending well beyond the "scapegoat movies" in which it is the central pleasure.

That spectators experience something like sympathy for characters is not a controversial claim, though some wonder about the propriety of responding emotionally to the plight of fictional characters as though they deserved fear and pity. Some viewers mistake actors for characters, or discuss a character's emotional life as though it had an independent existence outside of the fiction. Aside from these confusions, however, responding emotionally to characters is no more questionable than becoming interested in the solution to a mystery plot. There is nothing quaint about responding with sympathy to characters in a film that is not *also* quaint about responding to any fictional element of the film. Fictions are fabrications through and through, not merely in their portrayal of characters. It makes no sense to deride sympathy for fictional characters as naïve or unworthy of superior intellect, then go on to champion other kinds of mimetic response in relation to any element of the fictional world. After all, my sympathetic emotions in response to Lisa's fate in *Rear Window* are no less rational than my curiosity about whether Thorwald is actually a murderer.

Some would tell us that when spectators identify with a character, they feel and experience exactly what the character does. But this could hardly be the case; if it were true, it would be difficult to account for the pleasure of the film experience. Suppose that viewers feel exactly what Melanie Daniels (Tippi Hedren) does as she is attacked by birds in *The Birds*, or what Jo McKenna (Doris Day) experiences when her son is kidnapped in *The Man Who Knew Too Much* (1956). Why would viewers put themselves through that? If we assume the spectator's experience to be equivalent to the terror, pain, and grief of the characters, it would be unpleasant indeed, and certainly not something to actively seek out. Viewers can both sympathize with Jo McKenna and enjoy the experience in part because even while they sympathize, they are aware that they are viewing a fiction. Spectators do not "identify" with Jo purely and perfectly; they cannot have the same concern for her son that they presume she has in the world of the fiction. The spectator is not Jo, and moreover, the spectator has a different knowledge of Jo's situation than she does. Jo has no idea that her son will eventually be rescued, while the viewer, if familiar with the conventions of Hollywood, strongly suspects a last-minute reprieve. When spectators empathize with a character, they may or may not feel something similar to what she or he experiences (as I detail in subsequent chapters), but it is rarely the same affect, and it is always tempered by the implicit awareness of the institutions of fiction and the viewing situation. The implicit knowledge of mainstream film conventions, including the probable happy ending, also assures viewers that their sympathy will typically result in psychic rewards.

NARRATIVE SCENARIOS AND EMOTIONAL SATISFACTIONS

It is a film's narration, consisting of its narrative structure, style, and point of view, that shapes the overall experience it offers. Watching a film is a temporal experience, as we are drawn into mental activities and responses that flow inexorably onward, intermixed and building upon each other. Filmic narration determines the temporal processes of cognitive play, affective experience, and character engagement. It is obvious that *Rear Window*, for example, directs the mental activity of spectators in an ordered process. After learning something of setting and character in the exposition, viewers seemingly witness a murder and cover-up, engage in a process of discovery and questioning along with the characters, and finally have their hypotheses about the murderer Thorwald confirmed. The affective experiences the film offers are also structured temporally, often, as in *Rear Window*, in an ascending order of strength, until at the end the protagonist must engage in a rousing struggle for survival itself.

In everyday life, emotional experiences are often unpleasant. Sympathy may reward us only with pain or discomfort, since to sympathize or empathize can mean to share in another's disappointments and unhappiness. Therapists commonly hear the complaint that friends or family members are simply unable or unwilling to empathize because it is too threatening. In classical Hollywood films, on the other hand, conventions such as the happy ending, characteristic of comedies and other genres, make it probable that empathy will bring the rewards of an eventual favorable outcome for the protagonist; thus, emotional investment will likely yield psychically pleasing results.

Even endings not uniformly favorable for the protagonist offer some type of psychic reward for the viewer, whether intellectual, moral, or emotional. The resolution of *Witness* (1985), for example, has John Book (Harrison Ford) vanquishing the corrupt New York police but having to part with Rachel (Kelly McGillis), the Amish woman with whom he has fallen in love. Though the ending is mixed, the film implies that Book embodies an urban corruption that would taint the seemingly utopian society of the Amish. Though the lovers must part, the viewer can take comfort in the preservation of this rural Eden. In mainstream American film, the spectator's sympathy is typically expected to eventually bring a pleasant psychological experience.

That spectator emotion is so dependent on narrative makes sense in light of the nature of emotion. We sometimes think of emotions as static mental states, but emotions are a temporal process. While moods are thought to be pervasive and long-lasting, psychologists think of typical emotions as transient disturbances, initiated by the subject's construal or appraisal of a disruptive situation that relates to the subject's concerns. Emotions occur in time and have a structure; they ebb and flow according to the subject's evolving situation and response to it. Viewers' emotional experiences may change dramatically as their expectations are met or thwarted, and as the situation takes unexpected turns.

The language that philosophers and psychologists use to describe the structure of emotion is very close to that used by screenwriters speaking about narrative structure. Consider the screenwriting manuals, with their talk of catalysts and disruptive events, goal-oriented protagonists, conflicts and crises, expectations and reversals, rising action and climaxes, resolution, and a return to a state of calm. A film's narrative structure is clearly designed to cue emotional, visceral, and cognitive experience.

Some viewers, however, look for something more profound than the simple pleasures of happy endings and favorable outcomes. The stories that deeply move audiences and provide the kind of experience that make an indelible impression on their memories must intersect with their lives in significant ways. One of the attractions of psychoanalytic theory has been its explanations of the deepest attraction of mainstream movies, an attraction that was said to draw on the furthest reaches of unconscious desire, rooted in our most formative childhood experiences.

Later psychoanalytic film theory found desire and identification to be much more ambiguous and complicated than was previously thought,[25] but retained the assumption that films are at their essence a playground for unconscious fantasies that originate in childhood experiences. Linda Williams, for example, has developed a schema by which what she calls "female body genres"—pornography, horror, and melodrama—are said to stem from the largely unconscious desires (what she calls "perversions") of sadism, sadomasochism, and masochism, respectively, and obtain their power in large part as stories that replay originary fantasies of seduction, castration, and the loss of the mother.[26] Psychoanalytic theories share an appeal to film as a kind of fantasy that draws deep pleasures from the well of unconscious desire.

There exist many reasons to be skeptical of these kinds of explanations of our attraction to filmic and other narratives. Freud was undoubtedly a brilliant and imaginative thinker who made salient many important psychological concepts such as repression and the unconscious, even if he did not introduce them. Today, however, few psychologists accept Freud's particular accounts of how these and related processes function. In academic circles, psychoanalysis has the most influence in film and literary studies in part because Freud's intriguing theory of the interpretation of dreams also provides useful tools for the interpretation of narratives, including, for example, the notions of displacement, condensation, and manifest and latent content.[27] The fact that the vast majority of contemporary psychologists are skeptical of psychoanalysis does not necessarily imply its falsehood, of course. I would put my skepticism about psychoanalysis in check if there were stronger independent evidence for its claims, or if concepts such as the Oedipus complex, penis envy, or castration anxiety had any intuitive plausibility.[28]

A critique of psychoanalytic theory in film studies has been levied elsewhere, and there is no need to repeat the details here.[29] Suffice it to say that we need not turn initially to psychoanalysis to approach the issue of narrative pleasures, or even of the deepest satisfactions offered by narrative scenarios. Such pleasures and satisfactions are far too diverse to admit of genesis solely in infantile fantasies or indeed, in any single source.[30] Movies can offer audiences a sense of enlarged possibilities; movies can demonstrate what we can be like or how life might be. Their adventures, heroisms, strong ideals, and excitements can affirm individual identity and allow spectators to see possibilities, to feel again a sense of individual potency. Thus, movies are not mere distractions, they are also visions.

Movies can also take on ritualistic functions as celebrations or lamentations, offering the pleasures of seeing values or beliefs confirmed or questioned, or of celebrating ways of life. Even lamentations such as *Lost in Translation* (2003) or *21 Grams* (2003) might be taken as eliciting a pleasure in the confirmation or recognition of the listless ennui, drift, or lack of interpersonal connection that is said to characterize postmodernity, or the inevitable sadness that illness, death, and seemingly chance encounters bring to human life.

Many films oblige us with stories of the formation of the romantic couple, and these can be seen as ritual celebrations of romantic union. Such films extend beyond the genres of romantic melodrama and comedy; most classical Hollywood films include a romantic plot or subplot.[31] We also see this concern for romantic union in Bollywood extravaganzas and French comedies, together with countless literary narratives from the recent and distant past. We need appeal to no latent content in many of these cases; such films embody deep and sometimes obvious human needs and desires (however culturally inflected), and from this draw their power.[32]

REFLEXIVE AND SOCIAL PLEASURES

So far I have dealt with some of the *intratextual* pleasures of the movies—cognitive play, affective experience, character sympathy, and narrative scenarios that invoke emotion in satisfying ways. Hollywood has typically embraced an ethic of absorption, although reflexive and expressive stylistic flourishes seem to be much more common in contemporary Hollywood than in the past. According to many practitioners of the classical style, the purpose of film technique is not only to communicate narrative information, but also to rivet the spectator to the fiction. Any technique that draws attention to itself, and away from the story, is thought to transgress that fundamental convention. Yet although this was a common rule of thumb, it was also one that was often ignored, and as reflexive works become increasingly popular on both film and television, one wonders if the "invisible style" of classical Hollywood has been replaced with a kind of reflexive knowingness. Whether this is true or not as a characterization of a general trend, we can confidently say that the pleasures of film viewing go beyond the intratextual; spectators also enjoy the *intertextual* and *extratextual* pleasures of film viewing, critical appreciation, and fandom.

The reflexive and ironic interest in "bad" movies, for example, hardly admits the kind of illusionism sometimes thought to be characteristic of the spectator's experience. The release of *Ed Wood* (1994), a celebratory work about the man who gave us such curious failures as *Glen or Glenda* (1953) and *Plan 9 from Outer Space* (1956), speaks to this ironic distance with which spectators view some films. Another example is the current fascination with the spectacle of special effects. How many theatergoers saw *Jurassic Park* for its story as opposed to its supposed state-of-the-art use of computer-generated images? Similarly, the computer morphing in *Terminator 2: Judgment Day* (1991) was almost guaranteed to initiate critical distance, even while, ironically, the spectator marveled at the "realistic" but obviously unreal effects. *Sin City* (2005), *300* (2006), and *Beowulf* (2007) generated substantial interest due to their visual effects: the actors were filmed in front of green screens, and the backgrounds, colors, and other effects were later digitally added. Another sort of reflexive pleasure comes from the recognition of a director's style or other "signature." Hitchcock, a marvelously playful director, was very successful at self-promotion. A strong sense of Hitchcock as auteur is a component of viewing his work. This is most obvious in his cameo appearance in each of his films. The extent of audience participation in this game is evidenced in his usual placement of the appearances toward the beginning of his films, so that the audience could thereafter attend more to the story proper. Artifact-centered responses, of which I will say more later, are responses to both reflexive elements in the film and filmic elements other than content, for example, film technology, allusions to other films, and the status of a film as a "cultural event," and so forth.

Above, I argued that the particular emotional experience offered by films depends on the spectator's implicit assumption that film viewing is a conventional practice, and that what is seen is fictional. Film viewing is rarely so absorbing that, while viewing, spectators have no conscious, extratextual thoughts. Isn't this extratextual mental activity, whether it occurs during the viewing or not, among the pleasures films offer? For much of the audience, I believe, reflexive film viewing is a common practice and an important component of the pleasures of the cinema.[33]

Another sort of reflexive pleasure is the metaresponse. Our pleasure in a film can often be indirect, a second-order or reflective response to our initial reactions. To give a personal example, my initial response to the violence in *Unforgiven* (1992) was unease and revulsion; that response was gradually tempered by my reflection, while viewing the film and afterward, on how those feelings played into the film's thematic exploration of vengeance. In turn, such considerations radically altered my response during a second viewing.

To some degree, reflexive pleasures rely on an audience that, in part due to the increasing number of film courses in high schools and universities, is more sophisticated in at least one respect—they know something about films and filmmaking. But a film education isn't necessary to enjoy the reflexive pleasures. As early as 1915, Vachel Lindsay wrote of the "buzzing commentary of the audience."[34] And as William Paul writes, "Anyone who has experienced a movie in a . . . crowded urban theater (especially in the inner city, where audiences are often as vocal in their responses . . . as worshippers in Pentecostal churches) might even find the notion of a passive audience to be rather quaint."[35]

The pleasures of film viewing are also social in nature. We can see this, for example, in the various manifestations of fandom that create subcultures around "cult" movies, various stars, or genres of film. Another example is the social uses of horror films for adolescents, who may attend such films in part to reenact gendered roles as protector (males) and protected (females) within the context of courtship.[36] Viewings of "gross out" films such as *Jackass: The Movie* (2002), to take another example, might serve as "rites of passage" in the sense that groups of adolescent boys test their ability to withstand the viewing of repulsive or violent scenes in the context of a group of peers.

THE MULTIPLE PLEASURES OF THE SPECTATOR

Can we identify one final source or single essence of spectator pleasure in film viewing? Various theories compete to provide overarching accounts of movie pleasure. Psychoanalytic theories relate narrative pleasures to repressed wishes and unconscious desires that originate in childhood trauma. The proponents of evolutionary psychology claim that humans are fundamentally motivated by the need to reproduce their genes; thus, most human behavior is adaptively motivated, a means of equipping "the organism" for survival and reproduction. For the evolutionary psychologist, film viewing would have to be motivated by the adaptive benefits it offers. Among the benefits of viewing films we might find social instruction, the exercise of cognitive faculties, the exercise of the senses of hearing and sight, and perhaps cathartic physiological benefits stemming from excitement and calming. The evolutionary psychologist might claim that species members have evolved to enjoy activities that enhance survival and adaptation itself.

Others have suggested, in contrast, that film viewing is a form of cognitive play, a means of drive induction, of adding excitement and color to human life. Clifford Geertz, for example, claims that art, entertainments, and amusements offer an indirect means of dealing with the crucial conflicts and issues of life.[37] We have also seen that some cognitive theorists seem to assume that cognitive play is the primary motivating pleasure in film viewing.

Theories of repressed drives, unconscious fantasy, human adaptation, and play all have their attractions. But consider another alternative. Contrary to any broad theory, there may exist no final essence to the pleasures of mainstream spectatorship. Cinematic pleasures may be multiple and dispersed, depending on film, genre, viewer, and cultural and historical context. While screen theory posits a single, unitary pleasure as the fundamental motivation for viewing mainstream films, the account I offer here questions the existence of an essential viewing pleasure. Instead it recognizes various kinds of pleasures film viewing offers and doubts that any single theory can account for them all.

In this book, I propose a "cognitive-perceptual" account of the moviegoing experience. This approach will allow for a more specific description of the particular pleasures of individual films, of whatever genre or type. The means by which cognitive play, visceral experience, sympathy, narrative satisfactions, and reflexivity are played out differ markedly in individual films and genres, and between individuals and audiences. For example, we could make the case that while mystery emphasizes cognitive play and fantasies of intellectual mastery, the action/adventure genre appeals to visceral excitement and physical mastery, the melodrama genre to sympathy, and parody and irony to reflexive pleasures. Yet clearly no genre emphasizes one pleasure wholly at the expense of the others. Moreover, though films of a particular genre may share basic tendencies, each film presents a complex mix of intended pleasures, resulting in a unique spectator experience.

Screen theory has Brechtian roots; it sees mainstream film viewing as retrograde and pathological, steeped in illusionism and ideological subjugation. The account I offer, in contrast, paints a more benign picture of the pleasures offered by mainstream films. On the other hand, if those pleasures are often benign, they are not always or necessarily so. That some of our pleasures are rooted in psychological or social pathology, or the entertainment of unhealthy desires, is difficult to deny. How else do we explain, for example, the pleasure some audiences take in portrayals of violence toward women or in revenge narratives? Screen theory, as practiced in film studies, was so general that it seemed to locate an ideological problem in spectator pleasure itself, not merely in certain of its diverse manifestations. We need to account for spectator pleasure with an appreciation of its diversity. The pleasures of the cinema are multiple, and so are their psychological and cultural effects, as well as their implications for ethics and ideology.

MOVIE DESIRES

In psychoanalytic theories of narrative, a psychological phenomenon called "desire" plays a central role in the determination of spectator response. Given a Freudian account of the emotions, this is not surprising. Like cognitive theories, Freud certainly acknowledged the value of the emotions, and his theory is cognitive in that he connected emotions to ideas. But Freudian psychoanalysis differs from cognitive-perceptual approaches to emotion in an important way. For Freud, the root cause of an emotion was primarily within the individual rather than in a relationship between the individual and her or his environment. Freud assumes a "hydraulic" theory of emotions, such that emotions spring from an internal source that roils within and function as a kind of discharge based on overflowing energy. Where the cognitive-perceptual theory finds that emotions result from an individual's concern-based construal of an exterior situation, for Freud, object reference and the subject's relationship to the exterior world merely scratch the surface. In the deeper recesses of the psyche lies the unconscious world of instinctual drives and desires, or what psychoanalytic film and literary theorists sometimes simply call "desire." In psychoanalysis, emotions are linked to conscious ideas, because conscious ideas relate or refer to memory traces that have the potential to release psychic energy. Memory traces, James Hillman notes in an interesting metaphor, can be conceived of as "bombs," and affect as the explosive potential of emotion as repression is released and affective energy discharged.[38] Ideas and emotions are intimately related, but the discharge of emotion fundamentally depends on the storehouse of energy held in the body. Desire, then, can be conceived of as a general drive to release this fund of energy that builds up within the individual—to explode the bomb.

It is desire, as Peter Brooks writes in his book *Reading for the Plot*, that "carries us forward, onward, through the text."[39] For most psychoanalytic critics, desire—which bubbles up from the seething cauldron of chaotic energy in the unconscious—is thought to be that which motivates the viewing and reading of the spectator. Brooks writes at times as though a narrative were an engine running on the fuel of desire, granting the reader the pleasures offered by the indulgences that desire takes as its goal.

But desire is more than the need for a release of energy. Psychoanalytic theories of spectatorship often assume that narratives depend for their affects on the presumed human instinct to restore an earlier state of things. Narratives replay childhood fantasies and elicit conditions—in the realm of fantasy—that mimic early stages of childhood development. Christian

Metz holds that identifying with the camera allows viewers to experience the illusion of cohesiveness, reminding them of their earliest experiences of wholeness.[40] The repetitious nature of film narrative, both within the individual film and in the repetition of conventions, genres, and modes, replays ground already covered. It is similar to the child's *fort/da* game, in which the child repeatedly throws away and recovers an object, repeating the pleasure of mastery through recovery.

On this conception of desire, a fundamental psychic motivation of the spectator is to replay the originary fantasies in order to recover the lost plenitude of early childhood or to master the anxiety and fear arising from later stages of development. For Laura Mulvey, at least in her early writings, film viewing follows the contours of male desire, and film narratives are structured to diffuse the castration anxiety originating in the oedipal scenario. Psychoanalytic theories in film studies, then, have found narrative "desire" to be a drive for regression to psychic states that mimic and replay early stages of childhood development, thus granting a kind of illusory mastery.

But there are other conceptions of desire. Gaylyn Studlar has held that desire is not a sadistic fantasy of mastery, but is rather pre-oedipal and masochistic.[41] Todd McGowan, arguing that previous Lacanian theorists have misinterpreted Lacan, claims that the engine for desire is "the Other's seeming jouissance, not its mastery."[42] For Linda Williams, the so-called body genres—pornography, horror, and melodrama—have their roots in the originary fantasies of primal seduction, castration and the mystery of sexual difference, and the loss of origin, respectively.[43]

For Brooks, desire is something like Freud's notion of Eros; Brooks writes of developing a "textual erotics" of reading. Freud's notion of Eros, Brooks notes, cannot be limited to mere sexual desire. For Brooks, Eros, which seems to be used as a synonym for desire, is "polymorphous" and takes many other forms. In his book *Body Works,* for example, Brooks writes of epistemophilia, or what Freud calls *Wisstrieb,* the desire for knowledge or meaning. This instinct for knowledge arises, in Freud's "Three Essays on the Theory of Sexuality," from the child's desire to solve "The Riddle of the Sphinx," or the mystery of where babies come from.[44] In *Reading for the Plot,* Brooks writes of the "death instinct" as Freud's "master plot." Here Brooks claims (by punning on the word "end") that our desire for the end of the plot is motivated by our secret desire for our own end—our death.[45] But we are not done yet. Brooks also writes of another form of desire—the ostensible "primordial homicidal impulse."[46]

It is clear that for Brooks and other psychoanalytic theorists, desire is polymorphous indeed. Troubles arise when this polymorphous diversity is subsumed under the word "desire" or "Desire," as though it were a single Platonic entity. Desire then becomes, quite confusingly, both singular and plural, descriptive of many varied drives and yet, somehow, a unitary phenomenon. It becomes a clearinghouse for the entire panoply of unconscious and physiological drives, instincts, motivations, and pleasures. We are motivated by Desire when we are motivated by a need for release of energy, by the death instinct, by sexual attraction, by homicidal impulses, by curiosity, and by pleasure in looking.

We might initially be inclined to say that the theoretical formulations of desire are too broad to shed light on more specific processes of the elicitation of affect. Noël Carroll claims that contemporary film theory has a penchant for "Platonizing." As Carroll writes,

> All different sorts of desire, such as the male viewer's sexual desire for a movie character and any viewer's desire that the movie be intelligible, are slotted under the abstract noun *Desire*, whose laws the Lacanian then charts. One, of course, wonders whether, ontologically, there is such a thing as *Desire* per se, rather than particularized desires for this or that. Desires, that is, are individuated by reference to their objects . . . not as instances of some unified, univocally named force called *Desire*.[47]

Carroll's criticism here is slightly off target, it seems to me. There may certainly be a coherent and useful concept of desire per se, and it may be useful to chart the laws of desire apart from specific instances of it. Similarly, the concept of an emotion is useful to us apart from specific instances of emotion. Knowing what an emotion is allows us to better understand the various sorts of emotions and their instantiations. Yet Carroll is right that some scholars have written as though Desire refers to a distinct and univocal human drive or instinct, when in fact the word has multiple and sometimes conflicting meanings.

"Desire" is best taken to denote a psychic state in which the individual wants, wishes for, or craves something.[48] Thus, a desire only becomes interesting from a narrative standpoint in relation to its object, which may be specific or diffuse. In this book, I will write either of particular types of desires, such as erotic desire or desire for revenge, or of particular instances of desire, such as desire for a particular narrative outcome or for certain narrative pleasures. Thus I will not refer to "Desire" in itself (such a reference being a vestigial byproduct of apparatus theory) but always to particular desires or desire types.

As I have so far argued, narrative pleasures and desires come in many varied forms, such that discussion of Pleasure or Desire as though they are singular entities is bound to lead to confusion. I will, however, make a few general observations about the nature of our desires and pleasures. First, our desires and pleasures emanate from diverse psychic and bodily registers, and unsurprisingly, they sometimes conflict with or relate to each other complexly and ambiguously. For example, I may desire to see a character punished for a transgression. Yet if his punishment prohibits him from embarking on a promised journey that I am eager to see him undertake, I will have conflicting desires. The evocation of conflicting desires and pleasures is one of the dynamic tools of the scenarist and filmmaker.

Second, we may entertain desires and pleasures in the context of film viewing that we would scarcely allow ourselves in reality. One of the benefits, and perhaps dangers, of fiction is that it allows the spectator or reader to try on various desires, pleasures, and emotions—in short, to have vicarious experiences that would be impossible, unwanted, frightening, socially or morally unacceptable, or ill-advised in our actual lives.[49]

How do pleasures and desires differ from and relate to each other? A pleasure is experienced in the present, while a desire is oriented toward the future. A pleasure is something that we enjoy, while a desire embodies a wish for something anticipated. Pleasures and desires, of course, are related in various ways. The promise of a narrative pleasure can motivate our desires such that it can lead to our desiring a particular outcome. But as in the case of desires, one pleasure may interfere with the experience of another, such that the experience of the spectator becomes meld of pleasures, desires, emotions, and affects unfolding in a temporal process and building on and conflicting with one another in sometimes unpredictable ways. Such is the fascination of cinema.

MOVIES AS FANTASIES

Like pleasure and desire, fantasy is a term important in psychoanalytic film theory, in which it takes on a particular technical meaning. For some psychoanalytic theorists, fantasies are imaginary scenarios, intermixed with unconscious ideas, to which instinct becomes fixated and which become "stagings of desire." These scenarios, as we might expect, are said to be firmly rooted in childhood development. Thus, the deepest meaning of narratives—their deep structure—is thought to arise from unconscious, instinctual fantasies that have their roots in our earliest years of existence.

Clearly, much of human mental activity occurs beneath consciousness.

One common misunderstanding of cognitive theory is that it deals only in consciousness. In the next chapter, I describe what I call the "psychological unconscious," an essential element of the human psyche, but one that differs from Freudian conceptions of the unconscious in many respects. One can preserve room for preconscious and unconscious mental processes, while at the same time remaining skeptical about whether psychoanalysis provides a plausible account of them. But whether one is skeptical or not, it is clear that psychoanalysis oversimplifies the psychology of the appeal of film narratives. Movies, as narrative scenarios, do encourage fantasy, but these fantasies are the public fantasies of mass market familiar stories, generated from a source outside of the individual psyche rather than from within, and depending on the arousal of desires and pleasures, not from a single univocal source but rather from diverse sources. Even if psychoanalysis is deemed to be a plausible psychological theory (and of course this is certainly questionable), it must not be considered wholly adequate as a comprehensive account of the film viewing experience.

Movies often appeal to viewers not because they reflect experience, but because they idealize and exaggerate it. Movies are hypercoherent; they streamline reality, including in their narratives only what is needed to generate their desired effect. If melodramas or revenge films, for example, can be deeply satisfying to viewers, it is less because the films mirror the world than because they psychologically satisfy viewers by offering a means of psychically dealing with the world or responding to it. Movies offer narratives that elicit and satisfy desires, that comfort and placate, or that serve another function rooted in the individual and social psyches of the audience. This is what I mean by "fantasy." The remainder of this book develops a theory of just how movies appeal to the affective and emotional lives of spectators.

As in the case of "desire," then, I suggest that we decouple the word "fantasy" from the technical meaning it has taken on in psychoanalytic film theory. A fantasy, as I use the term, is any fictional scenario that draws on the deep social and psychic needs or desires of the audience. It derives its power from its ability to appeal to any combination of human desires—for power, admiration, communion with God, the attentions of attractive men or women, achievement, affiliation, intimacy, a better world, peace, and so on. Fantasies are scenarios that provide for the vicarious satisfaction of desires in the mental realms of fiction. Many fantasies have deep structures, some mysterious in their origin. Do the desires inherent in fantasies really get satisfied, or is it that there is pleasure to be had in imagining their satisfaction?[50] In Chapter 6, I consider this issue in relation to *Titanic* (1997) as a fantasy of transcendent romantic love. I think it legitimate to speculate and form hypotheses about the popular success of various film scenarios as fantasies. Yet we need not and should not limit the use of "fantasy" to the technical meaning derived from psychoanalysis.

MOVIES AND DREAMS

Some might want to preserve the technical use of the term "fantasy" as it is used in psychoanalytic theory because it captures the sense that watching a film is something like dreaming or daydreaming.[51] This comparison has the attraction of providing for critics the means and techniques that Freud advocated for the interpretation of dreams—the search for latent meaning through symbols, condensations, and displacements, for that mysterious bed of unconscious meaning lying hidden and repressed beneath the surface structure of the film. And some of the characteristics of the theatrical movie experience *do* suggest dreaming. As viewers enter the theater, they are prepared for a kind of inner mental and bodily experience, free, to some degree, from distractions. Ideally, they sit in comfortable chairs, the lights dim, and the images before them on the screen occupy a significant portion of the visual field. After the trailers and titles, spectators become gradually involved in the film's story world and less aware of the surroundings. Thierry Kuntzel has argued that *The Most Dangerous Game* (1932) lures the spectator with the forces of the primary processes (as conceived of by psychoanalysis), drawing the spectator deeper into its illusory hold. The opening of the film consists of a series of doors, openings, and enterings, as though we are traveling into a strange and forbidden world.[52] After waking from this film dream, viewers are gently nudged back into the universe of waking, ambulatory, active life.

Although there exist similarities between film viewing and dreaming, the analogy quickly becomes misleading if taken too far.[53] Both dreams and fantasies, as psychoanalysis conceives of them, arise from the unconscious of the individual and are experienced by individuals. Hollywood spectatorship, alternatively, is a public experience shaped from *outside* of the spectator's psyche. V. F. Perkins calls this a "public privacy,"[54] that is, a social "privacy" that is shared with other spectators. Moreover, unlike dreams, the images and sounds the film provides are *actually* perceived rather than imagined, and are orchestrated by other humans whose design is to affect us in some way, even if only to entertain us for a few hours.[55]

A film may appeal to our wishes and desires (as dreams sometimes do), but these are mass-produced appeals, not the spontaneous appeals of the idiosyncratic psyche.

Not only is theatrical viewing public rather than private, it is usually also both conventional and institutional. When a film is viewed at the theater, all of the elements of sociality as it impacts on psychology come into play. The spectator is typically aware of many of the conventions of film viewing, and unlike a dream, enters into the viewing situation willingly and with a measure of control over her or his response. She may choose a horror film or an art film based on the type of experience she or her companions desire. She is familiar with the conventional protocols for transportation to and from the theater; for purchasing tickets, food, and drinks; for proper behavior during the screening; and so on. She may hide her eyes or walk out if desired.

That spectatorship is a social and conventional activity further implies that there exists a kind of contract between the providers (filmmakers, distributors, exhibitors) and the audience. The French film scholar Roger Odin, who advocates what he calls a "semio-pragmatic approach" to film, writes that the film viewer adopts a social role, a "kind of psychic positioning . . . that leads to the implementation of . . . operations that produce meaning and affects."[56] The particular social role adopted by the spectator depends on many factors, not least of which is the film's genre or mode. Whether a film is indexed as documentary or fiction, a Western or a melodrama, a Hollywood blockbuster or a work of art cinema determines to a great extent the nature of the social role expected of the viewer, and conversely, also influences the viewer's expectations about the particular experience this sort of film offers. As Odin writes, it is only when the film director and viewer assume the same role that a "space of communication" is created and meanings and effects are harmoniously formed.[57] Needless to say, this doesn't always occur. A film does not require us to feel, or to feel in any particular way; as film scholar Greg M. Smith writes, a film is nothing more than "an invitation to feel."[58]

The point is that unlike dreaming and unlike the experience of private fantasies, the theatrical film-viewing experience is intentional, public, institutional, and conventional. For many viewers, its attraction is that it offers a relatively predictable experience that promises to offer certain pleasures and psychic benefits. Rather than rely too heavily on the film/dream analogy, it is better to explore the experience of film viewing itself as a conventional social and psychological experience, an experience that stands on its own and has unique characteristics separate from dreaming.

If a movie is a fantasy, then it is one of a particular sort, designed and screened for the viewing public in a remarkably visceral audiovisual array. We do not gain much by comparing a film to a Freudian-style fantasy, but as long as we strip "fantasy" of its technical meanings, the word does capture that sense that mass market narratives can powerfully tap into a wide range of human needs and desires and serve as a kind of vicarious wish fulfillment. With those observations, I have no quarrel.

2. Movies and Emotions

> Conceive yourself, if possible, suddenly stripped of all the
> emotions with which your world now inspires you, and try
> to imagine it as it *exists*, purely by itself, without your favorable
> or unfavorable, hopeful or apprehensive comment. It will be
> almost impossible for you to realize such a condition of negativity
> and deadness. No one portion of the universe would then have
> importance beyond another; and the whole collection of its things
> and series of its events would be without significance, character,
> expression, or perspective. Whatever of value, interest, or
> meaning our respective worlds may appear imbued with are
> thus pure gifts of the spectator's mind . . . . And as the excited
> interest which these passions put into the world is our gift to the
> world, just so are the passions themselves gifts.
>
> WILLIAM JAMES[1]

Movies have seemed to many observers to be excellent metaphors for, or approximations of, human consciousness. If consciousness is to some extent self-directed through the patterns of salience we impose on the world around us, then, as Oliver Sacks writes, a movie,

> with its taut stream of thematically connected images, its visual narrative integrated by the viewpoint and values of its director, is not at all a bad metaphor for the stream of consciousness itself. And the technical and conceptual devices of cinema—zooming, fading, dissolving, omission, allusion, association and juxtaposition of all sorts—rather closely mimic (and perhaps are designed to mimic) the streamings and veerings of consciousness.[2]

Sacks's insight derives in part from the work of other scholars whose writing straddles the boundaries of philosophy and psychology. The early film theorist Hugo Munsterberg had similar ideas,[3] as did his colleague at Harvard, William James. James wondered if consciousness, although it seems continuous, is actually discontinuous and subject to the same sorts of illusions as a zoetrope. Henry Bergson wrote that the "mechanism of our ordinary knowledge is of a cinematographic kind."[4] Given that the cinema, in some way, mimics human consciousness, then we can understand why it makes sense to understand a film as a "way of seeing." Similarly, V. F. Perkins describes film as "the projection of a mental universe—a mind recorder."[5] For our purposes, however, "seeing" may be far too restricted, and "mental universe" may suggest something cold or abstract; a film is not only a way of seeing, but also a way of hearing, feeling, thinking, and responding. It presents not just a mental universe (of perception and cognition), but a holistic experience connected to the emotions, affects, and the body. It offers a particular experience of what it displays, of the fictional world presented. This way of experiencing mimics the phenomenological contours of conscious experience generally, and thus is complex and multifaceted.

The attractions of such "ways of experiencing" are many and diverse, but chief among them is the ability of many films to elicit emotion in the spectator, to provide suspense, surprise, fear, screams, anxiety, tears, relief, and calm in a temporal order that is vivid and ultimately pleasurable. If films approximate conscious experience like no other medium, they do so also in their ability to elicit emotional responses to that experience. Those emotions, as they occur inside and outside the movie theater, are the subject of this chapter. Before writing about emotion, however, I first posit some basic principles of human psychology that lie at the heart of my theory. I then discuss the psychology of emotion generally, and go on to show how film-elicited emotions relate to general human emotion.

AUTOMATICITY AND
THE PSYCHOLOGICAL UNCONSCIOUS

I call my theory of the elicitation of emotion in film a *cognitive-perceptual* theory. This I distinguish from what might be called (somewhat archly) "cognitive fundamentalism," which could be said to overemphasize the role of consciousness and deliberate cognition in the generation of emotional and affective response. Some critics of cognitive theories have assumed that all cognitive theorists insist on purely conscious evaluations in the genesis of human emotion. That is, the cognitive theorist might be thought to claim, for example, that the experience of fear requires that the fearing subject consciously subsume the feared object under the category "seriously threatening" or "dangerous" to the subject's life or well-being, and that such conscious deliberation must *precede* having the emotion of fear. On the contrary, much of what leads a person to have an emotion must occur at the level of what I call, after Gerard O'Brien and Jon Jureidini, the "cognitive unconscious." The feeling of fear is felt consciously, of course. But the processes leading up to that feeling may or may not occur consciously. Most cognitive theorists reserve an important place for the unconscious mind and unconscious mental processes—for the cognitive unconscious. As O'Brien and Jureidini write, it "is the *sine qua non* of contemporary cognitive science that human cognition [requires] unconscious operations."[6] It is also true, I would argue, that human emotion requires unconscious operations.

O'Brien and Jureidini claim that a good deal of experimental work demonstrates the existence of unconscious information processing. Experiments with dichotic listening, in which subjects are simultaneously presented with two channels of auditory information, show that when asked to attend to information in one ear, the subjects cannot consciously remember the information presented in the other ear. Yet although the information given through the unattended channel is not remembered consciously, subsequent behavior of the subjects suggests that the information has somehow been processed. Other research in subliminal perception shows that many kinds of stimuli presented below the threshold of consciousness can influence a subject's subsequent behavior.[7] These studies both suggest that perceptual stimuli are processed unconsciously, at least in part. Additional evidence for this psychological unconscious comes from studies in automaticity, cognitive neuropsychology, and hypnosis.[8]

The idea of the unconscious mind predates Sigmund Freud and psychoanalysis. In the nineteenth century, in his *Treatise on Physiological Optics*, Hermann von Helmholtz argued for the existence of unconscious inferences:

> The psychic activities that lead us to infer that there in front of us at a certain place there is a certain object of a certain character, are generally not conscious activities, but unconscious ones. In their result they are the equivalent to *conclusion*, to the extent that the observed action on our senses enables us to form an idea as to the possible cause of this action. . . . But what seems to differentiate them from a conclusion, in the ordinary sense of that word, is that a conclusion is an act of conscious thought. . . . Still it may be permissible to speak of the psychic acts of ordinary perception as *unconscious conclusions*.[9]

The cognitive unconscious is not limited to cognition, however. Researchers are currently interested in discovering more about unconscious perception, unconscious affect, and unconscious conation (pleasure and desire).[10]

There is much about the unconscious mind that is poorly understood, but it makes sense to appeal to a contemporary view of the psychological unconscious over Freudian models. Berkeley psychologist John F. Kihlstrom, long a proponent of what he calls the "rediscovery" of the unconscious, writes that there exists scant evidence for Freud's view that the unconscious "is the repository of primitive, infantile, irrational, sexual and aggressive impulses, repressed in a defensive maneuver to avoid conflict and anxiety."[11] The presence of an unconscious mind, I would argue, does not require an acceptance of Freud's particular schematization of it, or indeed any account rooted in some variation of psychoanalysis. The psychological unconscious is generally directed toward personal well-being (or adaptation, if you will), and is driven by motives beyond Freud's libido and aggression, such as desires for achievement, power, affiliation, and intimacy. The psychological unconscious, moreover, is modular and fragmented, sometimes consisting of the activity of narrowly focused processing modules or components; in this way, also, it differs from Freud's unitary unconscious, which typically functions at an executive level to control psychological activity.

Much of our behavior and many of our responses to our environment are beyond conscious control. Most of the time, we do not consciously decide to breathe, yet we do so. A sudden loud noise can shake us to the core without, of course, any conscious deliberation. Charles Darwin famously recounted his experience by the reptile cages at the zoo:

> I put my face close to the thick glass-plate in front of a puff-adder in the Zoological Gardens, with the firm determination of not starting back if the snake struck at me; but, as soon as the blow was struck, my resolution went for nothing, and I jumped a yard or two backwards with astonishing rapidity. My will and reason were powerless against the imagination of a danger which had never been experienced.[12]

Our ability to exercise conscious, intentional control over our behavior and responses is limited. Much of our behavior and many responses occur as a result of unconscious mental processes. In other words, they are automatic and not mediated by deliberate consideration.

Automaticity has been the subject of much interest in recent psychological research, with serious implications for any theory of spectator response to films. I will explore particular automatic responses in film spectatorship more fully in Chapter 4, but here I will simply introduce the concept as central to the cognitive-perceptual theory of response. Automaticity refers to the idea that certain patterns of human response in relation to perceived stimuli occur without conscious deliberation. They are not carefully considered but rather immediate, as though they were programmed into us. Such patterns, whether innate, established through experience, or the result of cognitive "framing," enable humans to respond to their environment quickly and efficiently. Automaticity manifests itself in three major forms: (1) the automatic effect of perception on tendencies toward action, (2) the automatic pursuit of goals, and (3) the continued automatic evaluation of one's experience.[13]

For example, most responses to the environment are determined not solely by the information available in the environment, but by how that information relates to a person's goals. If my goal is to escape harm from a threatening beast, I likely won't stop to admire a magnificent landscape I happen to pass on my escape route. My escape-related behavior and mental processing become automatic in relation to my goal of survival. My attention is directed to the salient details of the environment to accomplish that goal, and my body readies itself for the appropriate physical responses required for the situation. The goal of survival, once established, automatically structures my perception until I perceive the danger to abate. Automaticity also functions in film viewing in relation to goals. One might say that if film spectators become intensely interested in a narrative outcome, they develop the goal of discovering that outcome. This goal becomes automatic, and in part governs their response to the unfolding narrative until the goal is achieved. I respond with anticipation, curiosity, and suspense, because the narration has successfully established my overarching concern to find out what happens.

(On a side note, it must be noted that conscious deliberation may over time become automatic, replacing what were once conscious, deliberate mental activities with automatic responses and behaviors.[14] The film viewer may thus become primed to respond in a particular fashion to types of characters or situations, either from conventions established within particular films or broader generic conventions of response-elicitation.)

To a remarkable degree, automatic responses outweigh conscious deliberation. Were we to have to consciously think about our every movement, action, and reaction, our conscious minds would be cluttered and we would be unable to live in the world. Automaticity allows us to attend to one thing at a time, while our unconscious minds perform a thousand tasks beneath the surface of consciousness.

"Conscious inessentialism" is the view that consciousness matters little in our moment-to-moment responses and judgments. Various considerations, however, make it difficult to accept conscious inessentialism. When we draw our conscious attention to our environment, we can exercise an element of control over our decisions and behavior. We can consciously form habits of mind and behavior that alter our automatic responses. We are not wholly free, but neither are we merely automatons. That we exercise some degree of self-conscious, active control is an assumption that we cannot dispense with, for on this belief in self-determination, even in partial self-determination, rests the entire edifice of morality and justice, not to mention our sense of a self with a will, intentions, responsibility, accountability, and the ability to plan for a better future. So although I assign an important role to the cognitive unconscious and automatic responses in the generation of emotion, I also reserve a place for conscious judgment and deliberation in emotional life.

If our goal is to discover the means by which the unconscious mind responds to cinematic representation, we need not turn to psychoanalysis. Although it is as yet insufficiently developed in film and media studies, a cognitive-perceptual approach is not only more plausible, it also fits with contemporary research programs in psychology, cognitive science, and many related disciplines.

WHAT IS EMOTION?

With this basic understanding of the cognitive unconscious and the nature of automaticity, we can now turn to the emotions. I begin my account of emotion with a hypothetical example. For ease of reference, I will call this story "Jack, Jane, and the Bear." A man, Jack, is hiking in the mountains. He has been warned of grizzly bears in the area and is primed for danger. As he rounds a bend, he sees movement and the flash of a furry brown animal in the meadow a hundred yards in front of him. Jack's reaction is automatic and nearly involuntary; he becomes motionless, and his attention is fully drawn to the moving object. He places his arms at his sides, elbows bent, at the ready; he positions his feet so that, if necessary, he can quickly turn and flee or climb a tree; he thrusts his head slightly forward to get a better look. He slows his breathing so that he might hear every sound. His entire body, it seems, is directed toward identifying this potentially threatening entity and preparing for possible action. Then he recognizes that the animal is a large, brownish bear, foraging among the wild blueberry bushes. The bear senses Jack's presence, rears up on its hind legs, and spots Jack.

At this point, Jack perceives that the bear poses an immediate danger to his safety. His respiration quickens, his heart pounds, his stomach muscles tighten, and his mind races as he calculates the best plan of action. His eyes open wide and his eyebrows arch upward; his mouth opens. He is experiencing the emotion of fear. The bear begins to charge forward, toward Jack. Jack lets out an involuntary yell, his arms extended outward, and begins to back away slowly. The bear, however, for whatever reason, breaks off its charge, turns, and ambles away, moving out of sight. Jack's fear slowly subsides as he realizes that he is no longer in imminent danger. Jack is at first relieved, then elated that he has escaped injury.

In this book, I define an emotion as an intentional mental state, or what I call a "concern-based construal," that is often accompanied by various sorts of feelings, physiological arousal, and action tendencies. Emotions are disturbances, departures from the normal state of relative composure. Jack's fear is complex, involving (1) a primal concern for survival, (2) a perception or construal that survival is threatened, (3) physiological and autonomic nervous system (ANS) changes, (4) the subjective experience of strong feelings, (5) a mental and physical state of excitement or perturbation, (6) a specific form of behavior or action readiness (flight, defense), and (7) other outward manifestations in behavior (body language, facial expressions).

Most of these elements have been thought at one time or another to be the essence of an emotion.[15] Philosopher Robert C. Roberts, whose work has been influential in the development of my theory, rejects the tendency of some theorists to seek exceptionless generalizations in their accounts of emotion. Such a compulsion, he writes, "often leads to a procrustean and reductivist denial of facts and a conceptual artificiality that serve obfuscation as much as understanding."[16] Ronald de Sousa, another prominent philosopher of the emotions, takes a similar position.[17] Yet while I would like to avoid talk of necessary and sufficient conditions in favor of a "family resemblance" account of human emotion, it is undoubtedly true that my account finds some elements of emotion to be central, or closer to necessary and sufficient conditions than others.[18] Most importantly in this regard, I will be considering an emotion to be a kind of intentional relationship between a person and the world. At the core, an emotion is a mental state that is accompanied by physiological arousal.

A COGNITIVE-PERCEPTUAL APPROACH

Why a mental state? A cognitive-perceptual approach to emotions claims that kinds of emotions are distinguished in part according to kinds of individual appraisals or construals of a situation.[19] To return to "The Bear," Jack was frightened by the bear because he perceived that the bear threatened his survival. That is, he appraised or construed the bear as dangerous. Suppose that along with Jack on that day is another hiker, Jane. Jane is packing a small-caliber pistol in a side holster. She confidently (and wrongly) assumes that this diminutive weapon will protect her from any large and hairy beast. Jane also sees the bear, but Jane's construal of the situation will be different than Jack's. Jane is enthralled at the sight of this magnificent furry creature and believes that her trusty gun will protect her if it attacks. She feels only a twinge of fear, a fear that is submerged underneath the confidence her skill with the pistol gives her. As the bear charges, Jane holds the pistol in front of her, ready to fire if necessary. Since her small-caliber pistol is likely only to anger the bear if fired, Jane is in as much danger as Jack, if not more. Clearly, what distinguishes Jack's and Jane's emotional responses is their differing construals of the situation, not merely the "objective" situation itself. The kind of emotion experienced, then, depends not on the nature of the situation but on the appraisal of the perceiver.

Neither can emotions be defined by particular physiological or ANS responses. In the well-known Schachter and Singer experiment, persons injected with drugs to simulate the physiological characteristics that accompany emotions interpreted their own emotional states largely according to cues provided by researchers. Though undergoing strong physiological changes (such as increased respiratory and pulse rates), they did not report themselves as experiencing a particular emotion until they were provided a context of euphoria or anger, or in other words, until they were supplied with the appropriate "cognitions."[20]

Again, this is evidence for the importance of construals or appraisals in emotional experience, as well as for the intentional nature of emotions. Emotions are intentional not in the sense of being deliberative and considered but in their "aboutness." They express a relationship between a person and the world. Thus fear, sadness, anger, jealousy, shame, and guilt are words we use to describe relationships between persons, on the one hand, and an object (person, situation, environment) on the other, in relation to the person's concerns.

Neither situation nor physiological response are sufficient to determine emotion; in many cases, the individual's construal of the situation determines the kind of emotion that is experienced.[21] Lest this theory be considered too individualistic, however, it should be noted that individual construals are not always subject to the whims of an individual. Emotional experience is heavily influenced by cultural context and social convention, so we must not neglect the sense in which emotions, though experienced by individuals, are often shared and in part influenced by cultural and historical conditions.

In this book, as I said, I consider emotions to be mental states that are often accompanied by subjective feelings, physiological arousal, and action tendencies. Roberts provides a good model for such mental states. He calls emotions *concern-based construals*. Two things need to be said immediately about emotions as "concern-based construals." First, the construals of an emotion are not necessarily conscious states or carefully considered, reflective appraisals. As Roberts writes, "Construals have an immediacy reminiscent of sense perception. They are impressions, ways things appear to the subject; they are experiences and not just judgments or thoughts or beliefs."[22] A concern-based construal is like a perception in the extended sense of the word. It is the experiencing of a situation in its import; it may be felt as much as thought, it may be pre-reflective as much as reflective, and it may be, but is not necessarily, automatic. Although an emotion can be described in terms of a deliberative and conscious appraisal, it often results from what are, at least initially, unconscious and automatic processes.

Whether such a construal can properly be called "cognitive" in every instance depends on one's definition of the term. Theorists such as Martha Nussbaum, Robert Solomon, and Richard Lazarus claim that emotions are judgments. If judgments are construed as deliberative and conscious, my view would not qualify as a cognitive theory. Taking a broader perspective, however, cognition is also associated with automaticity and the cognitive unconscious, and my view would qualify. The cognitive unconscious must play a central role in emotional response. The particular disposition of an emotion depends on a partly unconscious conceptual system that automatically structures a person's experience and directs his or her behavior. Events are perceived to be more or less significant to the welfare of the self, and emotions are experienced depending on the automatic assessment of events and responses. Unlike Freud's unconscious, the cognitive unconscious is available to consciousness through introspection (under strict conditions) and can be inferred in others via the observation of emotional behavior. Thus, an emotion may not be caused by conscious deliberation (a conscious construal), yet may nonetheless be justifiably described ex post facto as an intentional, cognitive state, because it can only be characterized accurately as a perceived relationship between persons and their environment in relation to their concerns.

Emotions may result not from conscious appraisals but from habits of mind, innate responses (the way that pigeons respond to shadows in the shape of a hawk, for example), or what might be called "affect programs."[23] These are judgments, I suppose, in a loose sense. Emotions can also result from the associations of memory, when objects or events remind us of an emotion-laden past. Emotions might be modular, emanating despite conscious attempts to think oneself out of having that particular emotion.

Remember Charles Darwin's response to the adder recounted above. All of these factors—associations, habits of mind, and memory traces—may figure prominently into the experience and intensity of emotion. Whatever the causal genesis of emotions, be it conscious appraisals or processes that occur in the cognitive unconscious, emotions are intentional states expressive of a relationship between a person and the environment; they therefore have objects, that is, they are directed at something or someone, whether real or imagined.

So far I have discussed the nature of construals. What about concerns? Construals are "concern based," that is, as Roberts claims, they are "imbued, flavored, colored, drenched, suffused, laden, informed, or permeated with concern."[24] I have an emotion because I construe that a situation relates significantly to one or more of my concerns. Jack experiences fear in part because he is concerned with his safety; if he lacked this concern, then he would not have been fearful. I grieve at the loss of a loved one; I would not grieve had I not cared for him. I am happy because my niece does well at a spelling bee; I would not be happy except that I love her and want her to thrive. We have emotions only if we have concerns.

In this book I refer to any felt bodily states as *affects* (what some call the "low road"), and to concern-based construals as emotions proper (or the "high road").[25] Thus moods, reflexes, mimicry, and felt physiological and bodily responses are affects, while fear, suspense, and pity, for example, are emotions. As concern-based construals, emotions are a type of affect that involve a higher degree of cognitive processing than the usual affects and are more clearly identified as intentional mental states. My jealousy has an object, for example, the person who elicits the amorous attentions of my spouse. My jealousy is an intentional state in that it expresses a type of relationship between me and the object of my jealousy. A reflex action, such as the doctor eliciting a "kick" by tapping you on the knee, for example, is caused by something, but its causality is mechanical and hardwired rather than cognitive and complex. A reflex action may be caused by the appearance of a snake, but it does not take the snake as an object. That is, my flinching is not a mental state that can be said to be intentional. This distinction between affect and emotion is not meant to carry any heavy theoretical weight, and little of what follows depends on any particular distinction between affect and emotion. The distinction is necessary for the purpose of recognizing that while both affects and emotions may be automatic and noncognitive in their genesis, the entities I call emotions typically employ a higher degree of cognitive processing and are intentional states.

Some emotion theorists contend that the evidence supports a claim that some emotion is prior to judgment, and does not result from judgment. R. B. Zajonc discovered what he calls the "mere exposure effect," by which people come to like or prefer some polygons more than others simply because they've seen them a lot.[26] Such findings would bolster Alfred Hitchcock's often-made claim that audiences prefer stars in movie roles because they are familiar with them. If spectators can so easily come to prefer and like certain polygons by mere exposure, then it is no great accomplishment to get them to respond emotionally to James Stewart or Halle Berry. I have already established that in some cases, the appraisals or construals that figure into the emotions are automatic, occurring at the unconscious level. What seems to be at stake here is that in some cases, as with the mere exposure effect, these "judgments" have the primitive simplicity that I have associated with affects such as reflexes. It is for this reason that the distinction between affects and emotions, although it is very useful, must not be taken to be absolutely rigid. Various affective entities bear a relationship to cognition that is as yet unclear.

Emotions occur in relation to stimuli that matter to the organism. They occur very fast, are automatic, and result in ANS responses. Yet if prior cognition is not always necessary to have an emotion, one need not deny its importance in many cases. Moreover, cognition may figure into the experience of an emotion at a "post-causal" stage. Philosopher Jenefer Robinson points out that affective appraisals, which she holds to be initially noncognitive, initiate a response, and for subsequent responses can take complex judgments and thoughts as input. I would only differ with Robinson in her contention that emotions, or what she calls "affective appraisals," are noncognitive.[27]

It is probably true that some types of affective responses do not require judgment, if judgment is thought of as conscious deliberation prior to the experience of the emotion. Note, however, that my taking an emotion as a concern-based construal does not require that a construal be this sort of conscious judgment. Our response, having perhaps once been a conscious judgment, might later become habitual, automatic, and nonconscious. But such responses are cognitively penetrable, that is, in principle accessible to consciousness, as, for example, in rational-emotive therapy, in which the therapist initiates new patterns of response in the patient by altering the cognitions associated with various stimuli. Moreover, in defense of a more central place for cognition in emotion, we should also recognize that those who think of emotions as automatic "affect programs" rather than mental states tend to choose their examples carefully and write about simple affects, such as the startle response, that most closely fit their theories. As we move toward more subtle emotions, such as jealousy and shame, or combinations of emotions that stem from the complex processing of ambiguous situations, cognition becomes a much more central element. My distinction between emotions and affects is meant to call attention to differences in processing between simple, automatic responses and those requiring more complex construals.

There is one further reason to emphasize the cognitive components of emotion. It is vitally important to conceive of emotions as mental states. Emotional responses, whether they occur in or out of the movie theater, are not merely physical, but also mental. Bodily states are not "about" anything, but emotions are. Emotions are states of mind that are intentional. Thus, in "The Bear," Jack's fear is about something; it is about the bear and the perceived threat to Jack's safety. My anger with a friend who twice misses a lunch date is not merely a bodily state but an intentional mental state. In addition, my anger can be justified or not. Bodily states such as gastrointestinal disorders or heavy perspiration cannot be justified; one either has this bodily state or not. Anger or jealousy, on the other hand, can be justified or not on the basis of the accuracy and measure of my concern-based construal of a situation.[28] Thus, I call my theory a moderate cognitive-perceptual theory because it emphasizes the cognitive elements of emotion while recognizing other influences and determinations as central elements of emotions as well.

BASIC CONCEPTS AND TERMS

Before turning to film-elicited emotion, we should consider some basic emotion- and affect-related concepts that will prove to be important later. For now I will list these and offer a few clarifying remarks:

> *Emotions are experienced in time.* Emotions and affects occur in time and, like a filmic narrative, have a temporal dimension. Emotions are temporal processes, not static entities.[29] It follows from this that concern-based construals are also temporal processes. Our appraisal of a situation changes as the situation unfolds. In "The Bear," we see that Jack is initially alarmed and curious at the sight of the furry animal, then later feels fear after he identifies it as a bear and it spots Jack, then experiences full-blown terror as the bear charges. When the bear leaves off its charge, Jack's fear subsides.

Emotions evolve in response to feedback. As concern-based con-struals, emotions are subject to continuous feedback. Our emotional life occurs in streams that continuously evolve in response to ever-changing construals, actions and action tendencies, bodily states, and feelings. Any of these factors can serve as input to affect our subse-quent response.

Emotions are related to stories. The type of emotional state that a person experiences is in part determined by the kind of story he or she would most likely tell in explaining it.[30] As discussed more extensively below, this is one element of the social construction of emotions. Movies are influential enough that they have the potential to attach emotions and affects to kinds of stories, thus regulating emotional experience.

Emotions vary in intensity and duration. Emotions may be mild and fleeting, or strong and long-lasting. Emotions can build in intensity or gradually attenuate.

Emotions may be mixed or ambiguous. Paradigmatic sorts of emo-tions (anger, fear, enjoyment, etc.) may occur discretely, but emotions often occur in seemingly contradictory or ambiguous combinations. For example, one can be both horrified and fascinated by a monster in a horror film. While one can easily imagine such a situation, the overall experience is mixed in that the emotions contrast in valence (negative and positive) and associated action tendencies (flight or fear versus attraction and lingering proximity).

Emotions should be distinguished from moods. While emotions typically have reasons, moods have causes. Moods can be brought on by fatigue, the weather, depressive or elative drugs, physiological changes in the body, and the sensory input common to the viewing of movies, such as sounds or music, high and low key lighting, the perceived energy of the on-screen activity, or various elements of the film's sets and decor. Moreover, emotions are often specified by the object to which they are directed, but moods need not have an object. I may be anxious about a public speaking engagement, but I may sim-ply have free-floating anxiety. On the other hand, I cannot be afraid without being afraid of something. That said, moods and emotions are closely related.

Moods influence emotion and vice versa. Moods may affect the priming of a subject to experience a certain emotion, or may affect the intensity of an emotion. Having a particular emotion can dispose one to being in a particular mood, and being in a certain mood can predispose one to having certain emotions. If I am in a depressed mood, for example, I might well be more likely to construe a situation more negatively than if I am in an elated mood. Conversely, when I experience joy in relation to some particular event, this may well put me into a happy mood.

Priming refers to our situational, short-term propensity to experience a certain emotion or emotions. We are primed (or not) to experience an emotion by diverse factors, including mood, mental set, and immediately prior or simultaneously experienced emotions. In "The Bear," Jack has been primed to experience fear by warnings he has received that dangerous bears are in the area. Jane, who has been told that her pistol will easily protect her from any bear, has been primed in such a way that she will less easily experience fear when confronted with a bear.

Disposition refers to our long-term propensity to experience certain emotions in relation to situations and construals. In "The Bear," Jack has been jumpy his entire life. He tends to think that all wild animals are dangerous; he flinches when he sees a spider and thinks that the squirrels in his backyard have rabies. Thus, he has a disposition to experience fear when he sees a bear. Jane, on the other hand, is a fearless daredevil, courting danger as a kind of fun. Very little scares her, and she is disposed to remain calm in the presence of a bear.

EMOTIONS INSIDE AND OUTSIDE THE MOVIE THEATER

So far I have presented a general theory of the human emotions. Now I turn to emotions as they are elicited in movie viewing. Film viewing and emotions have been paired since the early twentieth century, when Hugo Munsterberg, one of the early theorists of what was then a relatively new art form, wrote that to "picture emotions must be the central aim of the photoplay."[31] Munsterberg's idea was cutting-edge at that time, having strong affinities with the new expression theories of art being propounded by Benedetto Croce and Robin George Collingwood. Expression theorists typically held that art should be an expression of the mind of the artist and/or expressive of feelings or emotions generally. For Croce and Collingwood, such expression of emotion takes on striking importance because it is seen as distinct from and prior to conceptual knowledge. Art becomes an essential way of knowing, offering a means unavailable to philosophy, history, and the sciences.[32]

Some art theorists have held that the noblest experience of art is experience of the "aesthetic emotions." Such emotions, as Clive Bell writes, reach "the superb peaks of aesthetic exaltation" and constitute a "sublime state of mind." "And let no one imagine," Bell continues, "because he has made merry in the warm tilth and quaint nooks of romance, that he can even guess at the austere and thrilling raptures of those who have climbed the cold, white peaks of art."[33] Bell fails to adequately describe the source of such aesthetic emotions, appealing finally to a vague concept of "significant form."[34] One doubts, in any case, that Bell would have thought that aesthetic emotions had any place in the viewing of *Bonnie and Clyde* (1967), *Terminator 2: Judgment Day* (1990), or *Charlie and the Chocolate Factory* (2005). The emotions of which Bell writes are reserved for elite artists and critics. But even if we grant that such "aesthetic" emotions exist, they are not central to my attempts to shed light on the kind of mass emotions generally elicited by movies.

Rather than posit some entirely different breed of emotion, I argue that "art emotions," the emotions and affects elicited by narrative film and the other arts, have close affinities with the typical emotions of our extra-filmic lives. Emotions at the movies tend to result from similar kinds of concern-based construals. Moreover, emotions experienced in response to fiction elicit facial expressions very close to those one might have outside the movie theater. In many cases, the physiological effects will also be much the same. In the movies and in life, sadness and sentiment may well lead to tears, joy and happiness to smiles, fear to tenseness and the characteristic pursed lip, and relief to an expulsion of air in the form of a sigh and relaxation.

To find similarities between emotional responses to life and emotional responses to films is not to make the claim that movies are wholly realistic. Of course, movies are hardly transparent recordings of reality, but instead are conventional, expressive, exaggerated, or otherwise manipulated expressions. Yet they nonetheless draw on the structures of response spectators bring from their extra-filmic lives. Even in the apprehension of moving images that depict fantastical and even impossible fictional worlds, the viewer must make use of real-world perceptual skills.[35] When movie narratives are hypercoherent, exaggerated, and wildly distorted, the maintenance of viewer interest demands a connection to the real-world schemas for the concern-based construals that constitute emotions. Thus a sentimental or exaggerated romantic comedy, though hardly realistic in many senses, still plays in part on typical extra-filmic (and also genre-created) schemas about romantic love and happiness.

Some theorists hold that film-elicited emotions are entirely homologous with those we might experience in our outside lives. Ed S. Tan argues that due to the diegetic effect, or what some have called the "suspension of disbelief," responses to the events of the fictional world are "witness emotions" that are "comparable to affect evoked by the sight of nonfictional emotional events in real life." Tan goes further yet, arguing that the "natural audience of the traditional feature film" would have the sensation of "being in the film," entertaining the illusion that "I am present in the scene" and that "the adventures of the protagonists are actually happening to me."[36] For Tan, then, the spectator at times has the illusion that he or she is an invisible observer of actual events. According to Tan's theory, a spectator seeing Jack and the bear on the screen might imagine that he or she is witnessing an actual human-bear confrontation, and might presumably feel threatened by the bear.

Richard J. Gerrig and Deborah A. Prentice, similarly, claim that the film viewer is like a side-participant in a conversation, and that what they call "*as if* responses," that is, responses to the fictional events as opposed to responses to the film as an artifact, "approximate the types of responses viewers would have were they really participating in the film's events."[37] Thus, in relation to our film of Jack, Jane, and the bear, the viewer might respond with calls such as "Watch out for the bear!" or "Your pistol isn't going to help you, Jane!"[38]

There are several respects, however, in which the emotions of the spectator are different than those experienced outside the theater. Two elements of the viewing situation are problematic for claims to direct participation of the sort advocated by Tan, Gerrig, and Prentice. First, the film viewer, unlike an actual participant, is obviously unable to influence the fictional events in any way. That is, there is a radical and ineluctable physical separation between the viewer and what he or she sees on the screen. While an actual participant might be inclined to intercede and otherwise physically respond, the film viewer is wholly freed from the responsibilities of—and indeed, is denied the possibility of—physical response. This creates a serious difference between the responses of a witness of or participant in a real event, and those of a spectator of a fiction film.

One might object that it is still plausible to think of spectator responses as witness or "as if" emotions, with the proviso that the analogy assume a kind of witness who cannot interfere with or have any effect whatsoever on what she or he sees. This sort of invisible, silent, unnoticed, and powerless observer, much like a film spectator, would be unable to affect the outcome of the events, and thus would be freed from the responsibility to take action.

This leads me to a second point. The fiction film spectator, unlike a witness or observer of actual events, knows that what she or he sees is fictional. The world of the narrative is neither physically present nor a representation of actual events, and the audience knows it full well. Were spectators to believe, even for brief seconds, that the battles between soldiers and alien insects in *Starship Troopers* (1997) were actually occurring, or even less plausibly, were viewers to have the illusion that they were themselves in the battle, their responses would have an unpleasantly forceful and terrifying quality that comes when we witness or experience actual calamities. It is essential to realize that the spectator has an implicit understanding that fictional movie events are narrated and not actually occurring and that the film is designed for a viewing that presumes a knowledge of the conventional, gamelike nature of the experience. Only those viewers with significant mental illnesses, temporary mental lapses, and/or the rare inability to distinguish between imagination and reality ever mistake what they see for a reality that is tangible and malleable.

The mental set of the spectator incorporates an understanding of the theatrical context and the public, conventional nature of film viewing. Even if viewers thought the events were actually happening not to them but to other people, they might respond by calling the police or trying to distract the bear. Spectators typically do none of these things because their response occurs within the context of a mental set that assumes the viewing of a film that narrates fictional events. I take acknowledgment of the spectator's awareness of the fiction *as fiction* to be central to an understanding of spectator response.[39]

THE PARADOX OF FICTION

If spectators or readers know that the events and characters of a narrative are fictional, as I have argued, then why do they respond emotionally to them? Is not such a response irrational and absurd? This "paradox of fiction" is especially troubling for cognitive theorists who argue that emotional responses invariably occur in response to beliefs. If viewers of *The Wizard of Oz* (1939) do not believe that Dorothy exists in Kansas or in Oz, why should they have concerns about her? If they do not believe that there is an actual Wicked Witch of the West, why do viewers respond as though this crooked-nosed, green-complexioned character poses a threat to Dorothy? This, stated in rather loose terms, is the so-called *paradox of fiction*.[40]

In response, first note that according to the cognitive-perceptual theory advocated here, belief is not essential to emotion. As I am thinking of concern-based construals, emotions can result from impressions or ways things appear to the subject; they are sometimes automatic and only partially rooted in judgments, thoughts, and beliefs. In the original formulation of the paradox of fiction, Colin Radford argued that if emotions do depend fundamentally on belief, then perhaps our emotional responses to fiction are irrational and undesirable.[41] To my mind, such a conclusion by a reductio ad absurdum throws doubt on the judgment theory of emotion, at least in its more extreme forms. The paradox of fiction is not so much a philosophical problem as it is a psychological one, since emotion, by my lights, is rarely the result of solely conscious deliberation, is sometimes automatic, and may result from some mix of contagion, associative memories, and concern-based construals rather than simply deliberative judgments rooted in belief.

But why, one might ask, are "automatic" and "unconscious" incompatible with belief? If I instinctively avoid a blow by flinching, surely it was because I believed I was about to be hit. Well, not necessarily. I may flinch instinctively even in cases in which I manifestly believe I will *not* be hit, say, for example, when a good friend pretends for the twentieth time that he is going to strike me but stops the blow at the last second. Or when the adder behind the glass at the zoo strikes at the glass. Our affective life, I would argue, is certainly influenced by our beliefs, but it is not wholly determined by them. In many cases, our modular minds generate responses that are in part independent of belief. Spectators may respond with anger or fascination or pity for fictional beings, but spectators also recognize the fictional nature of the story and respond with actual emotions tempered by their knowledge of the story's status as fiction.

Three prominent responses to the paradox in the philosophical literature are illusion theory, which holds that we *do* believe propositions about fictional characters (and about which I will say no more); pretense theory, which argues that spectators have emotions within the context of a game of make-believe;[42] and thought theory, which holds that spectators can have actual emotions in response to propositions they do not believe to be true.[43] Of these, thought theory currently holds the most favor. Roger Scruton, perhaps via Friedrich Frege, introduced the term "unasserted thought" into aesthetics, arguing that imagination involves thought that is unasserted, hence going beyond what is believed. We can respond emotionally to unasserted thoughts, such as imagining losing a loved one or imagining winning the lottery. Imagine smashing your thumb with a hammer; the more vivid your imaginative picture, the more likely you are to respond. The fact that we respond to mere thoughts, as Noël Carroll writes, "is a naturally endowed element of our cognitive and emotive structure, one upon which the institution of fiction has been erected."[44] We have emotional responses to nighttime dreams, daydreams, imaginings, and ideas.

We also respond to mere perceptual impressions in both the visual and aural registers. Automatic perceptual response is heightened in film, which presents powerful visual and aural impressions. If much of our processing of the visual and aural world is automatic and unconscious, it is not unreasonable to suggest that much of our processing of the images and sounds of the motion pictures must be so as well. To respond with a startle to the image of a striking snake is neither rational nor irrational, strictly speaking, but is rather a built-in feature of our perceptual mechanisms. Our initial, automatic response is in the second instance tempered, evolving according to the cognitive processing that the initial response elicits. Perhaps the label of rational or irrational can be applied to secondary cognitive responses and metaresponses, but it makes little sense to apply it to automatic responses. Moreover, if the thought theory is right, as I believe it is, the so-called paradox of fiction is not so paradoxical after all.

I have no doubt that some philosophers, and especially those who find the thought theory to be problematic, will be wholly unsatisfied with this brief foray into the paradox of fiction. It does strike me that to take the paradox seriously as a significant problem, however, one needs to embrace what I would consider to be a simplified and rationalized picture of human minds and their workings. We respond to fiction with actual emotions because the human mind is modular. Fictions engage the low road and generate affective and emotional responses independent of belief, while at the same time eliciting higher-order cognitive and emotional responses that prevent viewers from responding as though the fictions were actual events. If human responses were solely the result of rationalistic deliberations and separate from automatic and unconscious "built-in" mechanisms, perhaps the paradox of fiction would seem more troublesome.

PLAY AND THE REGULATION OF EMOTION

There is a sense in which all art might be thought of as a kind of play. Wolfgang Iser demonstrates that reading fiction involves games of various sorts, including play with referential worlds of a text, assembled positions (or points of view) of a text, possible worlds, and reader's expecta-tions.[45] Given this conception of fiction as playful, it would not merely be experimental narratives such as *Sliding Doors* (1998), *Memento* (2000), or *Adaptation* (2002) that elicit playful behavior in their manipulations of time and of relationships between story world and discourse world. Classical realist films are also playful, since they too depend on conven-tional understandings of the playfulness of fiction.

In the previous chapter I mentioned Roger Odin's claim that films invite spectators to inhabit a kind of psychic positioning and to take up a social role.[46] The kind of affective experience spectators have at the movies depends on viewing conventions, and moviegoing is associated in most cultures with leisure and entertainment. A fiction film is thus a form of play, with the spectator as a participant who, very often, plays along.

What does this mean for emotional response? First, the concern-based construals that constitute emotions at the movies are colored by the context of play. The fictional situation represented, in most cases, has no direct, short-term consequence for the spectator. The spectator has no responsi-bility to act and respond. Whereas extra-filmic emotions involve action tendencies and often the social or moral expectation to act, the spectator is freed from any need or compulsion to take action. Fiction, like play, can sometimes be wholly serious in its intent, yet even morally and politically serious fictions provide the distance that comes with make-believe. This playful context, free of the immediate concerns of the outside world, allows the spectator to undergo emotional experiences and to entertain desires that are experimental, exploratory, varied, and sometimes far outside the range of "normal" experience. From this stems the exhilaration, and also the possible moral threat, of spectatorship.

Spectatorship is playful and also conventional. In other words, play is governed (sometimes ineffectively or imperfectly) by the rules of social convention. In mainstream American viewing, the spectator's experience is regulated by Hollywood, a culture industry with ideological and economic interests that packages emotions for various tastes and purposes, and by the institutions that provide for the exhibition of movies. Thus, the play of emotion is often controlled for pleasantness, intensity, and duration to ensure satisfaction by the film's end. Hollywood also provides intense and conventionally unpleasant emotions for the demographic groups who seek them out. This is especially true of horror films (which offer the extremes of terror, fright, repulsion, and horror) and "gross out" comedies, such as *Jackass: The Movie* (2002) and *Van Wilder* (2002), that blend ironic, "knowing" comedy with the evocation of disgust associated with close contact with various bodily effluents. Movie emotions are packaged and sold, and a variety of affective experiences are available to the consumer.

Yet even independent films and films produced outside of Hollywood are regulated in various ways, according to the dictates of independent film cultures, conventional mores and customs, and the localized conventions of filmmaking and viewing. Play serves a social function and is bound by social convention.

KINDS OF EMOTIONS

How can we categorize emotions to better understand those that films elicit in viewers? Below is a table listing and describing the seven types of film viewing emotions I introduce in this section and the next. It should be noted that many specific emotions can be examples of more than one type. Also, some emotions will not clearly fit into one category or another, but may straddle the boundaries between them.

Films elicit both emotions of extended duration—what I call *global emotions*—and those that last only for a few brief seconds, which I call *local emotions*. The global emotions, such as suspense, curiosity, fascination, and anticipation, are important in maintaining the spectator's focus and concern throughout the viewing of a film. For Alfred Hitchcock, it was suspense, that "most powerful means of holding onto the viewer's attention," that causes the public to ask itself, "What will happen next?"[47] Ed Tan finds "interest" to be the most characteristic emotion of spectatorship. For Tan, interest is the glue that holds the spectator's attention, motivating him or her to continue viewing. High emotion points (local emotions), such as marked sadness, exhilaration, or terror, help to sustain interest and are more enjoyable, memorable, and intense than interest. But interest, Tan claims, ideally covers the entire span of the narrative and can serve as a background for shorter emotion episodes of other, more intense types.[48]

Some psychologists, including prominent theorists of emotion Carroll Izard and Nico Frijda, for example, *do* find "interest" to be an important and even basic or universal emotion. Izard holds that interest, or what he terms "interest-excitement," is "the most prevalent motivational condition for the day-to-day functioning of normal human beings,"[49] and is fundamental to human constructive and creative endeavors. Frijda similarly finds interest to be a fundamental emotion. For Frijda, each emotion has an associated action tendency. In this regard, interest encourages us to attend to something for the purpose of learning about it and also encourages us to orient ourselves to our environment.[50]

TABLE 1. *Types of Spectator Emotions*

Kind of Emotion	Definition	Examples
Global	Long-lasting, spanning significant portions of a film viewing	Anticipation, suspense, curiosity
Local	Brief in duration, often more intense than global emotions	Startle, surprise, disgust, elation, excitement
Direct	Take as their object the narrative content and its unfolding	Curiosity, suspense, anticipation, surprise, startle
Sympathetic/ antipathetic	Take as their object the concerns, goals, and well-being of characters, either for (sympathetic) or against (antipathetic)	Compassion, pity, admiration, happiness (sympathetic); anger, disdain, sociomoral disgust (antipathetic)
Meta-emotions	Take as their object the spectator's own responses or the responses of other spectators	Pride, guilt, shame, curiosity, disdain, surprise
Fiction	Take as their object some element of the film's fictional world	Widely varied
Artifact	Take as their object the film as a constructed artifact	Admiration, fascination, gratitude, amusement, disdain, anger, impatience

Taking interest to be *the* overarching film-elicited emotion, however, is problematic. Many psychologists do not recognize interest as a discrete emotion, while others consider interest to be a cognitive state preparatory to emotion, not an emotion itself.[51] Although in my opinion Tan is right to distinguish between local and global emotions in film viewing, I have reservations about identifying interest as a discrete emotion that is the fundamental global emotional experience of film viewing. Interest, if we assume that it is indeed an emotion, is so broad and far-ranging that it is nearly shapeless. In its milder forms, at least, it seems to be a precondition for any kind of directed, conscious activity.

The emotions are typically defined in part by a particular kind of concern-based construal, a paradigm scenario that becomes associated with that emotion. Fear results when we judge that an object poses a threat; the object of our anger is an agent who has committed a wrong against us; we feel shame or guilt when we judge that we have failed with respect to some standard or goal. Interest, on the other hand, seems to require only that an object have some more or less intense hold on our attention, of any type whatsoever. The possible objects of my interest in film viewing would include just about anything—a gruesome car accident, a salivating alien, a futuristic cityscape, a hairy spider advancing on Little Miss Muffet, or a vague repugnance upon seeing a star whom I dislike.

My thinking with regard to interest is similar to what I wrote about desire. Instead of positing interest as a univocal, single entity—a kind of emotion—I contend that when we say we are interested in a film, this interest stems not from a single emotion but from a variety of sources, including global, long-lasting emotions (suspense, curiosity, anticipation),[52] local emotions (fear, surprise, disgust), desires, aversions, pleasures, and what have you. One of the tasks of the filmmaker is to preserve the spectator's interest, but I do not acknowledge interest itself as an overarching, single emotion that governs film viewing.[53]

Tan's contention that we must distinguish between what I have called global and local emotions seems right, however. This distinction is based primarily on duration and textual function. Local emotions are brief, their function confined to specific segments of the viewing process; in some cases, through repetition and variation they take on an intermittent function of promoting global emotions. When viewing a film such as *Alien* (1979), surprise and shock often accompany the sudden appearance of the threatening alien, but such emotions do not last long. Indeed, their intensity precludes duration, if the filmmakers expect viewers to endure such a film. Global emotions such as suspense, anticipation, and curiosity, on the other hand, are longer in duration and serve to focus spectator attention over time. Suspense and anticipation play a major role in *Alien* when the spectator begins to suspect that the alien's attacks are both imminent and unpredictable. Thus anxious anticipation motivates the spectator, through much of the film, to be on guard and to watch for the alien's next appearance. The global and local emotions also mutually reinforce each other. In the case of *Alien*, the viewer's suspense and anticipation are fed by periodic shocks and surprises, and both long- and short-term emotions work together to create the contours of the particular experience offered by the film.

Therein lies a major difference between Greg M. Smith's "mood-cue" approach to film-elicited emotion and Tan's and my approaches.[54] Smith argues that "the primary emotive effect of film is to create mood" (42). Emotions are brief and intense, he writes. They often require an orienting state that "asks us to interpret our surroundings in an emotional fashion" (42). Thus for Smith, mood is the primary global affect of a film, priming the viewer for the emotions that come only in brief interludes.

In response, I would first note that Smith is not clear about just what a mood is in his system. A mood, Smith writes, is an "orienting emotional state" that serves an adaptive function by priming us to attend to particular stimuli, creating expectations and inclining us to experience certain kinds of emotions. Moods, then, are not emotions themselves but "orienting emotion states" and "tendencies toward expressing emotion." A mood is "a predisposition that makes it more likely that we will experience emotion" (39). The filmmaker elicits a mood, then, to better enable the elicitation of brief "bursts of emotion." And an emotion episode consists of a mood (emotional orientation) *and* "external circumstances" (39) or narrative situations.

Smith's insight is found in noting the importance of such orienting states to the elicitation of emotion in film. Yet to call such orienting states moods is problematic. Smith writes of "cheerful" (38), "suspenseful" (45), "comic" (50), and "fearful" (51) moods. He describes the mood elicited at the beginning of *Stella Dallas* (1937) as "embarrassment for Stella" and "anticipation of impending class-based catastrophe" (89). Yet suspense, fear, humor, embarrassment, and anticipation are most often thought of as emotions rather than moods. And in the case of *Stella Dallas*, the embarrassment and anticipation are clearly the result of the spectator's appraisal of character and narrative situation, rather than the result of stylistic cues or associations that Smith favors in the mood-cue approach. The orienting states that Smith describes are complex phenomena that might best be described as synesthetic affect (see Chapter 5), consisting of a wide range of mental and physiological phenomena, including both moods and emotions.

Smith claims that all emotions are brief and intense, but this is not the case. Global emotions such as anticipation and suspense can extend through longer periods of the film-viewing process and may rise and fall in intensity over long stretches of a film.[55] Moreover, as I have just argued, global emotions are essential in priming the viewer's attention and generating the expectations that Smith wants to reserve for mood. In many cases, the expectations generated by a film narrative are better described as having been elicited by long-term emotion(s) than by mood. In my cognitive-perceptual approach, the mood created by a film is at times a notable experience in itself, of course, but it can also function to enable and intensify both global and local emotions.

DIRECT, SYMPATHETIC/ANTIPATHETIC, ARTIFACT, AND META-EMOTIONS

By far the most important distinction among types of emotions for my purposes is among the direct, sympathetic/antipathetic, and meta-emotions. First, let us consider the distinction between direct and sympathetic emotions. Aristotle, considering art as the imitation of life, proposed two kinds of emotions in response to literary works. One is the emotions associated with understanding or coming to understand what the story, or "imitation," is of. As he puts it, people "enjoy getting to understand something." The other has to do with ordinary emotions appropriate to the situation that is the object of the mimesis, or imitation.[56] I call these ordinary emotions *direct emotions*.

Direct emotions stem from the spectator's concerns about and interest in the content of the unfolding story. Responses such as anticipation, suspense, surprise, curiosity, fascination, and excitement are direct emotions. The spectator may, for example, be intensely curious about how the narrative will unfold, surprised at a sudden narrative turn of events, or suspenseful as he or she awaits the outcome of a precarious situation. Direct emotions typically arise as new narrative information is revealed and we come to understand the story.

Sympathetic or *antipathetic emotions* arise from the spectator's assessment of a narrative situation primarily in relation to a character's concerns, goals, and well-being. Such emotions as happiness, sadness, compassion, anger, pity, and fear are characteristically sympathetic emotions, as we are happy or sad *for* a character, or angry or fearful *with, for,* or *at* them. While through various forms of empathy (discussed more fully below) we can share these emotions in part, our response is always differently inflected, typically more sympathetic than empathetic. That is, I may empathize with a character, but my response is never purely and solely empathetic, for the reason that I perceive the situation from my particular perspective rather than "from the inside." (The essential difference between character and spectator response will be explored more fully in Chapter 5.)

When spectators sympathize with and "feel for" a character, their affective experience must be different from what they imagine the character's experience to be. We often say we "fear for" or have "compassion for" a

4.   The spectator's fear in *Jurassic Park* (1993) is for the characters, not for the spectator him- or herself. Thus, the nature of the spectator's fear differs from theirs.

character. The spectator's fear while viewing the climactic showdown in *The Silence of the Lambs* (1991) is not that Buffalo Bill will kill the spectator, but that Buffalo Bill will kill Clarice Starling (Jodie Foster). Thus my fear is for her rather than for myself, making the fearful experience of my viewing both qualitatively and quantitatively different than my fear might be for myself. And compassion is an emotion that also takes the experience of another, not the subject's experience, as its object.[57] Sympathetic emotions are "feeling for" emotions, while antipathetic emotions, such as anger or contempt directed at an antagonist, are "feeling against" emotions.

Some emotions are neither direct nor sympathetic, taking as their object either the spectator's own responses or the responses of other spectators. I call these *meta-emotions*. The spectator may respond emotionally to his or her own prior responses, thoughts, or desires while viewing a film. Such emotions may range from shame and guilt to pride and a strong sense of self-satisfaction. The viewer may become teary-eyed during a sentimental scene (due to sympathetic pity or compassion), and then become embarrassed at crying (a meta-emotion). Alternatively, viewers might pity a character (a sympathetic emotion), then take pride in being the sort of person who pities others (a meta-emotion). Or a viewer might wish for the death of a certain character, then later become guilty or ashamed for having so wished the death.

We can also distinguish emotions on the basis of whether they take

5.   A fascination with the technology used to depict the dinosaurs in *Jurassic Park,* for example, is an artifact emotion.

the fictional world of the narrative or the film as an artifact as their object. The former are *fiction emotions,* while the latter may be called *artifact emotions.*[58] Both direct and sympathetic emotions are typically fiction emotions. Artifact emotions are all of the emotional responses that can be solicited directly by the artifactual status of film as opposed to the content of the fiction. Artifact emotions may include exhilaration at a particularly brilliant camera movement, disdain for a hackneyed screenplay, anger at the seeming contempt the filmmakers have for the audience, or admiration for the excellence of a film. The increasing tendency in contemporary Hollywood toward allusions to previous films may elicit pleasure and amusement. According to most illusionist models of film spectatorship, the viewer has predominantly fiction emotions while viewing a film. My contention is that artifact emotions are quite common in the viewer's experience. This is hardly surprising given, as I have claimed, viewers' implicit assumption of the fictional nature of what they see.

It is important to note that audiences can have artifact and fiction emotions simultaneously. When the viewer self-consciously admires (or disdains) the famous opening tracking shots of Orson Welles's *Touch of Evil* (1958) or Robert Altman's *The Player* (1992), these are artifact emotions. The content of these shots can simultaneously elicit fiction emotions. Moreover, there is a sense in which the tracking shots, by the way in which they present the fictional world, also elicit fiction emotions. A static long shot presents fictional worlds and characters differently from a tracking shot; perhaps the former projects stability or solidity, for example, while the latter projects malleability, fluidity, and energy.

MEMORY TRACES AND ASSOCIATIONS

Viewer emotions are typically elicited by external stimuli provided by the film, but responses to such stimuli are often dependent on the memories and associations the viewer brings to the film. In this chapter, I developed a working conception of human emotion that considers emotions as concern-based construals. Construals become emotions in relation to powerful concerns. I use the word "concern" here in a broad sense: a concern is anything that involves us, has a bearing on our interests, or worries us. When viewing *The Silence of the Lambs*, the viewer develops various concerns, ranging from a desire to see and learn more about the evil but fascinating Hannibal Lecter to a sympathetic concern that Clarice Starling escape the clutches of the killer Buffalo Bill and prove herself to be a worthy FBI agent. The stronger the concern, the more intense the viewer's emotional response will be. The stronger my fascination with Hannibal Lecter, the greater my curiosity about and anticipation of what he will do next. The stronger my concern for Clarice Starling's well-being, the greater my suspense as she confronts Buffalo Bill in his dark basement.

The intensity of viewer response depends on other factors as well. Other sources of affective power are memory traces, learned associations, and affective contagion. I will discuss affective contagion in some depth in Chapter 4, so here I primarily consider memory traces and learned associations. The emotions viewers have in response to films are partly the product of learning. Various pieces of music, images, sounds, and paradigmatic narrative situations become associated with prior life experiences and take on some of the emotional associations that viewers have had previously.[59]

Mental associations and memory traces may be sparked by the viewing of a film or other artistic work. This suggestiveness of works of art figures centrally in the Sanskrit poetics of Anandavardhana and Abhinavagupta, who discuss *rasa*, the feeling component of experiencing a work of art. For Abhinavagupta (as recounted by Patrick Colm Hogan), memories are both representational and emotional.[60] That is, we do not merely remember events or persons (as images, in language, etc.); we remember them *emotionally*. Our memories are suffused with the coloring of affect. Abhinavagupta believed, in addition, that there are times when these emotional memory traces are activated such that the representational content of the memory lies beneath the surface of consciousness, while the affective component emerges and is felt consciously. In other words, we feel something without conscious knowledge of the object of the emotion. Thus, works of art may elicit feelings that stem from emotion-laden memory traces without the representational content of the memory having been made explicit.

For Abhinavagupta, aesthetic pleasure "results from the 'generalization' of emotion in rasa, which is to say, the removal from the self-interest that is part of the link between the affect and the representational content in memory traces."[61] Rasa is emotion that is in part isolated from self-interest, is empathic in nature, and is for these reasons comparable to religious enlightenment.

My response to such claims is this. It may be that in certain cases, film-elicited emotions are caused by memory traces, learned associations, emotional contagion, and the like. More often, however, such stimuli serve as intensifiers or enablers of emotions, rather than the objects of emotions. To illustrate my point, I will provide a personal example. More than twenty-five years ago, a month after the unhappy end to a romantic relationship, I viewed the Elia Kazan film *Splendor in the Grass* (1961). This drama, set in rural Kansas, is about a teenage couple whose families pressure them to break up, causing the pair excruciating emotional pain. Although their breakup had only superficial similarities to my own experience, this film threw me into a fit of strong emotion that lasted for hours. While I would still say that it was the particular narrative of *Splendor in the Grass* that was the object of my emotion, there is no doubt that my recent experience with a wayward romantic other perhaps enabled, and certainly intensified, my emotional response.

Thus emotions and affects are elicited in films by prefocused narratives designed to foster concern-based construals, but are in part enabled and intensified by associations, habits, dispositions, or conditioned responses that suggest either the reasons for the emotion or the emotion itself.[62] In film, of course, such suggestiveness may occur in many ways, through whatever objects, persons, events, or environments that can be represented visually or aurally. When one considers the vividness with which films may represent events and other phenomena, it would not be an exaggeration to say that the medium has a particularly strong capacity to elicit affects rooted in memories and associations and to both enable and intensify associated emotional responses. What I claim in the next chapter is that Hollywood presents narrative paradigm scenarios—basic stories rooted in common human concerns—that are likely to have emotional resonance with a significant cross-section of the potential audience.

SUMMARY: EMOTIONS AT THE MOVIES

In this chapter, I argued that emotions are best conceived of as concern-based construals. Fiction film–elicited emotions are in some ways similar to emotional responses to actual events in that they are also concern-based construals. Film-elicited emotions differ in fundamental respects, however. First, an element of any spectator's mental set, and thus of her or his construal of narrative events, is a thorough awareness of the fictionality of what is seen together with some knowledge of the conventions of fiction in the film viewing context. Film-elicited emotions occur within conventional contexts of play and its regulation, and within the context of the institutions of fictional movies. The so-called paradox of fiction need not pose an insurmountable problem for moderate cognitive theorists, since emotions do not necessarily depend on belief, and in any case, the argument that we can have responses to "unasserted thoughts," if correct, dissolves the paradox. Film-elicited emotions come in many varieties, and recognizing various types helps understand their functions. This chapter distinguished between local and global emotions, fiction and artifact emotions, and direct, sympathetic/antipathetic, and meta-emotions.

Many questions remain. If film-elicited emotions are concern-based construals, how does the film's narration prod or manipulate the viewer's concerns, and how are construals of situations emotively prefocused? How does style contribute to emotive prefocusing? How does character engagement, or what many call "identification," figure in this process? In the following chapter, I turn to the specific means by which films elicit emotion in relation to narration, narrative structure, and character engagement.

3. Stories and Sympathies

> In order to discuss [films] critically we have to find ways of
> defining the nature of our involvement.
>
> V. F. PERKINS[1]

This book examines the elicitation of affect in mainstream American films, or what might be called Hollywood movies. This begs a question about what constitutes a mainstream movie. The popularity of recent unconventional films such as *Memento* (2000), *Adaptation* (2002), *Thirteen Conversations about One Thing* (2001), *Being John Malkovich* (1999), *Magnolia* (1999), and *Eternal Sunshine of the Spotless Mind* (2004) makes it necessary to delimit my object of study. These films are marginally mainstream in their widespread distribution and popularity, but to one degree or another, they experiment with form and style to such an extent that they differ significantly from conventional filmmaking. In this book, I concentrate on films that illustrate significant conventional practices for the elicitation of emotion. Just as film production teachers often advise students to learn filmmaking conventions such as the 180-degree rule or three-point lighting in order to better understand alternative techniques, I think it is wise to first examine affect elicitation in mainstream films before turning to more formally daring and creative works.

In this chapter, I describe the ways movies in the "classical Hollywood style" are designed to elicit emotion through narrative structure, character engagement, and the employment of conventional narrative scenarios. This chapter identifies some of the primary structural features of the classical Hollywood cinema, or what I simply refer to as "movies," as they relate to affect and emotion. The classical Hollywood cinema is a mode of filmmaking designed to elicit strong emotions, and it does so in large part by means of identifiable conventions.

AFFECTIVE PREFOCUSING

Emotions have many roles in human life; one of these is the "searchlight function."[2] As we make our way through the world, we are bombarded with diverse stimuli, most of which we ignore and some of which we pay attention to. Emotions direct us to quickly and efficiently sort out what is salient from what is not, helping us organize these sense impressions into gestalts. Thus, we not only pay attention to certain details and ignore others, we also search the environment for specific types of stimuli relevant to our concerns about and appraisals of the environment in which we move. Emotions direct us to salient elements of our environment, bringing relevant perceptual phenomena to our attention.

When we watch a film, our attention is also at play, and we direct it according to our concerns about and construal of the fictional situation unfolding before us. Unlike the outside world, however, many fictions—and certainly mainstream movies—are *affectively prefocused*.[3] Built into a movie is a particular way of seeing events and characters, a specific order and duration to those events—in short, a built-in gestalt or perspective. Most mainstream films seem designed to elicit very specific emotional responses, such as fright and suspense in much of *Jurassic Park* (1993), or sentiment, tears, and laughter in romantic comedies such as *Sleepless in Seattle* (1993) or *You've Got Mail* (1998). Independent films of a certain sort are more likely to elicit ambiguous or contradictory affects or emotional distance. Jim Jarmusch's *Stranger Than Paradise* (1984), *Down by Law* (1986), and *Mystery Train* (1989) preclude the strong character allegiances and emotional responses of mainstream film, instead opting for an ironic and distanced response. Yet even this distancing is a type of emotive prefocusing that discourages strong sympathetic responses and encourages ironic amusement and a distanced curiosity.

All films are affectively prefocused to some extent. We might even say that many narrative films are in part embodiments of sequences of concern-based construals in the medium of film. That is, films represent characters and events but also embody or prefigure ways of responding to them. These construals may be unified and cohesive, or they may be ambiguous and even contradictory in valence. In whatever case, it makes sense to think of a narrative film as representing narrative events presented in such a way that they are prefocused to provide a particular complex of affective experiences.[4] This being so, the spectator's response to the film depends on a willingness to assent to the prefocused construals it offers.

The spectator may assent to or resist the intended responses embodied in prefocused narrations, and may do so in whole or in part.

PARADIGM SCENARIOS

To get at the relationship between film stories and emotions, consider this observation. Emotions, like film viewings, occur not as static events but as temporal processes. Emotions unfold in time according to the subject's evolving construal of situations. As psychologist James R. Averill writes, "Emotional feelings are not like snapshots that capture only events of the moment. Instead, they resemble motion pictures that depict a story."[5] The fundamental arena for study of the processes of emotions is the person-environment relationship, as the individual finds him or herself in situations that unfold in time. These person-event relationships might be called adaptational encounters, or episodes. Such adaptational encounters result in concern-based construals that are in transition from moment to moment as the conditions of our lives change. Emotions are a process; they change and flow over time. We experience emotions, then, in relation to the narratives of our lives as responses to unfolding situations and our concern-based construals of those situations.

Emotions and storytelling thus have clear connections. As concern-based construals, emotions can be communicated as stories—stories we tell ourselves about our experiences. Narrative films, simply put, are representations of concern-based construals not about ourselves, but about fictional events and characters. Movies tend to consist of hypercoherent narratives that organize experience to a much greater degree than we would normally face in our lives. Not only are movie narratives prefocused, exaggerated, and dramatic, but their subject matter is drawn from the kinds of scenarios that will be accessible to mass audiences.

As children mature, they are made familiar with the vocabulary of the emotions through "paradigm scenarios," types and sequences of events that are associated with certain emotions. As Ronald de Sousa writes, "our emotions are learned rather like a language and . . . they have an essentially dramatic structure. The names of emotions do not refer to some simple experience; rather, they get their meaning from their relation to a situation type, a kind of original drama that defines the roles, feelings, and reactions characteristic of that emotion."[6]

Small children learn to identify emotions through paradigm scenarios they see acted out in their lives. By the age of two or three, toddlers become aware of other people and of the fact that various participants in the same situation will respond differently to that situation depending on their role in it. By the age of three, children begin to understand that certain events are associated with particular emotions, and that their actions may lead to another's distress or delight. Most importantly, infants first learn to talk about emotions via stories, and by the time they are four or five years old, they associate stories with corresponding emotions. Stories, art, and culture continue to teach us about emotions later in life. De Sousa claims that "in literary cultures, [paradigm scenarios] are supplemented and refined by literature."[7] (It is perhaps a symptom of residual elitism that de Sousa omits mention of the influence of popular narrative in the visual media, which would seemingly play an important role in such processes in the contemporary world.)

We seem to be genetically programmed to respond with specific emotions to certain types of situations. Cross-culturally, a clear and immediate threat to one's survival—the impending crash of an airplane on which one is a passenger, for example—elicits fear. Culture and various forms of socialization influence responses to various paradigm scenarios, however. The same paradigm scenario—the theft of a valued object, for example—may elicit anger in both men and in women, but gender socialization might differ in regard to the expression of anger and its "criteria of appropriateness." Anger tends to be accepted more in men, while some may consider angry women as "bitches," or worse yet, "hysterical" (which denies the legitimacy of their anger altogether). Thus, a man may be socialized to experience an episode of anger as indignation, while a woman may be less inclined to assign blame, and instead feel sadness or frustration.[8] This is important to note not only for its revelations about this specific case, but also because it points to the flexibility of a cognitive-perceptual model in dealing with spectator differences. In this case, the cognitive-perceptual model of emotion can account for gender differences that might influence both the construal and the concern on which it is based, thus altering the nature of the emotion experienced.

Consider the paradigm scenario for fear. Fear occurs when the subject construes her or his safety or well-being as being significantly threatened, and the object of the fear is the source of the threat. The relationship of emotions to stories is a key to the ideological significance of Hollywood, because the movies show us how and what to fear by constructing and foregrounding objects of fear, formulating the nature of the threat, and demonstrating "proper" responses. Should we fear swimming due to the threat of sharks, or sleeping alone in dark bedrooms that might be haunted by ghosts? The movies have an influence in altering and exaggerating our fears, in part based on the scenarios for fear that are consistently repeated. We call scenarios that are consistently repeated until they become conventional "paradigm scenarios." Not all paradigm scenarios as portrayed in film are so simple and distinct as the scenarios for fear in the above examples. Film genres also embody combinations of paradigm scenarios, scenarios that are exaggerated, transformed, combined, and repeated according to various conventions.

Emotions, then, are drawn from scenarios, the very stuff of narrative. Frederick H. Lund writes that "fear, horror, disgust, repulsion, aversion, dislike, annoyance, anger, sadness, sorrow, despair, hopelessness, pity, sympathy . . . are not descriptive of so many internal or organic states. They are descriptive of objective situations and of accepted modes of handling and dealing with these."[9] Emotions are ways of interpreting the world, constructing and drawing from narrative paradigm scenarios that frame a situation as one for which a particular sort of response—anger, indignation, compassion, jealousy, for example—is appropriate. The prefocused narratives of movies, then, are also ways of interpreting the world, not only by what they show, but in their manner of focusing emotional response.

PRIMARY EMOTIONS AND THE MOVIES

What sort of paradigm scenarios does Hollywood draw from? Many scholars emphasize the place of emotions in organizing common behaviors that are necessary to all organisms to survive. These universal behaviors include, for example, protection of the self (fear), destruction of enemies or obstacles (anger), reproduction (love, affection, joy), rejection (disgust), loss and/or reintegration (crying, sadness), and exploration (expectation, surprise).[10] Each of these behaviors is a response to particular kind of adaptational encounter.

Most psychologists make a distinction between those emotions thought to be more or less innate and essential for human adaptation and those culturally conditioned to a greater degree.[11] The more culturally variable emotions, such as envy or jealousy, are greatly variable across cultures and not readily seen in other species. On the other hand, the basic emotions—fear, anger, sadness, joy, and love and affection—can be observed cross-culturally and even in other species. Psychologists differ significantly in their estimations about how many emotions are primary or basic and just which emotions those are. Rather than get into these debates, however, I am content to make use of the basic assumption that some emotions are more universal than others.

Most often, movies are made up, at least in part, of paradigm scenarios that correspond to primary emotions and to common adaptive behaviors. Although movies sometimes intentionally make appeals to segmented audiences, they typically represent scenarios to which people can respond across demographic lines and, increasingly, across cultures. My argument is not that people respond to the same scenarios in the same way; it is merely that the narratives consist of common emotion scenarios. These are often scenarios of coupling/mating, integration into the social group, and/or survival in the face of threat.

In *Beowulf* (2007), for example, the titular hero defends his tribe against the voracious Grendel and later a fire-breathing dragon, couples with two different women in addition to a womanlike entity (the alluring cave monster played by Angelina Jolie), and wrestles with shame for his ill treatment of his queen. The relevant paradigm scenarios here are survival, coupling and/or mating, and an integration into the social group that may involve conflicts between individual and group desires. *Titanic* (1997) embodies similar paradigm scenarios of coupling/mating between Rose (Kate Winslet) and Jack (Leonardo DiCaprio), integration into or departure from the social group (as Rose must decide whether to leave her family and fiancé for Jack, and Jack is invited to dinner among the social elite), and survival in the face of catastrophe (the sinking of the *Titanic*). In *Jaws* (1975), the protagonists battle for survival against a voracious enemy shark, but the story also centrally involves the formation of a social group in the face of grave danger, as the very different personalities of the sheriff, the shark expert, and the grizzled sea captain must mesh in order to form a unified front against their mortal enemy. *Do the Right Thing* (1989) explores the difficulties of integration within the group (family, ethnicity) and between groups (ethnicities). In *Pretty Woman* (1990), Vivian (Julia Roberts) not only finds romantic love (coupling/mating), but must explore, orient herself to, and incorporate herself within her new environment and social group (an elite, wealthy society).

These are all situations that correspond to common paradigm scenarios that are, to some degree at least, cross-culturally understandable and to which diverse individuals can respond. Aggression and survival, coupling and mating, integration into the group—all of these are subject to specific cultural and historical circumstances. Nonetheless, these scenarios retain core elements that are fundamental to human existence. The economic requirements of Hollywood filmmaking make the appeal to basic scenarios unsurprising.

If paradigm scenarios are understandable to large numbers of people, it is nonetheless true that particular types of scenarios will appeal to some more than others. Thus, Hollywood uses genre classifications to allow audiences to choose kinds of scenarios that promise specific kinds of emotional experiences. Action/adventure films appeal to the supposed masculine concerns of survival, acquisition of goods, heroic fantasy, and power and aggression, eliciting emotions such as suspense, excitement, anger, and vengefulness, but most importantly offering a fast-moving and strongly visceral experience. Romantic comedies replay scenarios of romantic union, and melodramas replay scenarios of social separation, union, and sacrifice among lovers and families generally. Both melodrama and romantic comedy underplay the visceral excitement of action and movement in favor of the sympathetic emotions and affective responses. The Western, of course, is set in a specific geographical and historical context, but nonetheless retains some cross-cultural appeal because its scenarios are more generally tales of masculine negotiation between the demands of wilderness and civilization, as well as a kind of ritual exercise of power (violence) for revenge or self-preservation.

Hollywood stories, then, do not simply report a series of events; movies elicit desires, aversions, concerns, and sometimes judgments, all rooted in variations on the most basic paradigm scenarios. Narrative literature and film are uniquely suited to expressing and embodying emotional experience of the prototypical kind, that is, they embody emotions as the concern-based construals spectators have in relation to the unfolding events of the narrative. This is not *only* a matter of expression, however. To comprehend a narrative, the spectator must not only recognize the expression but also engage with it by, at least to some extent, *having* something like the desires and affective responses initiated by the narration.

Hollywood fictions, so described, are commodified, prefocused construals designed for varied purposes—first and foremost, for pleasures and entertainment. Economically successful mass storytelling depends in part on the ability of the filmmakers to maintain interest; to delight; to arouse curiosity, suspense, and surprise; and to generate occasionally intense emotional responses such as fear, anger, pity, and relief. Narrative form, as Kenneth Burke writes, is "an arousing and fulfillment of desires."[12] Most typically, Hollywood narrative is an arousing and fulfillment of *mass* desires, rooted in narrative scenarios that are salient to a broad spectrum of persons.

HOLLYWOOD AND THE NEW HOLLYWOOD

Before exploring the formal means by which Hollywood films elicit emotion, it is worth briefly describing the "classical Hollywood cinema," for this is the model on which our analysis is based. The "primitive" period of cinema began in 1894 with cinema's origins and lasted until somewhere around 1906 to 1908.[13] This period, a "cinema of attractions"[14] in the words of Tom Gunning, was heavily influenced by vaudeville, and appealed to audiences primarily through simple comedy and melodrama, trick effects, exotic scenery, and other forms of spectacle. Around 1910, the classical style of narration began to emerge, and it was fully in place by 1917. The classical style embodies various stylistic and narrative conventions described below, in addition to the general aesthetic conventions of unity, transparence, clarity, and a balance of complexity and simplicity.

For many critics, the "new Hollywood" of the past three or four decades has forsaken the evocation of deep emotion characteristic of classical Hollywood for the surface amusements of spectacle. David Denby, film critic for the *New Yorker,* calls this new trend "conglomerate aesthetics":

> In contrast to films made before 1960, which seem to modern audiences to wallow in pathos, modern films provide spectacle and excitement without emotion. Blockbusters like *Kill Bill* and *Pearl Harbor* offer audiences the opportunity to be spooked, titillated, dazed, impressed, and blown away without giving them the chance to share in any of the characters' feelings.[15]

To put this in my terms, Denby is claiming that recent Hollywood films have forsaken both sympathetic emotions and the general complexity and depth of emotional response for the cheap effects of superficial direct emotions—the fascination and cheap thrills of mere spectacle.

Hollywood has changed, and for some scholars, the change has been epochal, allowing for the establishment of a new period or phase in the history of Hollywood film—the New Hollywood. The movie business has seen increased concentration of power, with 1990s Hollywood dominated by five companies that control the industry more completely than did the majors in the studio era.[16] For the first time, in 1990, Hollywood films earned as much box office overseas as they did at home, and by 1994, foreign box office surpassed American box office.[17] Hollywood films play to an international audience and cater to what is increasingly a world market for motion pictures.

Justin Wyatt describes what he says is "perhaps *the* central development" of "post-classical" cinema, what he calls "high concept," a style of filmmaking molded by these new economic and institutional forces.[18] This is a style in part determined by the demands of marketing, with an emphasis on easily sold premises or "pre-sold properties" (such as stars, adaptations from well-known novels, sequels, etc.), a visual form presentable in advertising, and marketable soundtracks. Those who make and market motion pictures have learned from advertisers, who understand that amidst the glut of material littering screens both large and small, an ad with "pop"—sexy models, kinetic action, or striking, easily comprehended images of any sort—is more likely to gain attention. Like advertisers, the New Hollywood often embraces such techniques, a tendency that has been exacerbated by computer-generated images and the ease with which filmmakers can now manufacture special effects that seem to have become the dominant focus in many films. The most extreme statement of the "New Hollywood" thesis comes from Christopher Sharrett, who sees a decline in Hollywood narrative as a sign of late capitalist malaise, arguing that "traditional notions of storytelling disappeared in the hyperactive montage of a new cinema that is essentially visual entertainment, the eye candy of image culture where the referent vanishes amid a whirlwind of spectacular editing."[19]

I would argue, on the contrary, that any claim that classical Hollywood narrative structures have disappeared is clearly false. To find that some recent films have become superficial spectacles, as David Denby does, is not to deny a remaining current of films with engaging characters, involved narratives, and strong emotions. To write of the New Hollywood as a clearly defined break with classical Hollywood is misleading. The changes should not be minimized, yet there remain marked stylistic and structural continuities between the films of classical Hollywood and those of New Hollywood.

In a survey of scholarship on "post-classical" Hollywood, Peter Kramer notes that most scholars identify significant departures from classical storytelling in contemporary Hollywood, but also acknowledge "that the majority of American films stay firmly within the classical tradition."[20] Kristin Thompson, for example, contends that modern Hollywood narratives "are put together in much the same way as they were in the studio era," and that the basic storytelling tenets of the classical cinema are alive and well.[21] To illustrate, this she analyzes narrative structure in ten mainstream Hollywood films of the 1970s, 1980s, and 1990s, including *Tootsie* (1982), *Back to the Future* (1985), *The Silence of the Lambs* (1991), *Amadeus* (1984), and *Alien* (1979). Classical narrative structure is clearly alive, and although we must be sensitive to the idiosyncrasies of individual films, it nonetheless still makes sense to consider generalizations about "classical Hollywood" and its use of narrative structure for the elicitation of emotion.

NARRATIVE AND CHARACTER

The overarching structure of classical Hollywood narrative is well known, and there is no need to repeat here what has been done well elsewhere.[22] A narrative is an emotively prefocused, structured set of evolving events, usually centering on one or more characters. The formalist toolbox of narratology will be immensely useful if the user remembers that the human significance of narrative fiction is not merely to enable comprehension (as some cognitive theories seem to assume), but to provide a rounded experience consisting of pleasures derived from the arousal, delay, and fulfillment of desires, as well as from affect, emotion, and a host of varied cognitive activities.

Let us first consider how the classical narrative elicits direct emotions. Direct emotions, the reader will remember, have as their object the development of the story events and, more broadly, the contours of the fictional world of the film. Direct emotions can be seen, in Aristotle's words, as responses to the viewer's getting to understand the content of the narrative as it unfolds. During the viewing process, the spectator continually surveys the film for unexpected changes and novel information. When a film does its work, the spectator responds to this "coming to understand" the story with surprise, curiosity, interest, anticipation, and fascination. Spectator desires come into play here in a wish to understand what has happened, to anticipate what will happen next, and to put new events into context.

The Royal Tenenbaums (2001), for example, presents the spectator with at least nine idiosyncratic characters whose lives all center around the Tenenbaum house, a rambling mansion peopled by a family of eccentrics and filled with strange items such as Dalmatian mice and the odd memorabilia of a quirky and talented family. One of the pleasures of this film is the satisfaction of the spectator's curiosity about these odd persons as the film gradually reveals details about their lives in an extended exposition that lasts well into the first half of the film.

Although the film is a network narrative following the lives of several characters, it gives the most screen time to Royal Tenenbaum (Gene Hackman), the patriarch who has been absent from the family for about twenty years. Royal is forced by circumstance (lack of money and home) to

6.   The emotional appeals of *The Royal Tenenbaums* (2001) in the end depend on the film's ability to elicit sympathy for Royal Tenenbaum (Gene Hackman).

attempt to reintegrate himself into the family. Simultaneously, he learns that Henry Sherman (Danny Glover) has been courting his estranged wife Etheline (Anjelica Huston). Royal notes to a friend that Etheline is still his wife, and that "no damned two-bit chartered accountant is going to change that." The spectator's curiosity and anticipation have been stoked; these are direct emotions, depending little, at least initially, on any sympathy or engagement with Royal or his family. The audience wants to know how Gene Hackman's troublemaking cad is going to accomplish his goals, or fail in the trying.

Next consider sympathetic emotions, which typically occur not in response to such "coming to understand" processes, but rather arise when the spectator assesses the narrative situation in response to a favored character's predicament and goals. When the viewer develops a concern that the goals of a character be met, this creates a desire for the attainment or maintenance of the character's desired state or the escape from or avoidance of an aversive state. In the case of sympathetic emotions, spectators typically align themselves with the character's concerns, and their construal of the situation is guided by this alignment. In this way, the emotive success of *The Royal Tenenbaums* depends on the film's ability to elicit spectator sympathy for Royal, despite his rather questionable behavior. After Royal fakes an illness to play on the family's sympathy, he is revealed as a liar by Henry Sherman and leaves the house in disgrace. But the experience has changed him; he says the six days back with his family have been "the best six days of my life." Royal begins to act to his family's benefit, offering his advice, staging an intervention for family friend Eli Cash (Owen Wilson), who is addicted to mescaline, getting to know his grandsons, granting his wife her sought-after divorce, and even saying a few kind words to Henry, her fiancé and his former rival. At this point, Royal's goals and those of the spectator become aligned. Royal wants to reconcile with his family and to make up for two decades of betrayal and failure as a father and husband. The spectator's emotional responses to the film, by its end, become wholly tied to an acceptance of the goals of Royal Tenenbaum. It is intended that his concerns become congruent with the audience's concerns, and the film's affective trajectory becomes more sympathetically rooted in Royal's experience and, to a lesser degree, that of the other characters.

Spectator response need not presume a wholesale acceptance of the goals of a character. Some films create an especially interesting friction between the goals of a sympathetic character and those of the viewer. I will explore this more fully in Chapter 5, so a few brief examples will suffice here. In Clint Eastwood's *Unforgiven* (1992), the viewer is meant to gradually distance him or herself from at least some of protagonist William Munny's goals and behaviors as he becomes increasingly violent and vengeful.[23] Such a process of misaligned goals is also common in romantic comedies, in which the spectator desires a romantic union of the two protagonists long before either member of the potential couple has such a desire. In *The Shop around the Corner* (1940), for example, two feuding clerks at a small Budapest shop unknowingly fall in love via a lonely hearts club that puts potential lovers in contact with each other through the mail. Since they've never met their correspondents in person, they continue to dislike each other in their work relationship. The viewer's desire that they form a romantic union generates a suspenseful tension between viewer and character goals, a tension that is relieved when the mistaken identities are cleared up and the favored romantic union is achieved. Sympathetic emotions form when the spectator judges a threat to the maintenance of a desired state for a character. Although the viewers may or may not share the goals of a sympathetic character, the viewers want the character to maintain or attain the desired state, or escape or avoid an aversive one.

The strongly emotional nature of Hollywood film does not preclude a third sort of emotion called artifact emotions. Artifact emotions, you will remember, take as their object the film as artifact rather than the content of the fictional world (although it is sometimes difficult to distinguish between the two). Time and again, contemporary Hollywood filmmakers have demonstrated that films can elicit strong direct and sympathetic emotions while incorporating reflexive markers that draw attention to the film as a film. The classical Hollywood film is moderately self-conscious, drawing explicit and implicit attention to its status as an artifact in various ways. Most obviously, the titles and credits identify the film as a manufactured product that has been given a name by its makers. Credits also identify the creative personnel and their functions on the film. Certain genres, such as comedy, maintain more instances of explicit reflexivity throughout the film. Think of *Wayne's World* (1992), in which Wayne and Garth (Mike Myers and Dana Carvey) directly address the camera at several points in the film. In most cases, however, self-conscious references to the film as artifact become less common after the titles, and spectators are encouraged to immerse themselves in the fictional world presented. Even here, however, I would argue that the spectator is often consistently reminded of the film as a discourse. This occurs during displays of filmmaking virtuosity, for example, a stunning montage sequence or some remarkable special effects. It occurs in cases of intertextual references that reward the spectator savvy enough to pick them up. It occurs due to the star system, in which the spectator never fully loses the sense that he or she is watching Katie Holmes or Tom Cruise, and not simply the characters they play on screen.

Again, *The Royal Tenenbaums* is a case in point. Not only does the narration self-consciously present its story as a book with chapters, but its gently ironic stance consistently draws attention to the film as artifact. Director Wes Anderson displays art and artifice in the quirky characters, occasionally ludicrous dialogue, and idiosyncratic production design. For an example of the latter, consider Eli Cash's house, on the walls of which are prominently displayed two obtrusive and disturbing paintings by Miguel Calderón, in front of which various characters conveniently pose as the camera makes the paintings a focus of attention. (The supplemental materials on the Criterion edition of the DVD include essays and interviews about the paintings.) For another example, after Chas chases Eli Cash and throws him over a brick wall, we see that Eli has landed squarely in a well-groomed Japanese garden. A few moments later, Royal knocks on the front door of an apartment to ask for permission to enter the backyard, and a traditionally dressed Japanese woman answers the door. Both the garden and the woman's exotic sartorial splendor seem incongruous in this urban American environment. One of the film's intended affective responses is laughter, humor, and perhaps admiration, artifact emotions directed at the imagination shown by the filmmakers. Thus, the film draws attention to its artificiality throughout, all the while attempting to elicit the strongly sympathetic emotions that depend on the spectator granting weight to the fictional characters and world of the film. This consciousness of the film as artifact plays a more central role in spectator response than is sometimes realized.

To sum up, I consider a fictional narration as the expression of an evolving sequence of concern-based construals that simultaneously take as their object the story content of the fictional narrative, the characters in relation to the narrative, and the work as a constructed artifact. Although we must appeal to the formal elements of the film to understand its workings, these formal elements do not constitute the ultimate significance of the film. My final goal is not to analyze form per se, and not to discover the means of comprehension, but rather look at how these elements influence and otherwise relate to the concern-based construals that lead to a wide range of affective phenomena. Ideally, we cannot stop with form, comprehension, and affect either, for these phenomena relate to ideas, to rhetoric, to ethics, and to ideology.

CLASSICAL NARRATIVE STRUCTURE AND EMOTION

The classical Hollywood cinema, in particular, has developed certain conventions of storytelling—many, no doubt, based on older conventions in drama, literature, and oral traditions—which have clear functions in the manipulation of audience emotion. Narrative form is not simply a matter of the organization of cues to facilitate story comprehension; it also encourages a chronological pattern of emotional response. (Of course, comprehension and response must often work in tandem.) Not all movies share the same narrative structure, of course, but within the classical paradigm, certain tendencies, or norms, appear frequently. These are well known, and here I mention the most central to demonstrate how an understanding of the emotions can account for their prevalence as conventional practices.

The exposition of a story consists of background information about setting, events, and character—information the viewer or reader needs to properly understand the story. In the Hollywood cinema, exposition is often concentrated (provided in one section of the narrative) and preliminary (coming before the main narrative action). It is meant to arouse the spectator's curiosity (a direct, global emotion) and typically initiates the process of character engagement by introducing the protagonist and her or his environment (thus preparing the spectator for the later elicitation of strong sympathetic emotions).

The story of *The Royal Tenenbaums,* for example, is literally introduced as a book with chapters. The film's first image shows a book titled *The Royal Tenenbaums* being checked out of the library. As the book opens, we see shots of the old brick Tenenbaum mansion, and a voice-over narrator (Alec Baldwin) intones: "Royal Tenenbaum bought the house on Archer Avenue in the winter of his thirty-fifth year." The voice-over, accompanied by illustrative, intentionally artificial tableaux, then goes on to describe the Tenenbaum family, the separation of Royal and Etheline Tenenbaum, and the accomplishments and sundry troubles of the three children (Chas, Margot, and Richie). By the end of this exposition, the spectator understands Royal's failures as a father and something of the effects his actions have had on his children. An emotion is a concern-based construal, and a construal quite obviously requires information. The exposition, which may initiate sympathies and antipathies for the characters, should arouse curiosity. It is only after this exposition in *The Royal Tenenbaums* that the viewer is given the intertitle "Chapter One."

The classical narrative usually begins with a stable state of affairs, a period of relative calm during which the exposition occurs. Though the affective processes may be aroused by simple acquaintance with the protagonist, stronger sympathetic emotions are often elicited later in the narrative. We can think of an emotion as a disturbance with both physical and cognitive dimensions; it is a divergence from the normal state of the person that involves changes in the body's physiological equilibrium. This relative lack of emotion characterizing the organism in a "normal" state corresponds to the stable state in the classical Hollywood narrative structure. The exposition is sometimes considered boring. Many spectators' capacity for curiosity is soon met and may be exceeded, requiring stronger emotions to maintain interest. (In some movies, exposition is delayed or distributed to minimize the possibility of audience boredom.)

The catalyst of a narrative consists of a violation of the stable state. A giant shark attacks a swimmer off the coast of New England in *Jaws* (1975). Thornhill is mistaken for a double agent and kidnapped by foreign spies in *North by Northwest* (1959). A tornado strikes Dorothy's Kansas farm and whisks her into the land of Oz in *The Wizard of Oz* (1939). A wife leaves her husband, forcing him to raise their small son on his own in *Kramer vs. Kramer* (1979). Martians invade Earth in *The War of the Worlds* (1953, 2005). A psychologist is shot and badly wounded by a former patient in *The Sixth Sense* (1999). In *The Royal Tenenbaums,* the catalyst is Royal

Tenenbaum's decision to reintegrate himself with his family and estranged wife, initially for purely selfish motives.

The catalyst functions in part to introduce a problem for the protagonist, throwing obstacles in the path of the achievement of her or his desires, and thus, often, is also a threat to the achievement of audience desires. With regard to the sympathetic emotions, the "concern" part of the audience's concern-based construal arises from the gap between the desired goals for the character and the actual, probable, or possible outcomes that conflict with those goals. The violation of the stable state in a narrative, then, corresponds to a physical disruption brought on by an adaptational encounter. The requisite emotional response depends on the spectator's assessment of the situation both in relation to her or his own desires, and in relation to the goals and predicament of the protagonist. The sudden or gradually emerging conflict raises a concern, and the viewer's construal of the unfolding situation leads to emotional experience. In mainstream films, what follows will be a consistent ebb and flow of emotion, rooted in clear and relatively simple paradigm scenarios, and kept simple and on course in what is commonly called a linear narrative.

To see the importance emotion elicitation holds for Hollywood film, one need only look at the elements of classical Hollywood story structure. All such conventions are employed for the manipulation of audience emotion and the construction of a salient affective experience. Small bits of exposition are scattered throughout the narrative. Since an emotion depends on narrative information, each scene must "bridge in," that is, carefully set the place, time, and mood. It must provide a minimum of exposition to enable basic understanding—just enough information to allow for a construal, but not so much as to bore the viewer. In addition, each scene should ideally reveal something additional about the major characters or expose some bit of new information necessary to understanding the narrative. All of this encourages the continuation of the global and direct emotions that keep audiences fascinated, curious, and interested, both anticipating possible future events and estimating the significance of new information.

The conventions of Hollywood screenwriting give evidence of an implicit concern with the proper spacing of powerful sympathetic emotions and for the maintenance of direct emotions throughout the narrative. The overall structure of the narrative is thought to consist of either three or four acts, each act punctuated by a major turning point or reversal that changes the direction of the narrative, or in other words, significantly alters the protagonist's goals.[24] The story structure maintains direct emotions with surprises, uncertainties, deadlines, or problems that lead to anticipation, suspense, and further curiosity about future narrative events. It maintains sympathetic emotions by altering the status of the major characters with respect to their goals and desires, thus creating the possibility for new kinds of emotions and mixtures of emotions.

The most obvious example in *The Royal Tenenbaums* occurs after Royal is kicked out of the house after lying to his family and pretending to be terminally ill. The experience has changed both his motivations and his goals (and thus constitutes a major turning point). He has previously been insincere in his efforts to integrate himself into his family and reconcile with his wife. His insincerity had made it difficult for spectators to respond to him sympathetically, and the emotions and affects elicited in the film up to this point are primarily direct and artifact emotions. One of the major turning points in the film occurs after Royal takes a sincere interest in his family's well-being and begins to act not in his own interest but in the interest of his family. At this point, the nature of spectator emotional response changes, allowing for strong allegiance and sympathetic responses that are gradually increased until they reach their climactic point at the film's end. Thus, major reversals not only alter the course of narrative events but also alter the nature of spectator responses.

While a conventionally structured film consists of three or four acts, it can also be divided into scenes, of which there may be roughly twenty to thirty. A scene is typically defined as a unit of action that occurs in a single location. In a conventional narrative, each scene must include conflict that blocks character goals and suggests possible outcomes that threaten the spectator's desires for the narrative and characters. For example, the spectator desires that Harry (Clint Eastwood) punish and perhaps kill the villainous Scorpio as the wounded Scorpio whimpers on the grass of the football stadium in *Dirty Harry* (1971). Yet Harry is constrained from shooting Scorpio because Harry represents the law, and to do so would break the law. Thus, many spectators experience frustration stemming from the lack of fulfillment of their desire, perhaps subjectively experienced as frustration with the law itself. From this kind of conflict between a desired and actual state (and sometimes from the resolution of the conflict) stems much spectator emotion.

To provide direction for the viewer's concern-based construal, each scene should have a direction, some favored goal for the character or narrated events that suggest to the viewer a favored outcome. The scene's direction specifies the desired goal or state, and conflict makes attainment or maintenance of that goal or state problematic. When the audience strongly desires an outcome for a character, and when that outcome is uncertain, the audience becomes concerned, and emotion is elicited.

Some screenwriting manuals also contend that each and every scene must have a reversal, although these minor reversals need not be as momentous as the reversals that occur between acts. Such reversals occur in *The Royal Tenenbaums*, for example, when Henry Sherman proposes to Etheline Tenenbaum, when Richie shaves his hair and beard and attempts suicide, when Chas and his sons move back to Archer Avenue, and when Margot leaves her husband, Raleigh St. Clair, and moves into the Archer Avenue house.

We often hear of the cliché of the Hollywood happy ending, but many films offer mixed endings that nonetheless manage to provide a moving emotional experience for audiences. *Witness* (1985) develops two plot lines, as John Book (Harrison Ford) must protect himself and his adopted Amish family against corrupt New York cops and decide what to do about his growing love for Rachel (Kelly McGillis), the Amish widow who nurses him back to health after he is shot. Book succeeds in vanquishing the cops during a shootout in the barn, but decides that it would be wrong for him to stay with the Amish Rachel or ask her to leave with him. Part of the success of this movie is the complex emotions it encourages in its bittersweet resolution. Corruption has been banished and the evil cops disposed of, dissolving fear and suspense into relief and a feeling of well-being. The Amish society, presented as Edenic and uncorrupted, has been preserved. Yet Book and Rachel, who love each other, must part, which may elicit sadness and regret. Although Book loves Rachel, he threatens the Amish society; thus, his departure preserves the integrity of the group, which has been lovingly represented as a homogeneous subculture uncorrupted by the outside world that Book represents. This encourages a return to normalcy and a calming of the emotional disturbances that the film has calculatedly provoked thus far. The conventions of closure and the happy ending aim to provide the audience with an experience ending in consummation, relief, and relative tranquility. Even if it is mixed with some negative emotions, such as regret and sadness, the audience rests easy in the belief that Book has acted admirably, as the traditional hero should.

To leave it at this, however, would be insufficient. A classical narrative must do more than simply ratchet down emotion by resolving all of its problems and answering all questions posed. Certainly, relief plays into a successful resolution, as the audience is released from its cares and is restored to a state of psychological and physiological calm. The most successful films do more than relieve us, however; they also move audiences, such that viewers are simultaneously relieved and exhilarated. The emotions generated by the film's end may be hybrid and complex—mixtures of admiration (for the insight the film provides or for the behavior of the protagonist), reflexive self-congratulation on the viewer's part (for having had the right sort of response), and joy or happiness that events turned out as the viewer had desired.

The Royal Tenenbaums has this sort of conventional ending, but with an interesting variation. If spectators have the desire that the dysfunctional Tenenbaums be healed and united as a family, then their desires are attained. After Chas's sons are nearly killed by Eli Cash's careening car, Chas responds angrily by chasing Eli Cash through the house, knocking a priest down the stairs, and throwing Eli over a brick wall and into a neighbor's Japanese garden. After considering what he's done, Chas jumps over the wall himself and lies next to Eli, in an apparent act of reconciliation. Chas's sons lose their pet dog in the accident, so Royal purchases a Dalmatian from the firemen responding to the accident and gives it to Chas as a replacement for the dead pet. Upon learning this, Chas shows his first signs of affection for his father, suggesting that their reconciliation has begun.

Like many comedies, *The Royal Tenenbaums* ends with a ritual community celebration signaling successful social integration (one of the most basic narrative paradigm scenarios). But it isn't a recommitment ceremony between Royal and Etheline; rather, it is Etheline's marriage to Henry Sherman. Royal grants Etheline a divorce, thus allowing her to marry a good man who promises to bring some stability to the family. Nonetheless, Royal has been invited to the wedding, has succeeded in integrating himself into the family, and has even begun to heal some of the brokenness that was in part due to his earlier actions as an errant father.

But there is even more going on here. The dramatic trajectory of *The Royal Tenenbaums* is also designed to foster a kind of emotion that we might call, after psychologist Jonathan Haidt, "elevation."[25] Of course, it should be noted that although Haidt claims to have identified this previously unnamed emotion, the very idea that psychologists can continue to identify new emotions is a fascinating and somewhat bizarre idea. Yet it is not implausible. It certainly suggests—and rightly so, I think—that our emotional lives are complex and nuanced, and that our language for speaking of the emotions can be elaborated on and improved. In any case, this emotion of elevation quite aptly describes the sort of emotional response generated by many narratives of the melodramatic variety. Elevation, Haidt writes, is the opposite of social disgust, triggered by the witnessing of acts of human beauty or virtue. In the epilogue of the movie, the spectator learns that Royal Tenenbaum died of a heart attack at age 68. All of the major characters are present at his funeral. As they leave one by one, the camera tracks to a close-up of his grave, with the epitaph Royal thought up himself: "Died tragically rescuing his family from the wreckage of a destroyed sinking battleship." The epitaph conveys a sense of Royal's histrionic personality and thus is partly ironic. It also demonstrates the film's preferred response to Royal as the protagonist, which is quite sincere in intent. Royal did save his family, though he was largely responsible for sinking the family ship in the first place.

Elevation, Haidt suggests, draws its power from a desire for moral betterment. In *The Royal Tenenbaums*, it is Royal who changes the most, beginning as a selfish cad and failed father and ending as a man who hopes the best for his family and expends considerable effort acting on their behalf. If spectators have come to have sympathy for the Tenenbaums, and if they strongly desire the family's reconciliation, then spectator desires are met—a happy ending. Moreover, the spectator witnessing and appreciating Royal Tenenbaum's moral improvement will experience elevation. However quirky or odd the characters are, *The Royal Tenenbaums* nonetheless provides a classic Hollywood resolution designed to both relieve and exhilarate audiences.

CHARACTER ENGAGEMENT

On seeing *Terminator 2: Judgment Day* (1991) at the theater, "cooperative" viewers—that is, viewers who allow the film to do its intended emotional work—develop a particular liking or disliking for various characters. Perhaps the spectator sympathizes with Sarah Connor (Linda Hamilton) and her desire to protect her son from the terminator assassins. Perhaps viewers admire the Terminator (Arnold Schwarzenegger) for his strength and tenaciousness. And the liquid metal T-1000 (Robert Patrick)—well, audiences fear and despise him for his lack of sympathy and the machine-like way in which he relentlessly pursues Sarah's son John. These sympathies and antipathies, as I will show, are an essential component of the film's intended emotional effect, and they encourage the viewer to develop deep concerns that lead to emotional response.

The very possibility of the audience's engagement with fictional characters rests in part on the human tendency to personify and respond to abstract, nonhuman entities, especially in the context of visual representations. Psychologists have demonstrated this in some intriguing experiments involving animated geometric representations. Subjects who are shown a short movie depicting triangles and circles moving around on a surface nearly always interpret these movements as the interactions of intentional agents.[26] The subjects attribute intentions to the triangles and circles, seeing their activity as self-directed. Small wonder, then, that audiences respond to animated characters such as Shrek or Snow White as though they were persons.[27] Given this human propensity, it is unsurprising that photographic depictions of fictional characters on the screen are taken to be personlike as well.

Not only do audiences see such characters as personlike, with intentions, beliefs, and desires, but they often respond to such characters empathetically, and sometimes strongly so. Eighteenth-century philosopher and economist Adam Smith writes, "However selfish soever man may be supposed, there are evidently some principles in his nature, which interest him in the fortunes of others, and render their happiness necessary to him, though he derives nothing from it except the pleasure of seeing it."[28] Smith called this "sympathy" or "fellow-feeling." When we sympathize, we tend to experience an affective state that is congruent with that which we observe in the character. The sympathetic observer feels pity for a homeless beggar, joy for a competition winner, sorrow for the bereaved, and so on. (This is in distinction to a hostile or antipathetic response, which would feel disdain for the beggar, jealousy directed at the competition winner, and smug satisfaction or *Schadenfreude* in the face of another's misfortune.)

Contemporary psychology and philosophy continue to investigate this complex process. It may be termed either sympathy or empathy, depending on one's preferred terminology. The idea of sympathy has its roots in eighteenth-century moral philosophy, while "empathy" derives from German aesthetics and the term *Einfühlung*, or a projecting of oneself into that which one observes.[29] Neither sympathy nor empathy are in themselves emotions, but rather a capacity or disposition to respond with concern to another's situation, and often an accompanying tendency to have congruent emotions, that is, emotions that share a similar valence. Depending on the character's situation, sympathy and empathy may arouse emotions as diverse as happiness, fear, anger, compassion, resentment, moral disgust, and so on.

It hardly needs proving that audiences respond with sympathy for fictional characters. Here Alfred Hitchcock's folk psychological observation about sympathy seems right (although he uses the term "empathy"); audiences tend to sympathize most strongly with those who are familiar to them and whom they like. Hitchcock insisted on the importance of obtaining major stars for his films because the public was familiar with them. When a major character is played by a secondary star, Hitchcock says, "the whole picture suffers, . . . because audiences are far less concerned about the predicament of a character who's played by someone they don't know."[30] Sympathy is key to strong audience response, Hitchcock says, because it is a means by which the audience becomes emotionally invested in the narrative situation. And note that Hitchcock uses the word "concerned." If emotions are concern-based construals, as I have argued, then the viewer's concern about what happens in the narrative is elicited in part through sympathy with the characters.

Before getting too deeply into the contours of empathy, sympathy, and antipathy, it might be wise to define these terms. It has become commonplace in aesthetic theory to sharply distinguish between sympathy and empathy.[31] I would argue, however, that such distinctions are counterproductive, for three reasons. First, they are stipulative rather than descriptive. Second, they fail to correspond to actual usage of the terms. Third, they tend to generate as much confusion as clarity. Empathy is sometimes thought to be the viewer's sharing of the emotions of a character, while sympathy, as Amy Coplan describes it, "involves caring about another individual—feeling *for* another," and "does not as such involve sharing the other's experiences."[32] Empathy, for Coplan, requires that the observer share identical or very similar emotions with the observed, while sympathy requires only concern and/or "feeling for," rather than "feeling with," and presumes no shared experience.

As I argue more extensively elsewhere, the distinction between sympathy and empathy is fraught with ambiguities and contradictions.[33] When an observer responds "congruently" to a character, that is, in such a way that demonstrates the observer's fundamental solidarity with a character's interests, it will typically be a response neither solely sympathetic nor empathetic, strictly speaking. Sympathetic/empathetic responses are usually mixtures of both shared feelings and "feelings for," and more often, they elicit congruent emotions that are not identical or even similar to those of the character. How often does one empathize with a character without also sympathizing? Or sympathize without also sharing some element of the character's presumed feelings? When my friend loses her mother to an illness, I share her sadness (to a diminished degree, perhaps), and I also pity her. My response is congruent in that it takes the same evaluative perspective, or valence, on an event, but nonetheless may involve somewhat different emotions than those my friend experiences. My friend grieves; I may grieve, but to a lesser extent. I feel pity for her, yet in her grief she does not necessarily pity herself. The emotions I experience, then, are affectively congruent but different in both strength and kind.

Just as in the example above, the film viewer will rarely, if ever, share identical and nothing but identical emotions with the emotions the viewer presumes a character has. I may share fear with a character as she faces grave danger, but my fear may be interspersed with pity (which the character does not feel) or suspense (because I know something about the situation that the character does not know). Those who strictly differentiate between sympathy and empathy may claim that this, as in the previous example, is a case in which the observer is both sympathetic and empathetic. If most such responses are mixtures of sympathy and empathy, however, then the usefulness of the distinction is thrown into question. Would it not be better to loosely use either "sympathy" or "empathy" to refer to this complex process, rather than multiply distinctions that play out only in the seminar room?

Another reason to remain skeptical of strict distinctions between sympathy and empathy is that such a distinction is stipulative and conforms neither to common usage nor to any solid consensus in current psychology. The words "sympathy" and "empathy" are often used interchangeably by regular English speakers. This is no wonder, since dictionary definitions often do not correspond to the stipulative definitions described above.[34] Moreover, there is very little agreement in the psychological literature about just how to think of empathy and sympathy.[35] Some define empathy as little more than cognitive role taking, without the feeling component. Some, such as Adam Smith, define sympathy to include the processes Coplan defines as empathy. Many psychologists have defined empathy as a process that does not require identical or even similar emotions with the object of our empathy, but rather merely congruent emotions (this is the conception of empathy I prefer).

These terminological difficulties and attempts to parlay subtle distinctions can sometimes be very confusing. Psychologist Lauren Wispé, for example, writes that empathy "is more likely to involve the same muscles and reactions as those in the sufferer, while sympathy responses may be similar rather than the same." On the other hand, to know "what it would be like to *be* [another] person" is sympathy, while to know "what something would be like for the other person is empathy."[36] But, one wants to object, if empathy involves the very same muscles and reactions as those of the sufferer, why would this not give us a sense of what it would be like to *be* that person? To maintain a strict separation between sympathy and empathy becomes a very troubling enterprise, and is probably more trouble than it is worth.

In this book I typically use the term "sympathy" rather than "empathy," and in line with the recent turn in psychology away from fine distinctions, conceive of sympathy as encompassing, depending on specific instance, vicarious emotion, role taking, and the ability to understand the situation of others.[37] The condition of sympathy, I argue, is typically marked by what I call *affective congruence*, a state in which the viewer is concerned for the plight of a character and may experience emotions that have similar orientation or valences with characters yet are rarely, if ever, identical. Thus, the viewer may sympathize with Maximus (Russell Crowe) in *Gladiator* (2000) when he finds his family slaughtered or when he is forced to fight for his life against great odds. We may even share some of the ostensible feelings of Maximus; spectators may be sad and moved to tears, for example, when he finds his family dead. Yet the viewer's external assimilation of his predicament cannot have the same affective charge we assume Maximus feels. After all, not only are these dead the family of Maximus (and not the spectator's family), but viewers have a background assumption of the fictional, gamelike nature of the viewing experience. In addition, the viewer may feel not only sadness but also pity for Maximus, while it is doubtful that Maximus would feel pity for himself (stalwart warrior that he is). The viewer's response will be congruent in that it is oriented toward the same general object, the death of Maximus's family, even though the emotions experienced will differ in degree and in kind.

Much more attention is generally paid to empathy and sympathy than to antipathy, indifference, and mixed feelings, as though viewers were prone to compassion and not to disdain and dislike. (It is unclear to me why antipathy and disdain receive so much less attention than sympathy and compassion, but perhaps it has something to do with a hesitancy to explore the darker side of human nature.) Hollywood assumes that most audiences prefer a strong and clear moral compass that assists them in developing strong desires and concern-based construals. Thus, many mainstream films offer characters who clearly embody good and evil to ensure that audiences will run on the same emotional track. If the spectator has sympathy for Maximus in *Gladiator*, she or he will strongly disdain the mentally warped emperor of Rome, Commodus (Joaquin Phoenix), and perhaps enjoy the emperor's violent demise at the hands of Maximus. If one of the pleasures of movies is compassion for the good, another is the satisfaction of disdain and hatred for evil.

CHARACTER GOALS AND ENGAGEMENT

The viewer's engagement with characters is complex, consisting of various cognitive activities and affective responses. It may involve sympathy, empathy, antipathy, neutrality, cognitive assessment, emotions, motor mimicry, and/or emotional contagion (discussed in the following chapter). Classical Hollywood cinema typically features one or more goal-oriented protagonists with whom the viewer is meant to have a kind of psychological allegiance. This is a feature designed to enable a clear orientation for the spectator and increase the likelihood that he or she will respond congruently with the film's prefocused concern-based construals. If the viewer grants allegiance to a character, and the character has clear goals, then the viewer is more likely to strongly desire that those goals be met. Strong desire leads to concern, and concern in the face of threats and obstacles elicits emotional response.

The international "art" cinema encourages character engagement of a different sort. Characters in the "art" cinema often lack the clear-cut goals that mark the protagonist in movies of the classical Hollywood paradigm.[38] Many times, characters in the "art" cinema undergo an existential crisis that leaves them paralyzed, uncertain, or unable to act. Modernist antiheroes are in conflict with themselves, have incoherent goals, and are often "victims" of this condition. Though these are no doubt also common human conditions (and thus may be "realistic"), such characters don't enjoy the mass popularity of the active, goal-oriented characters usually featured in movies, instead appealing to an audience that finds interest in a film despite (or perhaps, due to) the lack of a strong allegiance with a character.

In Fellini's *8½* (1963), for example, Guido, the protagonist, is hardly sympathetic, although the film allows some affection for him. In fact, many of the narrative pleasures provided by the film seem to stem from a kind of distanced, ironic evaluation of his character on the part of the viewer. Guido juggles the various women in his life, obsesses about his insecurities and lack of creative imagination, and negotiates the demands of his numerous coworkers on the film they are making together. But at the end of *8½*, rather than resolve these intractable difficulties (as a classical Hollywood film might), Guido seems to fantasize that he directs the entire menagerie with whip in hand, taking on the role of the ringmaster to a parade of his closest relatives, friends, and associates, represented as a group of eccentrics in a circus parade.

The Hollywood protagonist is usually more sympathetic, in part because Hollywood tends to take an optimistic, some might say idealized, view of human nature. Mel Gibson's character in *Braveheart* (1995) is not atypical. He wins the spectator's allegiance not only for his courage and tenacity in the face of the most barbarous enemies, but also because he is good-looking and kindhearted. Thus, spectators tend to align themselves unproblematically with his goals and are not encouraged to maintain any critical distance or to question any of his motives or behavior.

Hollywood in the late 1960s and into the 1970s produced several films that showed art cinema influences in this regard. In *The Graduate* (1967), Benjamin Braddock (Dustin Hoffman) plays the role of the listless, confused art cinema protagonist until he meets and falls in love with Elaine, after which his single-minded goal is to marry her. (Another nod to the art cinema is Elaine and Ben's obvious uncertainty as they ride the bus to their newfound freedom at film's end.) In *Shampoo* (1975) George (Warren Beatty) is a hairdresser who is unable to commit himself to any woman and has affairs with several. In general, he seems to lack a sense of direction, as his acquaintances point out throughout the film, and he often mumbles nonsense as though he isn't clear about what to say or what he believes. He seems to decide that he loves Jackie (Julie Christie) by the story's end, but by then she has chosen someone else.

The most popular term for spectator engagement with a major character is "identification," which sometimes implies that the audience has the illusion of "becoming" the character with whom it identifies, or that the audience thinks the same thoughts and feels the same emotions as the character does. Although viewers may think some of the same thoughts and share some feelings, the possibility of such a "Vulcan mind meld" form of identification is slight. "Identification" is commonly used in film studies by scholars who assume that the meaning of the word is self-evident. Berys Gaut notes that since the word "identification" seems to be firmly ensconced in critical discourse, we should sort out its meaningful uses to avoid talking at cross-purposes.[39] It may be better to dispense with this vague and polyvalent term "identification" altogether, as Noël Carroll argues, because it encourages simplistic ideas about the relationship between spectators/readers and characters.[40]

The viewer's "relationship" with a favored character is one of sympathy, together with an assimilation of the character's situation. That is, the spectator's interaction with the character is both internal and external. The internal part consists of the viewer's hypotheses about what the character thinks and feels, together with automatic processes such as mimicry and emotional contagion, which I describe in the following chapter. The external part involves an assessment of the character's broader situation, incorporating information at times unavailable to the character, and incorporating the character's assessment of and response to his or her situation. Given this simultaneously internal and external engagement with a character, then, neither the spectator's thoughts nor feelings can possibly be identical with those of the character, since the response necessarily involves that external portion of character engagement. The intended affective trajectory of a narrative, as I discuss more fully in Chapter 5, is guided on a path that sometimes diverges widely from that of any particular character.

Not all theorists of filmic emotion would agree with me on this. Torben Grodal, who has developed a comprehensive theory of emotion elicitation in film in his *Moving Pictures: A New Theory of Genres, Feelings, and Cognition*,[41] makes the viewer's identification and empathy with characters into a centerpiece of his theory. In viewing a film, Grodal argues, the spectator adopts the character goals, mentally simulates the character's situation, and responds to the film based on that simulation.[42] Grodal's model is a "flow" model in that it compares the temporal experience of the viewer to flowing down a narrative river. It is a compelling metaphor. The protagonist becomes the viewer's mental raft, so to speak. The viewer assesses the protagonist's goals, progress, blockages, and obstacles, just as the passenger might assess the progress of a raft on which he or she rides. The viewer responds accordingly as the viewer and protagonist float down the narrative river together. The viewer projects him- or herself into the protagonist, responding much as the protagonist would.

Grodal's model is close to the "Vulcan mind meld" conception of identification that Carroll rejects. I suspect that the disagreements between Carroll and Grodal on empathy and identification are in part terminological, however. Carroll's critical target is a theory of identification that would hold that viewers and characters *can* and in most cases *do* share identical experiences. Grodal does not hold this view, since when he defends empathy, his argument could be construed as a defense of "feeling for" as much as "feeling with."[43] Thus Grodal's conception of empathy is not the implausible entity criticized by Carroll. Moreover, it seems that Grodal's flow model, adjusted somewhat, would function even if the viewer's engagement with favored characters were primarily characterized by external assimilation rather than a strictly internalized projection into the mind of the protagonist.

Yet in the end, Grodal does shackle the viewer's mental life too closely

7.   The existence of several sympathetic characters in films such as *Casablanca* (1942) shows that the spectator's allegiances cannot be simply and wholly granted to any particular character, but are shifting and partial.

to that of the protagonist. We must recognize that the viewer has a mental and affective life, as well as a goal orientation, that is often quite different from that of any character. We can clearly see this in ensemble films or network narratives, such as *The Big Chill* (1983), *Steel Magnolias* (1989), *Grand Canyon* (1991), *The Usual Suspects* (1995), *Magnolia* (1999), and *Crash* (2004), which feature several major characters, requiring the viewer to negotiate the goals of and respond in complicated ways to multiple characters in varied situations. In such narratives, it is the viewer's sense of a separate self that enables him or her to evaluate and respond to such an array of characters. Moreover, in films with only one or two major characters, the viewer must often mentally part ways with the protagonist and desire narrative outcomes that differ from the protagonist's goals. This would be true for any cautionary tale in which the viewer is led to believe that the protagonist is making wrong choices. Consider gangster films such as *Goodfellas* (1990) or *The Godfather* (1972), in which the viewer does not see the goals of the protagonists in purely sympathetic terms. Or consider dramas such as *Casablanca*

(1942), in which the goals of sympathetic characters are partly in conflict—for example, the goals of Rick (Humphrey Bogart) remain hidden until the last scene.

It is for this reason that I distinguish between direct emotions (which take the content of the narrative as their object) and sympathetic emotions (which take a character's situation as their object), and insist that character engagement is essentially both external and internal. Although sharing character goals and emotions is an element of character engagement, the viewer must also negotiate the contours of the narrative independently of the character and view events in part from the outside. This is why the term "identification" has traditionally been so misleading. It implies the sharing of character goals and emotions and implicitly diminishes the importance of the spectator's independent engagement with the narrative.

THE STRUCTURE OF ENGAGEMENT

Murray Smith's formulation of what he calls the "structure of sympathy" has been very useful in explaining the centrality of character engagement to spectator emotional response. In Smith's model, the structure of sympathy consists of the viewer's recognition of the emotional experience of characters, a structure of alignment (explained below), and allegiance, or in other words, the viewer's moral and/or ideological approval or disapproval of characters.[44] The structures that Smith illustrates operate in cases of antipathy and indifference as well as sympathy; in addition, Smith's concept of allegiance seems quite close to sympathy. Thus, to avoid confusion, I will slightly alter Smith's terminology and refer to the structure of "engagement" rather than "sympathy." For our purposes, the last two elements of the structure of engagement, alignment and allegiance, are most important.

One of Smith's central contributions to our understanding of character engagement is his distinction between "alignment" and "allegiance." The spectator is aligned with characters in two fundamental ways: through *spatio-temporal attachment* and *subjective access*. By attachment, Smith means the way a narration may follow one or more characters though the course of the narrative. Attachment may be more or less exclusive, focusing on one protagonist; may shift between one character and another, or may disperse itself among many characters.

Subjective access refers to the degree to which viewers are given access to the subjective states of the characters. As Smith writes, attachment shows us what characters do, while subjective access reveals what characters desire, believe, think, and feel.[45] No particular degree of subjective access is necessarily entailed by attachment to a character, although attachment and access often correspond. Occasionally, the narration may grant spatio-temporal attachment and withhold subjective access (and perhaps even provide misleading cues about character subjectivity). In either case, alignment is a formal process that implies no particular evaluation of or emotional response to the character.

Smith does claim that alignment with a character, all things being equal, tends to increase spectator sympathy, but does not invariably do so. What Wayne Booth calls "the sustained inside view," or what we might call sustained attachment, may lead to a kind of "insider's sympathy" with the character and her or his allies and antipathy toward other characters portrayed as "out" group members.[46] Booth claims that such a process is at work independently from the reader's moral judgment of the character, or what Smith calls allegiance.

Allegiance with characters is another essential component of the structure of engagement. Allegiance has a stronger moral and affective component than alignment, and is less a structure of the text than a response of spectators to characters. Allegiance results from the spectator's moral evaluation of characters. These evaluations lead to the ordering or ranking of characters according to preference. For Smith, allegiance fundamentally depends on the spectator's moral approval of them, not necessarily in absolute terms, but sometimes merely in relation to our moral evaluation of the film's other characters. That is, spectators sometimes grant allegiance not to the character who is deemed morally spotless, but to the one who is the least morally objectionable.[47]

Two clarifications are in order at this point. First, allegiance and sympathy are related but not identical. It might be good to think of allegiance as a cognitive state that primes one to experience sympathy but does not necessarily lead to sympathy. Thus, one could have allegiance for a character yet fail to sympathize with the character in some circumstances, such as when the male lead in a traditional romantic comedy temporarily pursues the "wrong woman." Although spectators may lack sympathy with the protagonist in such a case, there remains an overarching allegiance with the character. Second, it would be wise to consider additional terminology. We might call lack of allegiance "indifference," and the opposite of allegiance "opposition," or an oppositional stance.

One caveat, however. I would maintain that the audience may give its allegiance to a character (thus harmonizing its goals and desires with the character) or maintain an oppositional stance for reasons other than moral approval or disapproval, in some cases lending allegiance, for example, because the actor is attractive, or the character small (we find children or small animated characters to be inherently sympathetic). Some spectators have a tendency to root for the underdog, for those who are familiar to them (as in the case of stars, or in the experiments detailed above, animated triangles), or for those who appear to be similar ("She's left-handed like I am!"), who share an affiliation (race, class, ethnicity, gender), or who have other complementarities of outlook that cannot be classified as moral per se. Moral approval or disapproval may lead to allegiance or an oppositional stance, but so may other characteristics.

Some might want to argue that the star system has as much to do with allegiance as moral evaluation does, and that audiences will lend allegiance to characters played by familiar and well-liked stars independent of any moral approval of the characters they play. This may be true to some extent, but to say that stars win audience allegiance completely independently of moral approval is clearly wrong. If audiences automatically granted all characters played by movie stars their allegiance, it would not allow liked stars to play the role of antagonist in a film. Consider Jack Nicholson's several roles as antagonist or otherwise unpleasant character, from *The Shining* (1980) to *The Witches of Eastwick* (1987) to *Batman* (1989) to *The Departed* (2006). Nicholson's star power fascinates spectators, but does not necessarily lead to allegiance with the characters he plays. One could make a similar case about Meryl Streep in *Adaptation* (2002) and *The Devil Wears Prada* (2006). Stars fascinate audiences, but spectators hardly lend their allegiance to stars automatically. In the cases above, moral evaluation, not merely star power, plays a role in developing degrees of spectator allegiance with characters.

Central to Smith's argument—and its significant insight—is his claim that alignment and allegiance are not necessarily coextensive. While a film may align viewers with one or more characters, allegiances may be conflicted or may lie elsewhere altogether. Similarly, a film may encourage allegiance with a single character but disperse alignment among many characters. Or a film may disperse both allegiance and alignment, as we see in various "ensemble" films or "network narratives,"[48] such as *Grand Canyon, The Big Chill, Thirteen Conversations about One Thing, Magnolia,* or *Crash.* Smith's notion of the structure of engagement, then, breaks down sympathetic engagement into smaller components, provides a useful means of thinking of its component parts, and offers a way to explain its sometimes contradictory and ambiguous nature.

CHARACTER ENGAGEMENT AND SPECTATOR DIFFERENCE

The problem of spectator difference is most striking in light of the structure of engagement, especially with regard to one component of that structure, allegiance. To what extent does spectator allegiance vary with spectator difference? It may help to briefly consider this question in light of gender differences. Of the many ways we can differentiate between spectators, gender differences are currently of great interest to film scholars. Early psychoanalytic film theory proceeded as though the formal characteristics of the film wholly determined spectator response. Laura Mulvey chiseled a crack in the "apparatus theory" monolith when she suggested that pleasure should be differentiated according to gender.[49] She preserved a fundamental tenet of apparatus theory, however, when she found cinematic pleasure in a unitary source, namely voyeurism and the symbolic dissolution of the threat of castration. For the early Mulvey, then, film pleasures were male pleasures.

Although I am skeptical of the psychoanalytic underpinnings of Mulvey's theory, to say that classical Hollywood film has often assumed a male viewer, at least in some regards, seems right to me. Take Hitchcock's *Rear Window* (1954) as an example. Much of the film seems designed to appeal most fully to a male heterosexual viewer. The protagonist, Jeffries (James Stewart), is male, of course, and for those who respond to the film, *Rear Window* offers male pleasures. The viewer is perceptually aligned with Jefferies when he "peeps" at the dancer, "Miss Torso," in her apartment or at the sunbathers on the building's roof. Although the film implicitly finds Jefferies to be morally at fault for his voyeurism, it simultaneously and somewhat contradictorily offers the pleasures of voyeurism in its somewhat provocative (at least for the 1950s) display of the beautiful dancer. Jefferies's little smile as he notices the helicopter descending to provide its occupants a better view of the two women sunbathing provides a kind of wink and a nudge at male sexual looking. *Rear Window* also plays to male desires in the way that the spectator is aligned with Jefferies (in both spatio-temporal attachment and subjective access), especially as the female characters dote on him. Stella, the insurance company masseuse, gives him massages. Lisa (Grace Kelly) participates in Jeff's journey of discovery in part because she wants to prove her worth to him. Throughout the film, Lisa caters to Jeff, offering to buy him a new silver cigarette case, modeling lingerie and an $1,100 dress for him, offering herself sexually, having dinner, wine, and champagne delivered to his apartment, and planting favorable "items" about him in newspaper columns. The film can clearly be seen as a male fantasy, in the nontechnical sense of "fantasy" discussed in Chapter 1.

To say that even such an obvious example as *Rear Window* offers *exclusively* male pleasures, however, would be wrong. Certainly, the pleasures it allows spectators fall in part along gender lines—but only in part. It is true that in many cases, spectators will find it easier to have allegiance for a character with whom they perceive shared similarities, such as gender, ethnicity, race, age, and class. Yet such affinities are hardly airtight. As many film theorists have since noted, women do sympathize with or have allegiance to male characters and men with female characters. The female spectator may also align herself with Jefferies's goals without granting him wholesale allegiance. Even were spectators to find Jefferies to be an arrogant cad, they could still align themselves with his desire to uncover the Thorwald mystery, and his desire that Lisa escape Thorwald's dangerous grasp when she sneaks into his apartment and is discovered.

Moreover, I would speculate that many spectators, both male and female, find Lisa to be more sympathetic than the somewhat cynical and demanding Jefferies, and it is certainly possible that the spectator's fundamental *allegiance* lies with her, though the film *aligns* spectators with Jefferies perceptually and in the subjective access to Jefferies's thoughts and reactions. It is Jefferies who initiates the voyeurism here, a voyeurism that the film itself questions, and it is Jefferies who dubiously resists the love Lisa offers because she is "too perfect." Lisa holds spectators' allegiance as much as Jefferies, though spectators are structurally aligned with him.

Moreover, many of the pleasures of the film have to do with the unfolding of the narrative and with the direct emotions of suspense, curiosity, and surprise, which do not depend wholly on allegiance to characters, and which are typically cross-gender pleasures. Women, like men, will be affected by the film's suspense and mystery. *Rear Window*, like many Hollywood films, is oriented toward a male viewer, but offers viewing pleasures that cross genders. Some might also argue that certain elements of Lisa's character are clearly designed to appeal more to women than to men, so that although Jefferies "controls" the narrative, viewing pleasures are also afforded to women through Lisa's interests and demeanor. Indeed, it could be argued that at the film's end, Lisa has taken control.[50]

Although Mulvey is right to claim that Hollywood has often presumed a male spectator, she is able to argue that mainstream films offer exclusively male pleasures only because her account of pleasure is too narrow and too firmly divided along gender lines. As Jane Gaines asks, "Is the spectator restricted to viewing the female body on the screen from the male point of view?"[51] If I am right that the pleasures films offer are more complex (as I argued in Chapter 1), then we must revise conventional accounts that posit a binary opposition between male and female spectatorship and admit that male viewers may have allegiance to female characters and vice versa. This is not a new suggestion, and is in fact gaining widespread acceptance.[52] To some extent, the pleasures of the movies, though differently inflected, are cross-gendered pleasures. To be sure, differences exist, for example, in the capacity of spectators to experience empathy and some of the specific emotions.[53] Yet many spectator allegiances, pleasures, and other responses cannot be drawn strictly along gender lines.

WHAT CHARACTER ENGAGEMENT IS: A SUMMARY

Character engagement is the trajectory of mental activities and responses viewers have in relation to film characters. Viewers sympathize with, have antipathy for, are conflicted about, and are indifferent to various characters. Engagement involves cognitive assessment, viewer desires for various outcomes, and sympathetic and antipathetic emotions in response to a character's situations. Most classical Hollywood films encourage strong sympathy for one or more characters. This sympathy is pleasurable in itself, but it also ensures strong emotional responses, since when the audience cares deeply about a character, it also has deeper concerns about the unfolding narrative. And deeper concerns often lead to stronger emotions.

4. The Sensual Medium

Film scholars and critics often talk about spectators "reading" films. Such talk is meant to imply, sensibly enough, that all films must be interpreted. Films are never transparent records of real events or people, but rather constructions with communicative and rhetorical functions. Some of the meanings of films are hidden and subtle rather than immediate and obvious. If this is true, then why not speak of film interpretation instead of "reading a film"? The phrase "reading a film" mischaracterizes the viewing process as literary, with the effect of distracting us from the medium's sometimes disavowed quality, namely, that film is a powerful sensual medium. Film gains its particular power from its direct appeal to sight and hearing. When critics talk about reading a film, they infuse film viewing with the patina of intellectual distance and implicitly ally film viewing with the ostensibly more active and legitimate activity of reading.[1] By using the language of reading, however, such critics also downplay the pre-rational elements of spectatorship, in other words, responses that are to some extent automatic, pre-reflective body responses, rather than the intentional and interpretive cognitions of the conscious mind.

This talk of reading a film is misleading not because film viewing is entirely passive or unworthy of such elevated discourse, but rather because films are primarily apprehended through nonlinguistic channels of communication. They are viewed and listened to, and whatever little reading the viewer might engage in is usually limited to titles, credits, and photographed written text. The ideas a film raises for a viewer are typically not read but perceived and inferred through a complex visual, aural, and linguistic experience that must be understood on its own terms. We can read film criticism, but—James Monaco notwithstanding—nobody reads films.[2]

SEEING AND HEARING MOVIES

The moving image media, while at times incorporating language in the form of dialogue, voice-over narration, and various forms of written text, are fundamentally visual and aural media. The moving image media rely on images and sounds that exploit innate perceptual capacities in addition to learned linguistic, visual, aural, and cultural competencies.

To say this is not to promote a naïve realism that assumes that films are simply photographic and aural records of reality. Such claims of simple reproduction of reality are deeply problematic, even for nonfiction films. In the case of fiction films, with their designed sets, costuming, actors playing roles, and scripted narrative and dialogue, one wonders how much reality is left to record. One can recognize the mediated, expressive, and stylized elements of film representation, however, and still note that spectators' experience of a film depends in large part on their real-world perceptual skills developed outside the movie theater. The perception and comprehension of computer-generated images, even of those that are fantastic, exaggerated, and distorted, employs such typical perceptual skills.[3]

We must distinguish between referential realism and perceptual realism. Traditional cinematography provides an indexical record of a scene *and* stylistically transfigures it. That is, the analog photograph is the product of a causal link between the photograph and that which the photograph is of, a link that has widely (and problematically) been thought to underlie the authority of documentary film.[4] Such an image may be referentially realistic due to its iconic and indexical link to the objects that were in front of the camera. Some computer-generated images (CGI), such as those created for animation or special effects, do not record the actual world but fabricate a fictional world. Despite this fabrication and fictionalization of the world, CGI can embody sights and sounds in ways that are *perceptually* rather than referentially realistic. A perceptually realistic scene, Stephen Prince claims, accurately replicates "valid 3D cues" such as collision responses (when, say, galloping dinosaurs bump one another while herding), the replication of light source illumination, directionality, and the rendering of light and shadow as light falls on complex surfaces such as fields of pebbles or human hair.[5] Perceptual realism, then, presumes only that the filmmakers present an audiovisual array that replicates the kind of real-world visual and aural cues that people make use of in natural perception.

To make such claims for perceptual realism does not deny the role of culture in the spectator's experience of the cinema. The claim is that elements of the spectator's response are not processed linguistically, but depend in some cases on more or less universal perceptual skills and in other cases on skills that are socially dependent but also relatively direct and automatic, that is, not mediated by language or conscious thought.

This sensual nature of the medium and its direct appeal to automatic response processes is most obviously manifested in the prevalence of sex and violence on the screen, which have been staples of the movies since their inception.[6] Such trends were visible in the popularity of boxing films such as *Leonard-Cushing Fight* (1894), designed for Edison's kinetoscope, or *The Kiss*, which was the most popular Edison film of 1896.[7] Sexuality in movies relies extensively on the eroticism of seeing, and much film theory has explored the relationship between the male gaze and sexual desire. The representation of violence and action is particularly suited to the movies not only because movies are well able to visually represent the kinetic energy of bodies and objects in motion, but also because sounds that suggest movement, impact, and physical power can be isolated and exaggerated for maximum effect.

Yet representations of sex and violence are only the most obvious manifestations of the sensual nature of the medium. Films are sensual to their very core, in ways that are not widely acknowledged. In Chapter 2 I drew a distinction between direct emotions—those emotions taking the unfolding story as their object—and sympathetic/antipathetic emotions that take as their object the plight or behavior or particular characters. In a similar way, I distinguish here between direct affect and affective mimicry. Spectators' real-world perceptual capacities and social skills will come into play in the generation of direct affect, that is, responses to screen imagery and sounds that are derived from movement, color, composition, sound, and so on. Direct affect would include startle in response to sudden loud sounds or "threat feelings" as, for example, a vehicle rushes toward the camera at high speed. Spectators' responses depend on homologies between the implications of space on the screen and in their extra-filmic lives, since certain uses of movement and space generate automatic responses. To this we can add the physical responses generated by shot composition, camera movement, montage, color, and sound.

On the other hand, affective mimicry is generated by the grain of the voice, subtle inflections of tone and cadence, facial expressions, gestures, and postures. Affective mimicry results from the spectator's experience of photographic and aural representations of the human body and voice. We are a species of mimics, and various sorts of motor mimicry strongly affect spectators without them being consciously aware of it.

A fiction film is presented to the spectator in a complex meld of image, sound, and language, drawing on many kinds of psychic processing. Perhaps those who speak of "reading" a film do this to defend the medium against those who would claim that viewing a film is mindless, and/or that making films is little more than recording a pre-existing reality. But are such defenses of the medium really necessary any longer? Should we not dismiss such naïve arguments against film out of hand? As I argued in Chapter 1, the sensual nature of film hardly precludes complexity or the need for active inferential or imaginative activity. But that sensual nature bears strongly on the kind of affective experience film provides and must figure centrally in any comprehensive account of film viewing.

FILM AND THE BODY

That the film spectator is not merely a conscious thinker but also an embodied, biological human being has been the subject of considerable attention in film theory recently. Linda Williams's essay "Film Bodies: Gender, Genre, and Excess" explores the excesses of violence, sex, and weeping elicited by horror, pornography, and melodrama respectively.[8] Williams calls these "body genres," which could be misleading since it implies that other genres do not involve bodily responses. In a sense, all films appeal to the corporeality of the viewer. As Williams rightfully notes, some genres and some films elicit more intense and obvious bodily responses than others.

Williams writes about mimicry, a vitally important element of embodied spectatorship. But she does not explain its functions or make reference to the psychological literature on mimicry or other forms of bodily response to stimuli. She instead limits her psychological references to psychoanalytic accounts of childhood fantasies. As others have argued, film and media scholars could learn much about media effects and the relationships between human perception and film viewing from the social sciences, cognitive and perceptual psychology, and neuroscience, but many have been reluctant to explore this literature.[9]

Closer to my approach to the study of film and the body is Vivian Sobchack's phenomenological theory of film experience. Sobchack claims that the cinema uses "modes of embodied existence (seeing, hearing, physical and reflective movement) . . . [and] the structures of direct experience (the 'centering' and bodily situating of existence in relation to the world of objects and others)." Sobchack concludes, "Thus, as a symbolic form of human communication, the cinema is like no other."[10] For Sobchack, psychoanalytic theorists such as Metz and Baudry disembodied the film spectator, presuming a "transcendental subject." Metz, for example, writes of the "spectator fish," an image that suggests passive observers who take in "everything with their eyes, nothing with their bodies." Sobchack reminds us that "the body and the eyes are not separate (in fish or in humans)," but are "part of the whole body, and what the eyes take in, the body does also."[11] In essence, Sobchack hopes to describe the pre-reflective experience of film viewing, an experience that emanates from the bodily existence of the spectator.

Sobchack's insistence on the corporeal nature of film viewing is leading to an important shift in the way film scholars understand spectatorship. After tipping my hat in her direction, however, I must note that my approach differs in some respects. In this chapter I take up some of the pre-reflective or automatic features of the spectator's experience, but I am also centrally interested in the spectator's cognitive activities and in reflective, conscious experience. It is for this reason that I put a good deal of emphasis on the importance of narrative as the governing element in eliciting emotional response; narrative scenarios are also central in the evocation of other bodily responses, as I argue below.

My approach also differs from Sobchack's in its characterization of the phenomenology of the film as experienced by the viewer. Sobchack claims that the film itself has a body. She writes: "What we look at projected on the screen . . . addresses us as the expressed perception of an anonymous, yet present, 'other.' And, as we watch this expressive projection of an 'other's' experience, we, too, express our perceptive experience."[12] For Sobchack, the film viewing experience is genuinely dialogical because it incorporates "two embodied views," that of the spectator and that of the film itself. The "two bodies and two addresses," she says, "must be acknowledged as the necessary condition of the film experience."[13]

In my view, we should not conceive of the film itself as a body, either literally or metaphorically. A film is constructed artifact designed to offer the spectator a structured experience that unfolds temporally. Except in the case of anomalous films such as the "first-person" *Lady in the Lake* (1947), the experience of a film is not, and is not presented as, the experience of another body, or of any particular "other." The film offers an experience that is affecting and sensual for the spectator, but not necessarily expressive of the experience of any particular person, whether a fictional "body" of the film or the actual filmmakers. (What person can alternate views of the world like a point-of-view structure, for example, in which a character's point-of-view shots are alternated with external shots of the characters looking? What person or body can jump back and forth, as in parallel editing, between two events occurring hundreds of miles apart?) In my theory, spectators have bodies, but films are structured artifacts in the viewing of which spectators are invited to have an embodied experience. Films invite spectators to see, hear, and experience their created "worlds" in particular ways, but these ways of experiencing are not necessarily those of any particular person or body.[14]

DIRECT AFFECT

Spectator responses to movements, sounds, colors, textures, and manifestations of space are in large part automatic and pre-reflective. The human brain did not evolve to interact with the visual media, or indeed with representations of any sort, but adapted itself to the more immediate environmental data to which we must daily respond for our survival and flourishing. Thus the spectator's responses to audiovisual media are rooted, in part at least, in those natural perceptual responses that have developed over long periods of human history. Some argue that the recognition of a picture as a representation (rather than as reality) is a "thoughtful," secondary response, occurring only after the initial, primitive response that would take it as real.[15] However, it is not always a matter of sequence, but sometimes one of simultaneity. The recognition of the artificiality of the media—that the picture is a representation of a bear and not an actual bear, for example—becomes a part of the spectator's background mental set and functions simultaneously with other automatic responses. I may flinch at the surprising close-up of a snake on screen, but I do not flee because I recognize that it is a film. This may be a case of sequential automatic and secondary responses. Yet there is a sense in which any further shots of the snake will be processed as a *representation* simultaneously with other automatic responses to the content, such as the alarmed "Snake!" response. And thus the alarmed or startled element of the response may be attenuated.

Most of the time, these physical, automatic responses occur beyond conscious control. Viewers flinch when surprised and recoil at the sight of vermin or filth. Although automatic, they are certainly conditioned by the bodily affordances of the theatrical experience. That is, spectators are positioned in the theater for receptiveness, with comfortable seating, climate control, darkened lighting, and a wide-screen image and digital multichannel sound to provide for ease of attention and maximum sensory stimulation. Spectators need not be distracted by bodily pangs of hunger or thirst, since concessions are easily available. In fact, one of the chief bodily pleasures for many spectators is the simultaneous combination of visual, aural, and gustatory stimulation.

On the other hand, if the theatrical experience is designed for receptiveness, it also diffuses any requirement for meaningful action or instrumental response. Spectators understand that under no circumstances will there be any actual threat either to themselves or to those persons represented. As I mentioned earlier, the relevant social context is "play" and "entertainment"; for those at the local art theater, the context may be "art" or "the art cinema." In any case, nothing immediate is required of the viewer, save the free rein of pleasurable response, which is inhibited only by social display rules, if, for example, the spectator is inclined toward inappropriate or disruptive vocalizations (moaning, incessant cackling, or loud screaming, for example), the flailing of the limbs (during scenes of startle or horror), or embarrassing emotional responses that must go unnoticed (such as excessive weeping for the American male, who according to conventional social display rules is "allowed" more pronounced expressions of anger than of sadness).

The physicality of film can sometimes aggressively assault the spectator. In 1997, about 700 Japanese children had seizures in response to a Pokémon cartoon. Most of the seizures occurred during a scene that featured the flicker effect, in which red and blue frames alternated at high speed for 4 seconds.[16] This is an extreme example, but we should recognize the possibility of potentially unpleasant physiological and affective responses to a wide range of filmic phenomena. Films can elicit anxiety and nervousness, shock and startle, disgust and revulsion, and such experiences sometimes lead the spectator to walk out of the theater. Filmic effects that cause discomfort through disorientation and surprise may seem intentionally aggressive toward the spectator. For example, when most viewers see *Un chien andalou* (1928) for the first time, the famous shot of the sliced eyeball is shocking and disturbing.[17] The amount of potentially unpleasant and aggressive effects will depend on genre conventions, with much more allowed in a horror film or experimental film, for example, than in a romantic comedy.

We can see the physicality of film very obviously in the startle effect, a staple of the action and horror genres. Startle is a response to any sudden and intense stimulus, such as a loud noise or a potentially threatening sudden movement.[18] *Alien* (1979) provides several particularly intense startles, as the carnivorous alien that inhabits the film's cargo ship and threatens its astronauts is skillfully made to emerge suddenly and threateningly at unpredictable moments. Startles are visceral responses, involving blinking of the eyes, vocalizations, and pronounced head and torso movements. Startles are resolutely bodily and physiological. They are universal to an extent, but as Robert Baird argues, the farther from the onset of the original response, the more learning, context, and personality influence behavior.[19]

Movement is another method of engaging the physicality of the spectator, and film theorists and critics have long recognized the physical effects of movement in film. Lisa Fehsenfeld has recently argued that two kinds of movement in film, what she calls technical movement (nondiegetic movement created through camera movement, editing, and special effects) and physical movement (diegetic movement of entities on the screen), affect the viewer's physiology directly and can initiate dizziness, nausea, motion sickness, autonomic reflexes, perception of effort responses, classic conditioning, mimicry, and basic stress responses.[20] Camera movement, object/person movement, and framing in a film are not simply about story and meaning; they also evoke marked visceral, physiological, and emotive effects in viewers.[21]

Aaron Anderson's work on martial arts films explores movement effects as well, and has much broader implications for the study of film movement in other genres. Anderson adopts what he calls a "kinesthesia-oriented analysis" in relation to the viewing of martial arts films.[22] Anderson argues, first, that martial arts films are not primarily about muscularity or the look of the static body, but a vicarious and romantic empowerment expressed through mastery in face-to-face fighting. Jackie Chan's muscles are not particularly rippling, but he nonetheless successfully provides the viewer with this sort of vicarious empowerment. The martial arts fight is typically stylized and musical, like a dance, and is several steps removed from actual violence. In fact, Anderson uses the techniques of dance analysis to examine the martial arts in film. He appeals to kinesthetics, the study of the aesthetics of movement that also incorporates an interest in the physiological effects of movement on viewers. Such physiological effects stem from "metakinesis" and "muscular sympathy,"[23] the latter of which is explored further below.

The idea of metakinesis derives from dance theorist John Martin, who writes that movement "is a medium for the transference of an aesthetic and emotional concept from the unconscious of one individual to that of another."[24] This transference occurs in part because human memories are "sedimented in the body," and bodily movement, or watching bodily movement, can evoke memories and responses rooted in such sedimentation.[25]

Sergei Eisenstein examined similar ideas in his exploration of "expressive movement," but Eisenstein, of course, also emphasized the physicality of the editing process. That is, he recognized the physical effects of editing apart from its specific cognitive content. Thus, he proposed metric and rhythmic editing, rooted in the temporal relationships established by joining shots of various lengths and rhythms together. He wrote of joining shots in relation to emotional tones and overtones. And finally, Eisenstein conjoined the physicality of editing with cognition, arguing for intellectual montage, a progression of shots according to an argument or thesis that is developed through the edited sequence of shots.

Consider also "proxemic patterns," those social conventions of closeness and distance by which we gauge the appropriate proximity of our bodies to those of others. Drawing on those conventions, the film can affect the viewer through framing, editing, and camera movement. The close-up can be used to create intimacy with a protagonist or to elicit disgust and revulsion toward an unsympathetic character. Through editing, the filmmaker can align us perceptually with a character through point-of-view structures that alternate between what a character sees and his or her reaction. The physical and affective effects of such alignments depend on context; it is well known that shots featuring subjects advancing rapidly toward a stationary camera produce a different physical effect than shots featuring stationary subjects or those moving away from the camera. The study of proxemics and kinetics has implications for the embodied response to films, but has so far been too little explored.[26]

These sorts of physical effects of a film are regulated with greater or lesser success, often alternating between excitement and calming, tension and relaxation, hot and cool. Too much stimulation becomes uncomfortable, while pure relaxation quickly becomes boring. As I discuss below, the rise of "intensified continuity" and the "impact aesthetic" in contemporary Hollywood can be seen as attempts to ratchet up the "energy" and affective impact of the movies in their sensual aspect.

REPRESENTING EMOTIONAL EXPERIENCE

In the previous section I noted some of the means by which films affect viewers bodily—what I call direct affect. In this and the following three sections, I focus on the unique capacity of the film medium to elicit various sorts of affective mimicry. Affective mimicry in the movies depends on the fact that viewers *see* the bodies of film actors/characters and *hear* their voices; they do not typically *read* about them. This is perhaps the single most important difference between filmic and literary narratives.

The ability to appreciate and interpret visual images is certainly learned, in that knowledge of various uses of symbolism, style, and artistic traditions is essential to a deep understanding of the visual arts. Nonetheless, in the case of motion pictures, the viewer need not learn to recognize objects in moving photographs. At the level of simple object recognition, photographs require no learning to be comprehended. If a mass untutored audience knows what a ship looks like, it can immediately recognize the photographic images of the ship in *Titanic* (1997). Moreover, empirical evidence shows that this ability to recognize familiar objects in photographs is shared cross-culturally. Anyone who remains skeptical of this claim to universal object recognition would have to account for the fact that not only humans but also various species of animals, which presumably have no visual education, are able to identify objects in photographs.[27] This untutored object recognition needs to be factored into the means by which the moving photographic image displays the human body.

Mimicry depends on the right kind of display of the human body. How does the film medium represent the emotional experiences of characters? To answer this question, I will briefly consider some of the means by which filmmakers display the body so that I can subsequently make some claims about how this leads to affective mimicry. The art of the actor is in part to mimic the behavior of human beings in the grip of emotions, to display the body and the signs of its passions.[28] The art of the cinematographer and editor is in part to display images and scenes of the body such that the impact on the audience will be maintained. At the climactic point of most movies, filmmakers aim to generate the most intense emotional impact. Accordingly, some of the most memorable scenes from American films are those in which characters are moved passionately at the film's climactic point. In *Stella Dallas* (1937), Stella (Barbara Stanwyck) stands before a picture window, on the other side of which her daughter is being married. For her daughter's good, Stella has imposed on herself a kind of self-banishment, but now she weeps openly in a bittersweet mixture of sorrow and joy. In *Mr. Smith Goes to Washington* (1939), when Jefferson Smith (James Stewart) pleads before the corrupt U.S. Senate at the film's end, his voice cracks, his face is weary, and his shoulders are stooped in exhaustion, but his determination and enthusiasm for his cause is both touchingly naïve and convincingly sincere. He finally collapses in an exhausted heap on the Senate floor.

Body language, including the use of facial expression, posture, and gesture, is one of the primary means of communicating emotion both in social reality and in the motion pictures. Through variable framing and point-of-view structures, a film can display the parts of the actor's body that are the most emotionally communicative. The close-up often foregrounds facial expressions or expressive gestures, while the long shot may show posture and the character's interaction with the environment. Moreover, in point-of-view structures the editor can show us, alternately, the character's facial expression, and then what he or she sees. The point-of-view structure not only provides information about the character's emotional state, but further clarifies the emotion by revealing the object of the character's emotional state.[29]

One element of the hypercoherence of the Hollywood narrative is its means of communicating character emotion clearly, powerfully, and often redundantly. This does not necessarily imply the *exaggeration* of gesture, facial expression, and posture, as in German Expressionist acting, for example. Johannes Riis argues that the move from broad and declamatory acting styles to a more naturalistic acting style in the silent era in Europe stems in part from a recognition that rather than merely expressing the outward signs of an emotion, the actor could suggest the object of the emotion, and thus engage in more subtle expression.[30] A simple glance or a mere twitch of the lip can be more effective than broad gestures meant to represent a particular emotion. Since a film can redundantly communicate the specifics of the situation (through music, point-of-view shots, variable framing, etc.), the acting need not be broad or exaggerated.

In addition, recorded sound gives not only the words of the character's voice, but also the sound of the voice as the words are being spoken. In *2001: A Space Odyssey* (1968), the ship computer, HAL 9000, has a voice that features vocal markers that suggest humanity and feeling. When HAL 9000 kills several astronauts and the surviving crewmember begins to dismantle the computer, bit by bit, HAL's voice gradually reverts to the primitive and mechanical acoustic qualities of its development as a machine. This scene is powerful in part because it suggests the slow death of an artificial yet intentional being. As HAL pleads for its life as it is being dismantled, its vocal qualities become progressively "inhuman" in a pathetic and somewhat uncanny devolution.

In his classic work on the expression of emotion in humans and animals, Darwin reserved an important place for the voice.[31] Researchers have determined that listeners can often accurately judge emotion solely by listening to the voice, picking up cues from variables such as changes in loudness, pitch, and temporal sequences of sound (utterance length, speech rate, and silences). The ability to decode emotion from the voice is remarkably consistent in studies conducted in various countries, in different languages, employing lay and professional actors, and using varied linguistic material.[32] Given our heritage as social animals, it is more than the identification of emotion at stake here. Humans have a built-in affective connection to the voices of other humans that is similar to the expressive and contagious effects of the human face, discussed below.

Given this, it is unsurprising that film composers and sound editors have learned to exploit the emotional power of the recorded human voice. For *The Sixth Sense* (1999), director M. Night Shyamalan and film composer James Newton Howard used recordings of voices in almost subliminal ways to create the sense of eerie human or spiritual presence. Instead of the typical ambient sounds for locations—the sound of traffic, street noise, air conditioners, and so on—the filmmakers used the sound of human (and sometimes animal) breaths and breathing. For certain scenes, Howard constructed a chorus of human voices, a cacophony of crying, groaning, and screaming, mixed at a low level such that no individual voice could be identified. The Oscar-winning documentary *Common Threads: Stories from the Quilt* (1989) mourns and celebrates the lives of those felled by AIDS, rails against government inaction, and features the Names Project Quilt, each panel of which represents one person who has died of the illness. The memorable musical score by Bobby McFerrin and Voicestra consists entirely of human voices, used most memorably at the end to suggest the voices of those who have passed away.

In summary, film communicates emotion particularly well in its use of photographic and sonic representations of the human body and voice in the grip of passion, in part because it relies on sensual channels of communication—the sight of the body and the sound of the voice—that people make use of in their everyday perceptual and social lives. Moreover, filmmakers have the ability to exaggerate, isolate, clarify, and otherwise manipulate such images and sounds to maximum effect without destroying their perceptual realism.

AFFECTIVE MIMICRY

So far I have claimed that the photographic representation of the human body communicates human emotion with a directness unavailable to literature. Filmic images do not merely *communicate* such emotion, however. They also *elicit* responses in the viewer, often in direct and automatic fashion. Humans are social beings to the core. Our sympathetic and empathetic responses to others, when we have them, come in many forms. We may mentally simulate the experience of another, making a deliberate effort to imagine how we might think and respond if faced with her or his circumstances. Many, if not most of our responses, however, are automatic and pre-reflective. One sort of reactive response is compassion and what some call "personal distress," a self-oriented response characterized by anxiety and unease in relation to a distressed other.[33] Or we may simply be fascinated by or curious about another's situation, distressful or not. But often our response to the represented body and voice is rooted in affective mimicry.

The recent interest in "mirror neurons" places mimicry as a central element of human sociality, behavior, learning, and response. Not only are humans social beings, but we learn by observing and imitating the actions of others. Neuroscientists have lately been implicating mirror neurons in this process. Most of the experimentation with mirror neurons has been performed with monkeys. Mirror neurons are a class of particular "visuo-motor" and "audiovisual" neurons that discharge both when a monkey performs a particular action and when the monkey observes or hears the sounds of that action being performed.[34] That is, the same neurons discharge when the monkeys perform an action (such as ripping a piece of paper in two) and when they observe that same action or hear the sounds associated with that action. It is thought that mirror neurons function to mediate imitation in primates, and that these neurons lie at the basis of the ability to understand others' actions.

Through indirect evidence, most researchers believe that such mirror neurons also function in humans. As two researchers claim, mirror neurons "represent the neural basis of a mechanism that creates a direct link between the sender of a message and its receiver." They conclude, "Thanks to this mechanism, actions done by other individuals become messages that are understood by an observer without any cognitive mediation."[35]

What is the relationship between mirror neurons and motor mimicry? Motor mimicry is the tendency of an observer to outwardly mimic the facial and body movements of another person. Mimicry results not only from observing the behavior of actual persons, but from looking at represented behavior in photographs and videos and from hearing the vocalizations of others.[36] The evidence for motor mimicry does not depend on the existence of mirror neurons, since researchers have observed mimicry as a behavior without necessarily needing to understand the neurological substrate of such behavior. Nonetheless, the existence of mirror neurons does contribute to the evidence for the psychological importance of motor mimicry.

Such motor mimicry may lead to various forms of *affective* mimicry and *emotional contagion*. Emotional contagion is the phenomenon of "catching" the emotions of those around us or of those who we observe.[37] This can occur when we view a film with a crowd of moviegoers. The laughter or screaming of a large movie audience can accelerate and increase the intensity of the individual viewer's reaction. Emotional contagion may also occur in our everyday social reactions. A group of friends sits in a room telling amusing stories. After one such story, you may laugh with the group, even if you don't find the story to be particularly amusing. Although a desire for social conformity may be at work here (and a desire not to offend the storyteller), the listener also may "catch" the emotions of those around him, affectively participating in the general mood of good cheer and merriment.

MIMICRY AND THE FACE

When it does occur, emotional contagion results in part from the observation of another's posture, gesture, voice, and/or facial expression. The classical film theorist Béla Belázs recognized this. He writes, "If we look at and understand each other's faces and gestures, we not only understand, we also learn to feel each others' emotions." For Belázs, the close-up of the human face plays a central role in the cinema because it feeds on the human propensity to respond to each others' faces.[38] But if it is true that representing the face is centrally important in the elicitation of emotion in film, it is also true that gesture, posture, and voice come in a close second.

Elsewhere I have written about the use of the face to elicit emotion, and here I will only briefly touch on the central importance of faces in the cinema.[39] Elaine Hatfield and colleagues, like many others, argue that humans have a pervasive tendency to mimic each other's postures, facial expressions, and vocalizations.[40] Much of this mimicry occurs beneath the level of consciousness, as a kind of automatic response.[41] At least one important study has shown that such mimicry occurs in viewers' responses to the human face on the screen.

The more controversial claim is the facial feedback hypothesis, the claim that one who mimics the facial expression of another actually catches the latter's emotions to some extent. Facial expressions provide us with proprioceptive feedback that at most causes an emotion and at least influences our emotional experience, especially our mood. In effect, if you want a brighter outlook on life, smile a lot. If you wish to dampen your mood, put on a frown for a while. I suspect that facial feedback is not *by itself* sufficient to elicit a full-blown emotion. Instead, I accept a weak version of the facial feedback hypothesis, which would hold that motor mimicry and facial feedback may affect mood or may contribute to the intensity of an emotion, but do not in themselves elicit emotions such as fear or sadness.

Motor mimicry and facial feedback may occur in relation to any close-up, but they tend to occur with the most frequency and intensity in relation to what I call scenes of empathy, in which the face of a favored character is dwelt on for some length in a close-up, and at emotional high points in the narrative, most often toward the end of a narrative. After the film has built sympathy for and intense interest in a character, the film's narrative momentum may pause to allow for a scene of empathy that encourages empathic response in the viewer. The viewer may actually "catch" some of the emotion the character is thought to be feeling through processes of motor mimicry and emotional contagion.

Such scenes of empathy occur often in any narrative that embraces the seriousness of a character's emotional life without irony or distance, such as *The Wizard of Oz* (1939), *Stella Dallas*, *Blade Runner* (1982), *Dead Man Walking* (1995), and *Schindler's List* (1993). The horror film also reserves a special place for the face, as the prevalence of close-up face shots of victims in anguish demonstrates. The vocal quality of the scream or the whimper figures into the effect, as can be seen in *The Blair Witch Project*, one the most financially successful films of 1999, in which a moving scene shows a horrified, sobbing Heather Donahue in close-up, looking directly into the camera and apologizing on screen for getting her mates into their wretched predicament.

Note that emotional contagion may occur in response either to onscreen characters or to the movie audience that surrounds the viewer at the theater. Thus contagion, strictly speaking, is not coextensive with empathy. (One can catch the crowd's response, sometimes beneath consciousness, without empathizing with the crowd.) When emotional contagion occurs in relation to a favored protagonist, however, it most often elicits some of the shared feelings definitive of empathy or sympathy. It is for this reason that well-developed scenes of empathy are nearly always reserved for sympathetic protagonists.

What has this to do with character engagement, which, as I have argued in previous chapters, is central to emotion elicitation in film? Affective mimicry complements and strengthens other processes that lead to allegiance, sympathy, and empathy with film characters. Character engagement, I have said, is both internal and external. It is external when alle-

8. The scene of empathy in *City Lights* (1931).

giance arises from the spectator's positive moral judgment of a character, when a more or less conscious judgment affects allegiance. Allegiance may also be affected by an artifact emotion that is a kind of judgment. Disdain for the perceived poor performance of an actor or for the actor her- or himself will nearly always interfere with allegiance for the character portrayed. Motor mimicry and contagion, on the other hand, are internal responses in that the viewer shares some of the experience the character is thought to have, possibly in an automatic and unconscious way. This hardly negates the viewer's exterior perspective on the character, however. It seems clear that viewers can both respond to characters emotionally and maintain some critical distance. It is also true that one may respond emotionally to a film and at the same time dislike or even disdain one's own response. Our modular minds are capable of multiple, ambiguous, and even conflicting responses.

The mind consists of a number of specialized mechanisms with particular functions. These specialized mechanisms, as Marvin Minsky argues, collaborate, negotiate, and ultimately perform executive functions in "societies": "The power of intelligence stems from our vast diversity, not from any single, perfect principle. Eventually, very few of our actions and decisions come to depend on any single mechanism. Instead, they emerge from conflicts and negotiations among societies of processes that constantly challenge one another."[42] Various processes in our minds work independently and perhaps negotiate with and/or conflict with one another. Emotional contagion may be a low-level automatic process that is only partially under our conscious control. This is why spectators can both cry in response to the plight of a character and disdain their own crying. Emotional contagion elicits crying, but the conscious recognition of the film's manipulation resents it.

Above I wrote that some of the most memorable moments in American film history occur during particularly emotional scenes. By this I don't mean to imply that intense expressions of emotion are always what the audience wants. The expression of emotion is governed by cultural display rules. That is, for any given culture, unwritten rules exist for the "proper" and "acceptable" expression of emotion, according to emotion type and the age, gender, and social status of the one expressing it. Thus, it is somewhat more socially acceptable for a male to express anger by intense vocalizations than to express sadness by crying, while for women the opposite is often true. Some stars have built careers, then, on their lack of outward emotion expression, their seeming calm demeanor, often in the face of extreme situations that would cause the mere mortal to feel and express intense fear. One thinks of Charles Bronson or the early Clint Eastwood, popular in part because they embody a conception of masculine stoicism as expressed in their *lack* of emotional expression in paradigmatic fear situations.

MIMICRY AND THE BODY

The importance of motor mimicry extends well beyond the human face to gesture, posture, and human movement generally. One psychological study among many relevant ones showed that adult subjects swayed in one direction or another while mimicking a model reaching for an object just beyond his grasp.[43] Sergei Eisenstein had a keen interest in expressive movement and what we now call "motor mimicry." Eisenstein believed that the film actor must first be trained to execute simplified and stylized movements, and the filmmaker needed to compose and edit shots of such movements to sharpen them and make them dynamic. When successful, the onscreen presentation would stir in the viewer's body a palpable echo of the actor's gesture. For Eisenstein, the power of expressive movement derived from motor mimicry, a process rooted in basic bodily responses.

He saw motor mimicry as susceptible to conditioning, however, such that filmmakers could create new associations—new links between movements and responses—and could thus manipulate the spectator's affective experience for persuasive purposes.[44]

Above I noted Aaron Anderson's emphasis on metakinesis, by which movement directly communicates with and viscerally affects viewers. Anderson also writes of "muscular sympathy," another form of motor mimicry. Anderson argues that with the exception of those with congenital paralysis, humans experience life in a human body that moves more or less like other bodies. "Every person who has a body," he says, "thus knows what it 'feels' like to move a human body through space. And every time a person sees another human body move, s/he implicitly understands what this movement might feel like."[45] These claims derive from Pierre Nora's contention that memory is not merely in the mind but embodied in autonomic reactions, sympathies, and all variety of learned reactions.[46] In part it is through this muscular sympathy that the spectator's experience of bodily movements on the screen can elicit physical, empathic feeling.

David Bordwell writes that Hollywood filmmakers, once "the world's leaders in portraying the dynamics of the human body," have been surpassed by Hong Kong filmmakers who understand the value of clarity and precision in the creation of "expressive amplification," whereby patterns of movement and their representation are orchestrated for maximum effect. Through all of the capacities of film style and technique, Hong Kong filmmakers working in the martial arts tradition have discovered how to enhance clarity, underscore rhythm, and amplify the expressive force of gestures, movements, and entire action scenes. Instead of the Hollywood pattern of "scattershot cataclysm," Hong Kong and other Asian action films often incorporate a "pause/burst/pause" pattern that makes represented action more precisely rendered and more powerful.[47]

In sum, then, the moving image media present to audiences a direct representation of human emotion, more accessible and more sensual than any other medium. Moving photographic images, as used in narrative film, display the human body in all its emotional expressiveness and depend fundamentally on the human tendency to respond strongly to others through motor and affective mimicry and various empathic responses. In the first chapter, I argued that one of the chief pleasures of the cinema is the affective, visceral experience it can offer. We derive these pleasures in part due to the pre-reflective means by which people respond bodily to the physicality of others. That is, the physical nature of screen representation affects the spectator directly and bodily.

MUSIC, SOUND, AND AFFECT

As I noted in the preceding chapter, the conventional narrative structures found in Hollywood screenplays seem specifically designed to elicit and manage spectator emotion. The same is true of the film music that composers and filmmakers compose and select to accompany films. Although film music has other functions, it is clearly used in movies to express and evoke particular moods and emotions. It is hardly surprising that composers and directors often discuss the many functions of music in terms of affect and emotion. How should the music make the audience feel? Would music or silence be more successful in generating response at a particular point? How can music communicate the emotions of the protagonist? Should the music strongly suggest the eerie feeling of the haunted mansion by striking a sudden dramatic chord? Or should the eerie atmosphere be evoked more subtly, subliminally? Disagreements between directors and composers may easily arise over the extent to which music should or should not bear the load of emotion evocation and expression. Randy Newman, for example, thought that director Penny Marshall used his music to excess in *Awakenings* (1990), unnecessarily "tugging at the heart strings." Less music would have led to a more subtle evocation of emotion, in his opinion.[48]

Most of those who enjoy movies can think of scenes in which the affective contribution of the music is unmistakable and essential. A popular example is Bernard Herrmann's shrieking violins during the unsettling and shocking shower scene in *Psycho* (1960), or the way Herrmann's score for *Vertigo* (1958) strongly suggests the physical condition denoted by the film's title and suffered by the film's protagonist. One also thinks of the astute use of evocative music in the films of Stanley Kubrick, ranging from Johann Strauss's "The Blue Danube" accompanying the "waltz of the spaceships" in *2001: A Space Odyssey* (1968) to the use of the fourth movement of Beethoven's "Ninth Symphony" to suggest Alex's "will to power" in *A Clockwork Orange* (1971). In all of these cases, the music carries meaning, certainly, but also an affective charge that colors the scene and infuses it with emotion. The overall experience of the scene depends in large part on the music.

One of the essential ways that Hollywood films prefocus emotional response to scenes is through music. In what follows, I discuss some of the means by which film music contributes to such prefocusing, ranging from affective and bodily influences to more cognitive and "idea-laden" effects. Let us begin with bodily effects of music on a listener. Music resonates with or otherwise impacts our very physiologies through rhythm, dynamics, tempo, and pitch. Music affects listeners and viewers in physical ways that researchers are only beginning to understand. For example, rhythm and tempo may lead to what researchers call the frequency following effect, or auditory entrainment, which is an auditory "mirror" effect. Physiological functions of the body, such as the heartbeat or brainwaves, tend to synchronize with the rhythmic patterns of audio, whether a complex musical score or heartbeats.[49] Heartbeats, slowly increasing in volume and/or tempo, can elevate suspense and anxiety in response to a film scene. And tempo strongly affects the spectator's perception of the calmness or excitement of a piece of music and the scene it accompanies. Filmmakers can also use sudden changes in dynamics to contribute to basic affects such as surprise and startle or merely to increase or decrease physiological arousal. The musical "stinger," a loud musical phrase that suddenly fills the soundtrack, has just such a function. In her analysis of how music is used to affect spectator physiology in *Vertigo*, Kathryn Kalinak shows how Bernard Herrmann juxtaposes *fortissimo* (very loud) and *pianissimo* (very soft) both successively and simultaneously, creating an asymmetry that "keeps us off guard musically."[50] The musical track, then, can elicit mood, strengthen or attenuate affect, and influence the spectator's affective experience by direct physiological means.[51]

Music can also elicit moods, those affective states that are said to lack a specific object and to be more lasting and diffuse than emotions proper. We all know that people sometimes use music to manage their moods or as a kind of affective therapy. Music can counteract or soften bad moods or intensify or prolong good moods. The moods elicited by music in film are often poorly described in language, their "color" and "feel" often complex, perhaps ineffable. Camille Saint-Saëns' "The Aquarium (Carnival of the Animals)" in Terrence Malick's magnificent *Days of Heaven* (1978) was perhaps chosen in part in response to Malick's fascination with nature and the myriad animals he displays around the Texas wheat farm that serves as the film's primary setting. Yet the viewer need not know the music's "extra-musical associations" for this piece to set a mood of delicate wonder, of awe at the mysterious order of natural things. One might object that words like "awe" and "wonder" used in relation to *Days of Heaven* are better described as emotions than moods. In part, this results from the inability of language to fully describe the riches of human experience. Linguistic determinists notwithstanding, it often seems that language, far from circumscribing conscious experience, is desperately trying to keep up with it.

It is also true that it can be difficult to tell where mood leaves off and emotion begins. This is hardly surprising (given that both mood and emotion are fuzzy concepts) and need not be of major consequence. Unless we describe moods in the vaguest of terms (good, bad, anxious, relaxed), many of the words we tend to use are emotion words (happy, sad, excited anticipation, morbid dread, etc.). Moods and emotions often do interact in film, and in fact, as Greg M. Smith convincingly shows, moods can prime emotions of a similar valence.[52] Thus, the rapid tempo of the driving techno-pop in *Run, Lola, Run* (*Lola rennt*) (1998) creates a mood of anxious anticipation that increases the likelihood of suspense, excitement, and other discrete emotions.

Some of the affects elicited by music scarcely qualify as moods, as though they were almost "felt ideas." The majestic rhythms and stately tempo of Franz Schubert's "Piano Trio in E-Flat, Op. 100" in Kubrick's *Barry Lyndon* (1975) during the courtship of Barry and Lady Lyndon not only suggest the rigidly ordered social structure of their milieu but positively enable the viewer to feel it. The music also contrasts nicely the outward polite behavior of the lovers (which conforms to the expectations of the social order) with their inward desires and the scandalous nature of their adulterous affair. Through synesthesia, that is, a kind of cross-modal fittingness between images, sounds, rhythms, and so on (discussed in the next chapter), and through association, music can suggest ideas. This is another way in which music serves to prefocus emotional response. Ideas, of course, are essential elements of the spectator's construal of a scene, and thus, assuming the film's successful evocation of concern, music can prefocus the emotions that I have defined as concern-based construals.

In an earlier chapter, I made a distinction between affect and emotion. Emotions, as concern-based construals, were said to have a marked cognitive component, while many affects, on the other hand, are cognitively impenetrable. Can music elicit the "higher," more cognitive emotions, or at least contribute to such elicitation? That music plays into the communication and elicitation of emotion in film is hardly a controversial claim for most of us. Yet it is one that needs unpacking, since the issues are more complex than they might first appear. Music that is composed for a film is most often program music—in other words, music designed to accompany another text, in contrast with "pure" music, which is designed to stand alone. Taking a strict cognitive view of the emotions, it is difficult to see how music alone could be said to elicit emotion. We have an emotion based on our construal that some state of affairs bears significantly on our concerns. Yet sad music does not constitute such a state of affairs in the way that the misfortune of a loved one does. If the music is strictly instrumental (with no accompanying narrative, lyrics, or images), it is not about anything; it arguably has no representational content. Thus, many music theorists insist that while music may be expressive of emotion states, it does not itself elicit emotions in audiences.[53]

While at a concert a few years ago, my companion and many other members of the audience wept through much of a particularly fine performance of Henryk Górecki's "Symphony of Sorrowful Songs." Audiences, quite obviously, are often moved by music and musical performances. What is it about the music that elicits such strong emotions? It could be argued that it is not the music itself that elicits emotion, but rather the memories suggested by the music that make people weep or swoon. That is, while the music is played, listeners remember sorrowful incidents in their lives and respond to those remembered incidents rather than to the music itself. Or rather than memory traces, it may be associations that music suggests. Music often accompanies the most important rituals of our lives, including weddings, funerals, and religious services. It is common for a romantic couple to identify a piece of music as "their song," or for old folks to nostalgically associate pieces of music with a more youthful past. Pieces of music accrue emotional impact through association, on both a personal and societal level. Musical associations are also developed in the viewing of a film itself, most typically by some variation on the leitmotifs that come to stand for characters, events, or places. In all of these ways, pieces of music can carry an immediate emotional charge. Through association, then, films can build on learned responses to music. In this way, strict cognitive theorists could maintain that it isn't the music itself that elicits emotion. What elicits emotion is a representational memory or association that the music suggests. Music, then, prefocuses concern-based construals in part by suggesting associations or common types of memories with particular emotional valences.

In my cognitive-perceptual theory of emotion, it is less important to decide whether emotion is elicited by music itself or by music in tandem with memories and associations than it is to acknowledge the brute fact that by either explanation, music plays a vital role in the expression and arousal of emotion in movie viewing. Yet it must be noted that film music is not pure music but program music. Thus, it faces none of the objections against emotion elicitation directed toward pure music, since music in mainstream films is always presented in tandem with images, other sounds, and a story, all of which supply the cognitions supposedly necessary for music to elicit emotion. Film music is carefully placed, through "spotting," at temporal intervals in the unfolding of the narrative. The narrative of movies, as I have argued, embodies prefocused, concern-based construals that unfold in time. Thus music may serve to both enable and intensify an emotional response that has been initially elicited by other elements of the discourse, most specifically the narrative paradigm scenarios. While the American helicopter cavalry attacks a Viet Cong village in *Apocalypse Now* (1979), Lt. Colonel Kilgore (Robert Duvall) turns on a sound system with massive speakers and plays Richard Wagner's "The Ride of the Valkyries" from *Die Walküre*. The music itself is strident and warlike in its use of horns (which are often associated with the military) and building crescendos of sound. Thus, it serves to intensify the excitement of the battle and to suggest the glory and honor of the battlefield and the brave warrior. (The functions of the music here are more complex than this, as I will argue below).

Noël Carroll has argued that one important function of film music is to serve to modify or characterize what a scene is about "in terms of some expressive quality." The example Carroll gives is from *Gunga Din* (1939), in which characters played by Cary Grant, Douglas Fairbanks Jr., and Victor McLaglen are ambushed in a seemingly deserted village and engage in a rousing battle with thugs. Alfred Newman's musical score during this fight scene is jaunty, its horns "bouncy, light and playful." Thus, while battle scenes might often be thought to be suspenseful and anxiety-producing, this one is presented as a lark, a playful charade.[54] Music that serves this function, Carroll argues, *modifies* the movie. If instrumental music is expressive of emotive qualities, the qualities are ambiguous and broad. For this reason, the explicitness of the movie—its visuals, narrative, dialogue, and sound effects and ambient sound—work together with music. The movie indicates explicit objects and events, while the music "modifies or characterizes what the scene is about in terms of some expressive quality."[55]

Carroll notes that, apart from the music, the scene itself may also be expressive (and not merely indicative). His point is not that *only* music can "modify" in this sense. Music is one technique among many used as a means of expressing emotive qualities. One function of music, then, is to suggest the way in which a scene should be construed, the intention being to generate or modify particular sorts of emotional responses.

Film scholar Jeff Smith brings us further toward an understanding of how film music emotively prefocuses a scene in his discussion of the musical expressiveness of film music. Smith argues that empirical research on musical affect suggests that the expressiveness of film music involves at least two processes: polarization and affective congruence. Polarization occurs when music influences response in directions not expressed in the scene, while affective congruence occurs when music is used to heighten and intensify the existing emotional characteristics of the scene. When music is used congruently, it tends to deepen the viewer/listener's impressions of the affective meaning of the scene to an extent greater than the impressions of either the music or the movie individually.[56]

A piece of music can function in complex ways, and in some cases, the same piece of music can be affectively congruent in some regards and polarizing in others. Consider once more "The Ride of the Valkyries" in *Apocalypse Now,* played while the American helicopter unit attacks a Viet Cong village. The emotional tenor of the music is congruent with the excitement of the attack and is congruent with the rest of the scene. But the use of this music also fits with the ironic and somewhat critical narrative stance of the film, since Wagner is associated with extreme nationalism and is often regarded as "Adolf Hitler's favorite composer." The artifact emotions elicited here may stem from such associations as much as from the qualities of the music itself. This is a case in which the ironic and distanced artifact emotions may interfere with the direct emotions of excitement and anticipation. It is also a case in which the music's associations with rampant nationalism seem at odds with the suggestions of heroic action the music evokes.

The use of Wagner in *Apocalypse Now,* it could be argued, is an example of simultaneous polarization and affective congruence. It is polarization in the association of the music with ardent nationalism and with Hitler's well-known special liking for Wagner; this suggests that perhaps Kilgore is guilty of similar mindless nationalism and warlike tendencies. But the music is affectively congruent in that it expresses the excitement of the attack itself and of the soldiers participating in it.

In sum, film music has a number of affective functions. First, it elicits affect through direct physiological effects on audiences. Second, it elicits moods, which prime audiences for certain kinds of emotions. Third, it modifies the scene by suggesting its emotional valence. Music modifies, intensifies, and complicates the affective experience of a scene through polarization, affective congruence, or both simultaneously. In other words, it can move the expressive interpretation of a scene away from that inherent in the nonmusical elements, it can strengthen the scene's existing emotive qualities by adding to them, or it can elicit affect in ambiguous and complicated ways.

When film music suggests emotive qualities, it contributes to the cognitive framework for how the scene should be interpreted and for how the viewer is invited to formulate a concern-based construal. When the music elicits affect or emotion, that affect/emotion in turn causes the viewer to attend to particular elements of the scene that correspond with the framework suggested by that emotion. Eerie music in a horror film, for example, does not merely *elicit* fear or unease; it also leads the viewer to *expect* and *anticipate* possible additional objects of fear and unease in the fictional world of the film. In either case, music does not merely elicit feeling but also influences the spectator's concerns and construals, perceptions and cognitions. It is one of the central means by which films marry thinking and feeling.

AFFECT AND CONTEMPORARY HOLLYWOOD STYLE

How do Hollywood films in particular marshal stylistic techniques such as editing, framing, and camera movement to affect the spectator physically or sensually? The classical Hollywood style, consisting of norms for the use of film technique at least through 1960 (and arguably still in existence in an altered form) is widely varied in effect, and its stylistic techniques are used for diverse purposes. The style is meant to be transparent or "invisible," that is, it is used to transmit story information and to allow the spectator to focus on story. Although classical Hollywood style has always been moderately self-conscious, especially at the beginning and end of films, the classical style is not meant to be obtrusive. Techniques of continuity editing (for example the match on action and the "180-degree rule") are designed to maintain this transparency and to ensure that the spectator is not distracted from attending to character and story.

The baseline style for a scene consists of an establishing shot and a series of closer shots to get into the action, with an occasional reestablishing shot to remind the spectator of spatial relationships. Shots were once longer in duration than today, and editing more leisurely. In 1930s Hollywood films, the camera moved, but usually only to follow characters or reveal new information. Of course, all of these tendencies could be overruled when the action called for it. Editing could pick up in pace for a chase scene, an unsteady camera could suggest frenzy or chaos, and camera movements could become more pronounced to follow an elegantly-dressed woman down a spiral staircase, for example, or to track back in front of a protagonist who makes a mad dash away from danger. Certain directors—Orson Welles, for example—are known for baroque styles that pushed the baseline style to its limit with virtuosic camera movements, exaggerated camera angles, shock cuts, and flamboyant montage scenes. The classical style can become expressive at times, but its primary function is to keep the spectator firmly focused on the story and to maintain clear spatial and temporal orientation. The baseline style is not meant to convey "energy," as today's "intensified continuity" is.

The use of style for intense physical effect has always been related to genre conventions. Genre films tend to elicit similar emotions, such as pity and admiration in melodramas, fear and revulsion in horror, and (arguably) nostalgia and regret in films noir. Similarly, the affective arc of style can be characterized in relation to genre. David Bordwell notes that the post-1960s move toward intense and extended physical action in contemporary Hollywood coincides with the contemporary revival of certain genres such as crime, horror, science fiction, comic book stories, and in general, action films.[57]

We should take note of three recent changes in Hollywood style as they affect the spectator's relationship to the screen and the story world: the "impact aesthetic" that dominates action films and has influenced style in other genres; what Bordwell calls "intensified continuity" as the new baseline style; and the increased obtrusiveness of style that accompanies an expanding self-consciousness in overall narration. Together, these signal an increased reliance on spectacle, or in other words, on images, sounds, scenes, and techniques that are valued not primarily for their place or function within a narrative but for their inherent fascination and entertainment value, as well as for the visceral and reflexive pleasures they afford.[58]

The "impact aesthetic" has become more influential with the rise of the action film in the new Hollywood. Geoff King, who coined the term, suggests that perhaps Hollywood has been driven to this aesthetic by the need to compete with music videos and video games for the attention of a certain segment of the audience, teenaged and twentysomething males.[59] The impact aesthetic consists primarily of two stylistic elements: rapid editing and pronounced movement toward the camera (of flames, large objects, careening vehicles, blast debris, smoke, and human bodies). As King notes, in such films a fireball is a must. The scale of the mayhem increases as the film reaches its climactic point, with flames and explosions, fast-moving vehicles, smoke, dust, and other debris moving toward the camera (or the camera moving through them). In *The Rock* (1996), for example, various devices are used to create a sense of speed during the car chase scene. These include fast-paced editing, unsteady shots of drivers (suggesting the extreme difficulty of filming vehicles traveling at such speeds), objects flying toward the camera, shot compositions featuring blurred foreground items such as trees or fence posts, and the Doppler effect noise of a racing car passing at top speed.[60]

By contrast, the British film *Pride & Prejudice* (2005), aiming at a much different audience, begins with a 45-second stationary title shot of a rural landscape as the sun almost imperceptibly rises. Thus, the film quietly but proudly insists on its difference from the Hollywood action film. Other scenes in the film begin or end with stately long shots or elegant tracking shots, befitting the sense of solidity that is associated with an adaptation of a classic Jane Austen novel. Yet even in this film, with its scenes featuring several drawing room conversations, one can see the director's eagerness to provide the visual and aural energy contemporary style demands. This is most displayed in the ballroom dance scenes, which feature either quick cutting or an elegant camera tracking through corridors and rooms filled with people, the latter reminiscent of Renoir's camera in *The Rules of the Game* (1939). In either case, the shot compositions are crowded and somewhat anarchic and the soundtrack elaborate and multidimensional, sometimes picking up on several layers of conversation and other sound. Like the impact aesthetic, *Pride & Prejudice* also repeatedly has the camera tracking back as characters walk or trot toward it, providing that sense of energy so sought after.

Hollywood films in general give evidence of a change in style that likely is having a worldwide influence. Bordwell claims that such changes have resulted in "intensified continuity," a style that has not so much replaced traditional continuity as "amped" it up, raised it to "a higher pitch of emphasis."[61] Whether intensified continuity is a break with classical style or not, it clearly results in an altered physical relationship between the viewer and the film. Bordwell characterizes the style as consisting of rapid editing and lower average shot length, bipolar extremes in lens lengths (alternating between wide angle and telephoto), a reliance on close-ups or "singles," and wide-ranging camera movements. The aim of the style is to create "energy," a more dynamic and riveting physical relationship between viewer and screen. What is essential from our standpoint is to recognize that intensified continuity is not reserved for scenes of special energy or emphasis but has become the baseline style for contemporary Hollywood films and is used for ordinary scenes.

The third important facet of contemporary style as it relates to viewer affect is its increased obtrusiveness. Contemporary style is not only more likely to draw attention to itself in its self-conscious artfulness, but it is also not afraid of the small spatially or temporally ambiguous inconsistencies that classical Hollywood tried to avoid. In classical continuity, for example, filmmakers were loathe to cut during a camera movement unless the succeeding shot maintained a match on movement. In the style of intensified continuity, such prohibitions are no longer in force, and cutting during camera movements has become common. The narration of contemporary Hollywood has in general become more self-conscious, and can in fact be characterized as a cinema of allusions and playful knowingness.[62] Such playful knowingness can be found in the popularity of "puzzle" films such as *Eternal Sunshine of the Spotless Mind* (2004), *Adaptation* (2002), *Memento* (2001), and *The Usual Suspects* (1995), which prompt the spectator to ask what really happened and perhaps to re-view the film for a better understanding of it. This heightened self-consciousness does not imply a loss of interest in the pleasures of fictional worlds and stories. Bordwell notes that contemporary filmmakers have become interested in creating more intricate fictional worlds through visual, aural, and narrative detail, through density of production design and props, complex webs of sound, and reflexive reverberations within the narrative.[63]

We might say, all things being equal, that the design of contemporary Hollywood films favors their visceral and reflexive pleasures to a greater extent than in the past. But such pleasures have by no means eclipsed the cognitive pleasures of narrative and comprehension, as the puzzle films amply demonstrate. Perhaps the classical detective film, in which a detective's goal is to unravel a mystery, has been eclipsed by a new sort of mystery. In these new mysteries, it is the spectator's role to investigate and come to understand the narrative as an intricate puzzle with complex or difficult temporal/spatial, subjective/objective, and story/discourse relationships. For some contemporary films, the pleasures of direct emotions such as curiosity and fascination are clearly emphasized over the sympathetic emotions.

In general terms, intensified continuity has increased the dynamism of seeing and hearing at the movies. The baseline style has become more visually and aurally dynamic in an attempt to rivet the attention of the spectator and to maintain energy through intensified continuity. Whether such stylistic changes actually result in a more physically moved spectator is a good question, since once intensified continuity becomes the baseline style, it is more difficult to distinguish the ordinary "restful" scene from action scenes. If nervous movement and dynamic editing become the norm, then their effect becomes normalized and less pronounced.

In this chapter I have explored what might be called film affect, the means by which motion pictures influence the spectator bodily by eliciting the sorts of affects that are typically not thought of as "emotions" proper. The following chapter puts it all together, showing the means by which affect and emotion function within the context of narrative and spectacle.

5. Affective Trajectories and Synesthesia

> The narrative artist is a conductor of the free reader's feelings.
> The narrative is not rigid tracks but a walking path that . . . guides
> the flow of feeling, even if wandering from it is frequent and easy.
>
> ROBERT C. ROBERTS[1]

Now that we have explored the spectrum of human affective responses as they relate to film viewing, the task remains to say how these affects interrelate in the spectator's overall experience. How should we think of that "walking path that . . . guides the flow of feeling," as Robert C. Roberts describes it in the above quote? The spectator's viewing experience is complex, consisting at least of the varied activities and responses I have so far identified. A list of these would include cognitive processing (inference making, question asking, etc.), visceral responses, character engagement (including sympathy, primitive empathic responses such as emotional contagion, and antipathy), emotional responses to unfolding narrative scenarios and both artifact and meta-emotions, emotions elicited by the viewer's idiosyncratic associations and memories, moods, pleasures, desires, sexual arousal, various kinds and degrees of kinesthetic turbulence, affective mimicry, and reflex actions and other sorts of affect in response to narrative, spectacle, setting, music, and the spectator's own prior subjective experience. With such an array of affects, can we speak of the unity of affect in the film-viewing experience, and if so, what are the mechanisms through which affects are unified? What trajectories do intended affects take in a film?

In this chapter, I claim that these questions must be approached from the perspective not only of broad narrative scenarios but also of associated elements of style and subject matter that are seen as fitting in the creation of a coherent response. In this book I focus on film-elicited responses that I have called "intended" responses. (If the notion of intention is problematic to the reader, we may alternatively think of such responses as broadly intersubjective, as opposed to idiosyncratic.) Ultimately, I argue, a film's intended spectator response is guided by a film's narration and, more particularly, by narrative structure in relation to point of view. This may seem obvious, but if so, it is often denied by those who would gauge the possible affective responses of spectators. Instead, those who assume a simple relationship of "identification" or "empathy" between spectator and protagonist often conflate character and spectator response, as though the designed arc of spectator response closely follows that of a protagonist. My central point at the outset is that the spectator's affective arc is sometimes congruent with that of a sympathetic protagonist, but never wholly congruent and sometimes widely divergent. It is the filmic narration that guides the film's intended elicitation of affect, and sometimes in such a way that this affect will differ markedly from that we presume any character to have in the film.

With regard to coordinated affective experiences elicited through various stylistic registers, the relevant term in this chapter is "affective synesthesia." The skilled filmmaker combines affective elements of diverse sorts in the creation of an overall experiential mix that is fitting or appropriate to the effect she or he is trying to achieve. Particular stylistic choices in editing and camera movement, for example, might be "exciting" or "energetic." An audiovisual combination of languid tracking shot and music may be experienced as peaceful and relaxing. Certain lighting and shot compositions may be fitting with guilt or shame. Although such effects are orchestrated by the narration, they depend on a spectator that experiences the effects as fitting, working together to produce a coherent affective experience and response. To demonstrate this point, I explore the psychological phenomenon of synesthesia and what I call Alfred Hitchcock's synesthetic guilt and shame.

NARRATIVE FOCUS

The perception of films, like natural perception, is both synesthetic and synoptic, eliciting "bottom-up" and "top-down" activities and responses.[2] Let us consider the top-down activities first. What are the mechanisms by which spectators make sense of the film in global terms and by which the film encourages affective responses that are congruent and unified? How is it that the spectator's responses are guided, managed, and made coherent by the art and craft of narrative filmmaking? In the most general terms, it is film form in relation to content that shapes intended response. The content must be appropriate to the generation of fear or suspense or sentiment, while the form in which it is presented shapes the trajectory of emotions in regard to intensity and duration. More specifically, I claim that narrative scenarios are the most important structuring mechanisms in the movies.

Before defending my position here, let us briefly consider some alternative theories as to the global means by which spectator affect is organized or unified. Greg M. Smith, as I mentioned earlier, proposes that mood is the orienting state that "asks us to interpret our surroundings in an emotional fashion." Smith offers a "mood-cue" approach to emotion elicitation in film, which holds that "the primary emotive effect of film is to create mood."[3] As I argued previously, Smith asks too much of moods here. Moods can certainly contribute to emotional experience, but by themselves cannot qualify as the basic orienting state that determines overall affective response.

To understand my objection to Smith's claim, let us undertake a thought experiment. Suppose that a filmmaker designs a film scene to create the emotion of suspense. To borrow the example given by Alfred Hitchcock,[4] imagine that a long shot shows an intruder, having snuck into a stranger's house, opening and sifting through the drawers of a dresser in a bedroom. We are shown the owner of the house, returning after having been away. The owner approaches the room in which the intruder stands, and unbeknownst to either, a confrontation will soon occur. Suppose that Hitchcock shows this by cross-cutting between the intruder in the upstairs bedroom and the unsuspecting homeowner, climbing the stairs. All things being equal, this scene may well elicit suspense in a spectator.

What is the genesis of this suspense? Hitchcock might carefully set the mood for the scene through program music, lighting, and other means. Yet it isn't the mood that causes the suspense, and suspense itself is not a mood but an emotion. If the scene is successful, it is the narrative situation that elicits suspense. Unless the spectator understands that an impending confrontation between intruder and homeowner might occur (a possible narrative outcome), and unless the prospect of such a confrontation creates anxiety, there will no suspense.[5] That is, suspense, like the other emotions, depends primarily (but not solely) on concern-based construals that are provided through a narrative framework. This narrative framework may be fictional or nonfictional, but without the spectator's sense of a probable but feared outcome— a sense that can be developed only through story-telling—no suspense can occur.

One might object that Hitchcock could create suspense merely through low-key lighting, sinister music, and a tracking shot that slowly moves across the scene. This may be true, but such suspense is still an emotion, not a mood, because it is a concern-based construal. In this case, stylistic techniques create narrative expectation. The lighting, sinister music, and so on, create an expectation that "something" unpleasant or shocking may soon occur. Moreover, for the impatient Hollywood audience, at least, such techniques will quickly lose their power if this expectation is not soon either met or dispelled by evolving narrative events. Stylistic techniques by themselves cannot generate suspense in the absence of any narrative concerns. That is, the creation of suspense depends in the final analysis on narrative and on the concern-based construals that narratives elicit in the spectator. Mood, then, cannot be the orienting state that guides the trajectory of affects in film viewing.

Another possible answer to the question of what unifies intended affect in movies is that for contemporary Hollywood, and certainly for action films, some spectators are basically thrill-seekers who are uninterested in narrative altogether. Such spectators employ few top-down mechanisms by which to make sense of a film, but are rather interested in films only as a series of shocks or attractions. Such an argument is made by Martin Barker and Kate Brooks, who claim that, for certain audiences, the film's story is like a "carrier-wave" that is necessary only to string together the spectacular images and effects that are the conscious focus of spectator pleasure.[6] We might extrapolate from this to say that for the action film spectator, at least, the affects themselves are the source of pleasure and not any sort of formal trajectory they might have. One could take the shocks, jolts, thrills, and titters, shake them up in a hat, and lay them out one by one in random order. The action film spectator could not care less about order, as long as the shocks are there.

Yet Barker and Brooks, in their reliance on research techniques such as interviews and questionnaires for their conclusions, are far too willing to take what spectators say at face value in displacing the importance of narrative in action films. If some spectators *say* they are interested in spectacle rather than story, this may mean only that story structures in action films have become an element of the spectator's automatic, nonconscious responses to films. Spectators may consciously attend to explosions and car chases without considering the preconscious importance of narrative in providing the conditions for the full enjoyment of such spectacular scenes.

As Geoff King argues, even in the case of the action film, which is often accused of narrative incoherence (lack of narrative unity, little character motivation, etc.), what is offered are not mere "random and contradictory items but some kind of *negotiation* between the two extremes"[7] of narrative coherence and unrelated spectacular bits. In the vast majority of films, and for most spectators, it is narrative that offers the top-down coherence most spectators require; without it, most spectators will dismiss even the most mind-bogglingly spectacular action film. Were this not the case, we might see more films that dispensed with narrative and offered a series of unrelated shocks and attractions. It is worth noting that even in the rare instance of an episodic movie such as *Jackass: The Movie* (2002), which consists of a series of stunts related only by their vulgarity, physical danger, and/or intended appeal to teenaged and twentysomething males, most of the individual stunts are given in a story structure of the type I identified in Chapter 3, with a setup, developing action, climax, and sometimes an epilogue. Thus, although there is no macro-narrative governing the film as a whole, several micro-narratives structure the episodes individually. Narrative storytelling as an overarching framework is endemic to Hollywood films.

A similar alternative to my insistence on the importance of narrative depends on the force of what film scholar Barbara Klinger calls "the arresting image," which she examines in relation to the art film. Arresting images function something like attractions or spectacle. The narrative seems to momentarily slow to a crawl and an affect-laden image is foregrounded, allowing time for "the ripple effect," by which the spectator's associations and memories reverberate with the image, suggesting connections with other texts and with personal experiences such as dreams and memories. Klinger suggests that one routine element of art film spectatorship is arresting images that allow for "the occurrence of digression through a chain reaction of associations" that are "a law in any textual encounter."[8]

Klinger does not argue that narrative and other textual strategies have no affective power. Rather, she usefully highlights the affective power of the arresting image, a fascinating concept that has not been sufficiently recognized. Nonetheless, given the current tendency in reception studies to favor the personal, culturally specific, and idiosyncratic spectator response over the formative strategies of the work itself, I think it useful to remind readers that such arresting images gain much of their power from their narrative context. That is, they are not merely random images with affective force, but images that gain force primarily through their meaning within a story, and only secondarily through personal memories and associations that typically ripple out from that narrative meaning.

To see this, let us examine a scene that figures prominently in Klinger's analysis. In *The Piano* (1993), Ada (Holly Hunter), Baines (Harvey Keitel), and Flora (Anna Paquin), Ada's daughter, sit in a boat being rowed to their new home and new life. Ada has escaped the oppressive husband who has earlier chopped off a bit of her finger in a fit of jealous rage. Ada's beloved piano, which has become a symbol of her need for autonomy and self-expression, is in the boat also. Ada unexpectedly demands that the piano be thrown overboard, and in an apparent attempt at suicide, intentionally entwines her feet in the rope that had connected the piano to the boat. She is pulled into the sea and under water. As she descends into the deep, however, she decides to choose life, disengages herself from the rope, and counteracts her previous suicidal impulse.

As Klinger suggests, in such an art film, the image of Ada and the piano in the sea is highly aestheticized, ambiguous, and affectively powerful for many audiences. Klinger downplays an important element of affective response here, however. Even the personal associations viewers have in viewing this image depend in large part on a narrative context that is not personal but provided by the film. The image does not affect spectators merely due to its visual beauty and formal dynamics (movement, composition, etc.), considered apart from what the image actually pictures (a woman underwater, tethered to a piano). Neither is it affectively powerful simply as the image of an unfamiliar woman curiously tethered to this underwater piano. Affective response depends in large part on an understanding of Ada's situation (given by the narrative) and on the spectator's sympathy with Ada (in large part constructed by structures of engagement). Ambiguous though the image may be in narrative terms (why does Ada attempt suicide when she has recently won her freedom from her oppressive husband?), it is the narrative context for the images that circumscribes and suggests possible associations for this ambiguously motivated action. The narrative context suggests associations with feminist concerns including oppression, identity formation, and the freedom to control one's destiny. Even the *ambiguity* of the image depends on narrative context, because given Ada's story of apparently breaking free of her oppressive husband, Ada's motivation for this feint at suicide is unclear. In another narrative context—say, that of a character who has not escaped oppression and has little to live for—perhaps the image would lack the ambiguity this image contains. The difference is in narrative context.

Without a narrative context, the images of Ada underwater would have a far different and lesser affective impact. To put it in the terms I have developed, the spectator's initial reaction to these images fundamentally depends on concern-based construals that arise from a familiarity with the character and her situation. These reactions are enabled and intensified by conditioners such as the personal characteristics of the spectator (perhaps gender and culture, for example) and are also inflected by personal associations and memories. Again, however, the essential role of narrative cannot be dispensed with in the generation of affect. If narrative context is fundamentally important for the affective power of images in an art film such as *The Piano*, then how much more will this be the case for most Hollywood movies, with their driving linear narratives?

The Hollywood film offers a narrative scenario, together with character engagement, as the primary formal means by which the spectator's mental activities and responses are directed. The mainstream narrative is designed to encourage the spectator to develop specific concerns for characters and to construe events in accord with its constructed parameters. The spectator wants to understand the narrative as it unfolds; such a drive to understand is a unifying impulse. The classical Hollywood narrative directs such inferential activity by linking causes and effects, posing problems for which the spectator is led to desire solutions, and asking questions to which the spectator desires answers.[9]

Narrative events do not necessarily require causal motivation to generate this sort of inferential and evaluative activity on the spectator's part. In a melodrama, for example, a coincidence might put the protagonist in an awkward or embarrassing situation, or lead to a chance meeting of two former lovers destined to love and then tearfully part ways again. Yet whether the situation is motivated causally or is coincidental, the spectator in either case perceives the situation as it relates to the protagonist's goals and the spectator's desires. That is, the spectator's concern-based construals of the narrative situation govern the spectator's response, whether the narrative events are caused or coincidental, coherent or relatively incoherent.

In Chapter 2, I defined affects as any felt bodily states, while emotions, as a subset of affects, are concern-based construals that are thus intentional and have a more pronounced cognitive element. Affects such as moods, pleasures, motor and affective mimicry, muscular sympathy, auditory entrainment, facial feedback, emotional contagion, and visceral stimulations such as startle are vitally important in the film's overall affective mix. If affects are sometimes less complex and less cognitive than emotions, this does not diminish their importance. Affects may serve at least these functions in storytelling:

- as providers of affective color and tone in their own right, for either aesthetic or rhetorical purposes;
- as intensifiers and enablers of emotion;
- as distancing devices that reduce or minimize the spectator's concerns or alter construals, and thus diminish emotional response.

In relation to the suspense scene previously mentioned, for example, the filmmaker can intensify elicited suspense by creating the right mood, priming the spectator for suspense through anxiety elicited by small startles and surprises (a mouse in the dresser drawer, for example), heartbeats on the soundtrack that increase in volume and pace as the house's owner approaches the bedroom, or music that is expressive of concern or anxiety. Alternatively, the filmmaker can decrease suspense by using comic markers, by creating a light mood, or with jaunty music. In either case, the suspense itself depends fundamentally on the narrative scenario, and only secondarily on intensifiers and enablers.

To say that affective and emotion-eliciting devices are always unified in the Hollywood film is clearly wrong. The skilled filmmaker may provide intentionally ambiguous or contradictory affect cues, typically for a specific effect such as the elicitation of suspense or curiosity. Some filmmakers, on the other hand, may seriously mistake the effect of a device for spectators, or lack the skill or resources to successfully put the device into play. But it would be true to say, nonetheless, that the spectator of the classical Hollywood film will attempt to unite the disparate visual and auditory stimuli into a coherent whole. Film communicates multimodally, making use of images, graphic material (titles, credits, intertitles, act markers), ambient sound, sound effects, music, and language. The spectator perceives the film multimodally as well, then attempts to unify the perceptual input. In the usual scene, all of the imagistic and auditory information is taken to have originated in a single "world," typically in a single narrative event or related events, and viewers attempt to relate the stimuli to that.

The spectator looks for ways to unite sensory stimuli. Joseph Anderson calls this tendency toward unification "cross-modal checking," and appeals to Eleanor and J. J. Gibson, who suggest that as perceivers make their way through the world, they seek "invariant properties of an event across modalities"[10] as an essential survival strategy. The film spectator, similarly, seeks invariant properties of film stimuli according to the schemata supplied by the film's narration. And the emotions and affects the spectator experiences, in turn, further amplify the tendency to top-down processing and congruent response.

If the suspense scenario actually succeeds in eliciting suspense, then the spectator will be more likely attend to narrative details that correspond to the concerns embodied in the suspense. Noël Carroll calls this the "searchlight" function of the emotions.[11] The emotions organize perception, directing our attention to what we consider salient or what we desire to learn based on the emotions or affects we currently experience. In functional terms, the emotions draw our attention to what is most salient to the person, often quickly and automatically. But the emotions may also lead to specific cognitive activity.

This searchlight function is illustrated in Adam Smith's account of the workings of human sympathy. In his treatise on the "moral sentiments," Smith suggests that what we now call motor mimicry is the most primitive form of "sympathy" (or what most contemporary aestheticians would call "empathy"): "When we see a stroke aimed and just about ready to fall upon the leg or arm of another person," Smith writes, "we naturally shrink and draw back our own leg or our own arm; and when it does fall, we feel it in some measure, and are hurt by it as well as the sufferer." A more complex sympathy, however, and a sympathy that will extend in time, requires a measure of understanding on the observer's part:

> Even our sympathy with the grief or joy of another, before we are informed of the cause of either, is always extremely imperfect. General lamentations, which express nothing but the anguish of the sufferer, create rather a curiosity to inquire into his situation, along with some disposition to sympathize with him . . . The first question which we ask is, What has befallen you? Till this be answered . . . our fellow-feeling is not very considerable.[12]

Smith posits not a passive perceiver, but rather one who actively seeks out meaning, much like J. J. Gibson's perceiver, who seeks out invariants in the perceptual environment in relation to adaptive goals or needs. And what directs the perceiver's questions here is a particular sort of affect that is rooted in a situation that can be stated in narrative terms.

We might see the film spectator in the same light. The spectator is motivated in part by a desire to understand. He or she is curious about the unfolding of the narrative and will relate disparate sensory experience to narrative concerns that are often felt as strong emotions and marked sympathies and antipathies toward characters. This is not to deny "excess," ambiguity, conflicting interpretations, or filmic elements that simply cannot be plausibly integrated.[13] Nonetheless, a cognitive-perceptual theory of spectatorship must assume a spectator who attempts to make sense of a narrative by relating disparate elements into a coherent whole, and whose bodily and cognitive experiences are understood as synoptic as well. The Hollywood cinema is clearly designed to encourage such sense-making activity. The spectator is invited to make sense of and respond to the film, guided by the film's prefocused narration and in accordance with the representation of concern-based construals that are built into the film through the film's narration, as expressed in narrative structure, point of view, and style.

CHARACTER GOALS AND NARRATION

If a spectator has no concern about a film or its story, the spectator will have a markedly tepid emotional response, or perhaps a negative response of boredom and disdain. If emotions are concern-based construals, as I have argued, how do films generate and maintain the strong concerns that are necessary for powerful emotional responses? To a certain extent, the film's narration may depend on the spectator's natural curiosity and fascination, but this will not last long. The narration might also create suspense and elicit surprises in order to maintain spectator interest. One of the most powerful and common means by which films create concern, however, is through sympathy, empathy, and antipathy for film characters. Sympathy for a character leads the spectator to take a strong interest in the character's well-being and develop strong concerns about story outcomes.

It is not controversial to claim, then, that spectator response is aligned, to a certain extent, with the fortunes of certain characters, and most centrally with characters for whom the film encourages sympathy or empathy. In this section, I more deeply explore the nature of spectator response in relation to such favored characters. In doing so, I want to steer my way between two opposing views of this process, two extremes in the formulation of the spectator's psychic relation to a sympathetic character, most often a protagonist.

The first view we might call the "identification hypothesis," a view that we have briefly discussed previously. The identification hypothesis holds that spectators share the thoughts and emotions of the sympathetic protagonist through processes of simulation and empathy. This view has been associated with film theory of the psychoanalytic school (screen theory), and also, to some extent, with Torben Grodal, as I have discussed previously in the "Character Goals and Engagement" section in Chapter 3. The second view, which is diametrically opposed, we might call "ineliminable egocentrism." This is the position that the viewer's cognition and responses are not the same as the assumed thoughts and emotions of the protagonist or any other character. The viewer's response to characters, then, cannot be properly considered to be empathetic, if by empathetic one means that the spectator will have the same responses as the protagonist or protagonists. As I detailed at some length in Chapter 3, Noël Carroll, for example, argues that the proper term to describe the spectator "relationship" with a character is not "identification," which implies a projective immersion in the subjectivity of the character, but "assimilation," which holds that the spectator maintains a sense of external "critic" or separate subjectivity even in the case of following the actions of the most sympathetic protagonist.[14]

Neither of these extremes—the identification hypothesis or ineliminable egocentrism—is plausible, it seems to me; I argue for a position between the two, a position that recognizes that intended spectator response is guided at the highest level not by the response of any particular character, but by the film's narration. Spectators often respond incongruently with even sympathetic characters, making the "identification hypothesis" too simplistic. But spectators are also capable of sharing some of the imagined emotional experiences of characters through emotional contagion and other empathic processes. Moreover, even if spectators do not share exactly the emotions of sympathetic protagonists, their responses are very often congruent in valence. To put it colloquially, spectators root for favored characters. This cannot be described as mere egocentrism.

This being said, I think the latter position—ineliminable egocentrism—is more accurate than the identification hypothesis. To demonstrate this, I would like to consider the relationship between character and spectator concern-based construals. That is, if I can demonstrate that the spectator's concern-based construals are not aligned with the presumed concern-based construals of sympathetic characters, then it would be quite easy to see that the presumed character responses to narrative situations will often be different—sometimes radically different—than spectator responses. And if this is true, then we must maintain that spectator response, although dependent to some extent on the response of favored characters, must be conceived as having an independent trajectory.

Protagonist Structures

First, consider the several *protagonist structures* that are found in Hollywood films.

1. *Single protagonist.* This is the most common protagonist structure, in which a single character's goals, concerns, decisions, and actions, along with those of minor characters who function as "helpers," drive the narrative forward. Examples: *Jerry Maguire* (1996), *Indiana Jones and the Temple of Doom* (1984), *Gladiator* (2000), *Casablanca* (1942), *Dances with Wolves* (1990), *Mr. Smith Goes to Washington* (1939).

2. *Single protagonist, partially sympathetic antagonist.* A film with a traditional protagonist, but an antagonist who is partially sympathetic and of close to equal stature, perhaps played by a major star. Examples: *The Boys from Brazil* (1978), *Heat* (1995), *Runaway Jury* (2003).

3. *Aligned dual protagonists.* Two or three protagonists who share a goal or goals. *Lethal Weapon* (1987), *Lethal Weapon 2* (1989), *Butch Cassidy and the Sundance Kid* (1969).

4. *Parallel dual protagonists.*[15] Interacting protagonists with differing but not opposed goals. Examples: *Handle with Care* (1977), *Desperately Seeking Susan* (1985), *The Hunt for Red October* (1990), *Crimes and Misdemeanors* (1989).

5. *Initially misaligned dual protagonists.* Protagonists who are opposed initially but who come to share a goal by story's end. Example: *His Girl Friday* (1940), *The Lady Eve* (1941), *You've Got Mail* (1998), *Catch Me if You Can* (2002).

6. *Opposed protagonists.* Example: *Amadeus* (1984).

7. *Three protagonists.* Examples: *On the Town* (1949), *How to Marry a Millionaire* (1953), *Three Coins in the Fountain* (1954), *It's Always Fair Weather* (1955), *The Philadelphia Story* (1940).

8. *Network narratives.* Multiple protagonists given roughly equal stature. Examples: *Grand Canyon* (1991), *Smoke* (1995), *Hotel Berlin* (1945), *Plaza Suite* (1971), *American Graffiti* (1973), *Drive-In* (1976), *Dazed and Confused* (1993), *Do the Right Thing* (1989), *Crash* (2004).

To understand the ways in which spectator and character concern-based construals differ, we must also consider various *types* of protagonists. Below I describe four sorts of protagonists in regard to the textual construction of their goals and character. More types of protagonists could be listed, of course. This list is meant not meant to be comprehensive.

Protagonist Types

1. *Conventional hero.* Laudable goals and superior character. Examples: Clark Kent/Superman in *Superman* (1978), William Wallace in *Braveheart* (1995), Sarah Connor in *Terminator 2: Judgment Day* (1991), Jefferson Smith in *Mr. Smith Goes to Washington* (1939).

2. *Flawed hero.* Partially flawed goals and/or character. The charac-
   ter often, but not always, is redeemed by story's end. Examples:
   William Munny in *Unforgiven* (1992), Ethan Edwards in *The
   Searchers* (1956), Rick in *Casablanca* (1942), Jerry in *Jerry
   Maguire*, Frank Abagnale Jr. in *Catch Me if You Can*, Erin in *Erin
   Brockovich* (2000), Royal in *The Royal Tenenbaums* (2001), Henry
   in *Regarding Henry* (1991).

3. *Warped protagonist.* Warped goals and/or character, unredeemed
   by story's end. Examples: Salieri in *Amadeus*, Jack Torrance in
   The Shining (1980), Carrie White in *Carrie* (1976), Don Michael
   Corleone in *The Godfather: Part II* (1974), Scottie in *Vertigo*
   (1958).

4. *Conflicted or confused protagonist.* The protagonist has conflicting
   goals and is troubled by ambiguity or conflict, sometimes having to
   make a difficult choice. Examples: Deckard in *Blade Runner* (1982),
   John Book in *Witness* (1985), Johnny Cash in *Walk the Line* (2005),
   Benjamin Braddock in the first half of *The Graduate* (1967), George
   in most of *Shampoo* (1975).

Relative to these varied protagonist structures and types of protagonists, the spectator can have varied concerns and construals. Some or all of
these responses may be present in the same film at various points in the
narrative development.

Spectator Alignment with Characters' Concerns and Construals

1. *Congruence.* The character's and spectator's concerns and construals are relatively congruent. For example, Jerry in *Jerry Maguire*
   acts to keep Rod Tidwell as his client after Jerry is fired by his
   agency. The spectator also desires that Rod Tidwell remain Jerry's
   client, and thus Jerry and the spectator share a concern and a construal. The concern is for Jerry's success as an agent and for his
   general well-being. The construal is that if Rod Tidwell fires him,
   he will have no clients and this will harm his well-being.

2. *Benign incongruence.* The spectator's concerns and/or construals
   are congruent, but do not match character concerns and construals. For example, Jerry intends to marry his fiancée, Avery. The
   spectator desires that Jerry marry not Avery but Dorothy, who
   needs Jerry more than Avery does and will be a better mate for
   Jerry. This sort of misalignment of character goals and spectator

desires is characteristic of romantic comedies, at least until the narrative's end, when the favored couple unites romantically and the story comes to a happy conclusion. For the bulk of such narratives, character and spectator concerns are similar, but the construals of the narrative situation may be markedly different.

3. *Movement from incongruence to congruence or vice versa.* In *Unforgiven,* the spectator is initially aligned with William Munny's goal to capture and punish the cowboys who assaulted a prostitute. (This is in part due to expectations having to do with Clint Eastwood's star persona; he should not be a mere pig farmer, as he is as the story begins, but a heroic figure engaging in adventure.) As one of the cowboys, Davey, apologizes and wishes to make restitution for his part in the crime, and as the spectator learns that the accounts of the assault have been exaggerated and falsified, the typical spectator does not desire that William Munny shoot Davey. When Munny does shoot him, it is intended to be a negative, even painful emotional experience for the spectator due to sympathy for Davey and the spectator's desire that he not be shot. Here the movement is from congruence to incongruence. The spectator gradually becomes alienated from Munny's concerns and behaviors.

4. *Mixed, ambiguous, and conflicted congruence.* In *The Searchers,* Ethan has the goal of finding his niece, Debbie, who has been kidnapped by Comanches. But the spectator suspects that Ethan will kill Debbie rather than save her because he hates Native Americans and loathes the idea that she has married Scar, a Comanche chief. The spectator desires that Ethan find Debbie, but fears that he will kill her. One of the greatest moments of relief in the film occurs when Ethan finds her and takes Debbie into his arms to rescue her. Spectator concerns are in alignment with some of Ethan's concerns (to find Debbie), but are opposed to other of his apparent concerns (to kill Debbie). Thus Ethan's presumed emotional trajectory will differ from that of the spectator.

5. *Distanced and/or ironic observation.* In many of the films of Jim Jarmusch—for example, *Stranger Than Paradise* (1984), *Down by Law* (1986), and *Mystery Train* (1989), the narration encourages neither congruent nor incongruent concern-based construals, but rather a distanced, somewhat ironic perspective toward the characters and their situation. This stance is more common in films of the "art cinema" than of Hollywood, at least with regard to the

narration's perspective on the protagonist. Perhaps the goals of the characters are unclear, irrelevant, or meant to be merely amusing or curious rather than the object of sincere spectator concern. In any case, the film encourages not sympathetic emotions, but rather emotions that do not depend on sympathetic response, such as ironic amusement, fascination, disdain, and so on.

With these basic categories in place, we can draw a few conclusions. If spectator emotion is a concern-based construal, then a spectator can never entirely share the character's presumed emotions. This is most easily seen in the last four types of spectator misalignment, in which spectator desires are incongruent with character goals or the spectator lacks the concern about the goals that the character is presumed to have. The most consistent congruent alignment occurs in single-protagonist films with conventional heroes. Fewer films than might be assumed, however, have flawless heroes. Such films tend to be along the order of superhero movies or the sort of morally unproblematic tales favored by Mel Gibson or Sylvester Stallone. Even here it is essential to separate protagonist goals from congruent spectator desires. In *Superman*, Superman's goal is to prevent Lex Luthor from destroying the world. The spectator's appraisal of the situation is congruent in that he or she generally approves of Superman's goal. Yet the spectator does not want to prevent Lex Luthor from destroying the world; the spectator desires that in the world of the fiction, Lex Luthor be stopped from destroying the world. With such radically different standpoints and appraisals of the situation, the spectator's emotional response must be different from the assumed response Superman will have (assuming that Superman has humanlike emotions).

More realist drama favors the flawed hero, as in *Erin Brockovich*, for example, which foregrounds the crusade of uneducated single mother Erin Brockovich (Julia Roberts) to successfully win a huge lawsuit against the polluting Pacific Gas and Electric Corporation. Although Erin is a sympathetic hero and spectator desires are aligned with her goals, her flaws require that the spectator's response will typically not be wholly congruent. Erin's passion is responsible in part for her success, but her red-hot temper and foul mouth cause her problems. When Erin loses her temper, the spectator's response is hardly congruent; rather, it is likely amusement, fascination, or especially at the film's beginning (and before strong sympathies have developed), disdain.

Other flawed protagonists include Jon Voight's naïve cowboy, Joe Buck, and the homeless New Yorker Ratso Rizzo (Dustin Hoffman), whom he

9. The troubled protagonists of *Midnight Cowboy* (1969), Ratso Rizzo (Dustin Hoffman) and Joe Buck (Jon Voight).

eventually befriends in *Midnight Cowboy* (1969). Full of optimism and good cheer, Buck leaves the small Texas town where he works as a dishwasher to become a hustler or gigolo in New York. The viewer is led to believe that his optimism is misplaced, his good cheer a result of his simple naïvete. This perspective on the man ensures that the spectator's responses will rarely be completely similar to his, but rather focused on him from an exterior viewpoint in part determined by the film's narration. It is only in the film's second half that viewer and protagonist goals become congruent.

In the case of network narratives, spectator desires may be more or less aligned with various characters in various degrees of congruence. But the congruence will be different from character to character as the spectator develops complex responses to each one. When sympathetic characters clash or their goals conflict or compete, the spectator must negotiate which of the character's goals to maintain alignment with in what measure; such alignments may alter dramatically through the course of a film. *Crash,* for example, follows several Los Angeles residents of various races and ethnic origins during the course of a few days. Its thematic intent is to demonstrate the power of racism to cause misunderstanding, hurt, and even death. Throughout the film, the spectator's sympathy for the various characters ebbs and flows according to the filmmaker's careful calculations. Early in the story, racist Officer John Ryan, for example, assaults Christine by caressing her against her will in the guise of a weapons search. Christine is the wife of Cameron, whose Lincoln Navigator Ryan has stopped. Ryan assaults Christine as a way to humiliate the black man and exercise his power as a policeman. Later, however, the film increases sympathy for Ryan, as we see that Ryan is powerless to get proper medical care for his suffering father. Later still, Ryan risks his life to save Christine after she has been in an auto accident. Similarly, two articulate young black men, Anthony and Peter, walk a swanky L.A. street discussing racism and their perceived racially motivated lack of good service at a restaurant. Then, surprisingly, they steal the car of a young white couple.

Moreover, sympathetic characters come into contact with each other and clash. Christine berates Cameron for allowing her to be humiliated and for his lack of righteous indignation. Farhad, the Iranian shopkeeper, confronts Daniel, the Mexican-American locksmith, and nearly kills Daniel's daughter. Anthony and Peter attempt to carjack Cameron's vehicle. Jean, an affluent white woman, accuses Daniel of intending to rob her house after changing her locks. The point is that the spectator's responses do not simply correspond with those of sympathetic characters, because sympathetic characters have conflicting, contradictory, and/or seemingly flawed responses, goals, and construals to which the spectator cannot entirely assent.

What guides intended spectator response is not merely the response of favored characters but, more centrally, *the narration* that establishes preferred modes of judgment and response. A film's narration, to a greater or lesser extent, presents the story from a perspective exterior to that of any character, protagonist or not. And it is the narration that forms and guides intended spectator response. That focusing or guidance may elicit emotion that is independent of and in some cases quite different from the responses of sympathetic characters. Thus, intended spectator response and character response should not be confused, although for many films, at least much of the time, such responses will be congruent, that is, oriented toward similar outcomes and goals.

SYNESTHETIC AFFECT AND FITTINGNESS

So far, we have come to some conclusions about spectator emotion in relation to character emotion, and I have claimed that the affective trajectory of a film is guided by the narration and not necessarily by the emotional response of any particular character in the fiction. Thus, for example, while a film character may experience extreme fear, the spectator may be privy to superior information and know that he or she is in no imminent danger.

The spectator may experience something like mild pity and amusement at the character's fearful response. Although the spectator will not typically have the *same* emotions as those experienced by a character, a film scene may nonetheless provide for an affective experience that participates in the affective shading or color of that experience, or that is *fitting* with it. Thus, a fear scenario (in which a character experiences fear) may not necessarily elicit fear in the audience but may elicit affects associated with fear or fearlike experiences.

This claim must seem vague at this point, so I will explain. Spectator comprehension and response are unified in part through the top-down mental activities and emotional responses elicited by filmic narration. Perception is not only synoptic, however, but also synesthetic, in that spectators often find their response to stimuli in one modality to fit with the responses to stimuli in another. Disruptive editing may fit with chaotic music; conversely, a slow, smooth tracking shot could fit with the elegant movements of a ballet dancer. We might call this *synesthetic affect.* Certain elements of a film have affective charges that are congruent in tone and valence, fitting in the means by which they express and elicit a "feeling tone" that the spectator experiences as unified and coherent. This is bottom-up processing, because the viewer may find the elements to be fitting in their felt similarities prior to or independent of any narrative coherence imposed from above.[16]

In using this terminology, I am making reference to what some psychologists call "weak synesthesia."[17] Strong synesthesia, which affects perhaps one of every 2,000 persons, is a phenomenon in which in the mind of a subject, words or sounds are accompanied by vivid images of colors or shapes. Weak synesthesia, on the other hand, is a form of cross-modal fittingness that is experienced by most people. Thus, particular sounds might be perceived to fit with shapes or line-shapes, such as a soothing melody with a softly curving line. It is highly likely that some associations between various elements, such as the association of fast editing and movement toward the camera with "energy," are to some extent universal, due in part to their powerful physical effect on spectators. Other associations between elements are no doubt idiosyncratic to particular cultures and subcultures, or to particular individuals. For example, the association of various human gestures with ideas or attitudes is culturally variable to a significant extent, while the effect of objects apparently rushing toward the screen (and toward the spectator) at high speed will be more universal.

Since film is such an eclectic art form, one of the chief skills of the film-maker is the ability to combine cross-modal elements that will be affectively congruent and working in tandem, or that will elicit the right kind of affective friction in appropriate dramatic circumstances. A consideration of the nature of synesthetic affect is vital to a full understanding of the affective experience offered by narrative film. It also further demonstrates that all considerations of spectator emotional response must distinguish spectator from character response.

NARRATIVE SCENARIOS AND SYNESTHETIC AFFECT

Charles Dickens loved to give public readings because he could directly observe how his stories affected his listeners. After an 1845 reading of *The Christmas Carol,* attended by an audience of 2,500, Dickens observed: "They lost nothing, misinterpreted nothing, followed everything closely, laughed and cried. . . . I felt as if we were all bodily going up into the clouds." Another reading by Dickens was attended by the famous Shakespearean actor William Macready, an audience member whom Dickens was particularly interested in affecting. Dickens observed, "If you had seen Macready last night, undisguisedly sobbing, and crying on the sofa as I read, you would have felt, as I did, what a thing it is to have power."[18]

Many filmmakers have shared Dickens's deep satisfaction in the ability to move and manipulate audiences, to exercise the techniques of their craft to orchestrate powerful affect. Dickens played on his audience's sympathies, but Alfred Hitchcock was more interested in eliciting suspense and an experience something like the "existential emotions"—fright, shame, guilt, and more generally, anxiety and self-conscious unease. Hitchcock was fascinated with and proud of his success in manipulating the audiences of *Psycho;* he was "playing them like an organ," he said.[19] As Hitchcock summed it up:

> My main satisfaction is that the film had an effect on the audiences, and I consider that very important. I don't care about the subject matter; I don't care about acting; but I do care about the pieces of film and the photography and the sound track and all of the technical ingredients that made the audience scream. I feel it's tremendously satisfying for us to be able to achieve something of a mass emotion. It wasn't a message that stirred the audiences, nor was it a great performance or their enjoyment of the novel. They were aroused by a pure film.[20]

In popular opinion, Alfred Hitchcock is often associated with suspense and thrills, but the emotions elicited by his films are more complex and oddly chilling than these words suggest, having something to do with shame, guilt, and social anxiety in general. Hitchcock often put his characters into classic scenarios in which they experience shame and/or guilt. Joan Fontaine, who in *Rebecca* (1940) plays a character known only as "the second Mrs. de Winter," becomes the mistress of Manderley, but cannot escape the feeling that she is an inadequate imposter who cannot take the place of the first Mrs. de Winter. In *The Wrong Man* (1956), Manny Balestrero is arrested for a robbery that he did not commit and suffers both guilt and shame despite his innocence. My question is this: can the spectator be made to experience these emotions him- or herself? To put it another way, do Hitchcock's films produce shamed and guilty spectators, or merely shamed and guilty characters? And if only the characters might be thought to experience shame or guilt, what sort of affective response do spectators have to these narrative scenarios?

Scholars of emotion and the arts sometimes assume that film and literature can elicit the full spectrum of human emotions. Yet in such accounts, one rarely hears the claim that a novel makes a reader jealous or that a film elicits shame in a spectator. Certain emotions and affiliated affects—for example, suspense, pity, fear, and anger—are mentioned far more often than shame, guilt, and jealousy in accounts of narrative and emotion. Could it be that narrative film and literature are incapable of eliciting certain kinds of emotions? Why is it that narratives regularly elicit some human emotions and rarely elicit others? My argument is that narrative scenarios of guilt and shame usually elicit not shame and guilt per se but rather a synesthetic affect that is congruent or fitting with paradigm scenarios of shame and guilt. The various affects that Hitchcock intends to elicit and arouse do not constitute shame and guilt themselves, but do approximate the affective color and valence of paradigmatic guilt and shame—through a process of affective synesthesia.

SHAME, GUILT, AND THE SPECTATOR

First, let us examine shame and guilt as paradigmatic emotions, in order to determine whether and under what conditions a film spectator might have these emotions. Emotions are rooted in construals or appraisals of events and situations in relation to the concerns of the subject; I have called emotions "concern-based construals." Shame and guilt occur when one evaluates one's behavior in relation to some standard, rule, or goal, and finds that one has failed to meet the goal or transgressed the rule. Thus, shame and guilt have at their heart the evaluation of the self. These standards, rules, and goals are in part culturally constructed, and therefore, like disgust (an emotion dealt with in Chapter 7), shame and guilt are gatekeeper emotions that can serve to regulate social behavior. Hitchcock is not interested in exploring the social implications of the existential emotions, however, but rather invokes shame and guilt primarily to increase suspense and engender various self-conscious anxieties. Hitchcock invokes scenarios of shame and guilt as tools to affect the spectator, and for Hitchcock, producing such affect is his ultimate goal.

Many have noted Hitchcock's interest in guilt, but often it is shame or embarrassment that is best associated with the scenarios Hitchcock constructs. Shame is rooted in a concern about respectability, both being intrinsically worthy in some sense (for example, worthy in physical appearance, social grace, religious piety, athletic skill, or intellectual aptitude) and having the social appearance of such worthiness. Shame typically implies the perception of defects in the self, or in a person or group with whom one closely associates, with respect to some standard or goal one would like to have attained. Unlike guilt, however, in the case of shame, the defects are not construed as morally blameworthy. The concern of shame is for respectability; the relevant construal is that one has failed to maintain respectability in some respect.

Iris in *The Lady Vanishes* (1938) may appear to be disrespectable because she insists that Miss Froy has disappeared, even while those around her consistently claim that Miss Froy never existed. Alicia in *Notorious* (1946) has much cause for shame, ranging from her father's traitorous past to her expedient marriage to a man she detests; her shame is magnified by the distrustful and disapproving attitude of her lover, Devlin (Cary Grant). Certainly, some of the suspense of these films stems not merely from danger to the character's lives but also from the spectator's interest in their respectability and the preservation of their self-image as socially worthy.

Guilt, unlike shame, occurs when one finds moral fault with one's own actions or the actions of an individual or group with which one is closely associated. The concern of guilt is to avoid blame with regard to some moral standard, and the construal that leads to guilt is that one has transgressed such a standard, and that one is in fact to blame. The guilty person believes that he or she has transgressed a moral imperative that is perceived as legitimate or authoritative.[21]

Shame and guilt often accompany one another. Typically, according to Susan Miller, wrongdoing experienced as voluntary produces guilt, while wrongdoing experienced as involuntary produces shame "both in relation to the action itself and to the failure of self-control."[22] Yet one's construal may be uncertain or conflicted with regard to the volition involved in the wrongdoing, or the wrongdoing may be seen as only partly voluntary.

Moreover, if one commits an act of wrongdoing, one will often experience guilt for having violated the standard and shame for the diminishment of self-esteem that follows from what one has done.

Can narrative films elicit shame and guilt in spectators, and more particularly, do Hitchcock's films elicit such emotions? I would like to put aside for the moment the very real possibility that some viewers may feel shame or embarrassment for the act of moviegoing itself. In some cultures, where the act of moviegoing is morally proscribed or at least strongly suspect, the very act of being seen in a theater or viewing a particular kind of film (pornography, horror, sentimental melodrama, or inspirational film, for example), might cause embarrassment. My question assumes a culture and an audience for which moviegoing is seen as normative and socially acceptable, and asks whether spectators can feel guilt or shame not for moviegoing per se, but in relation to the particular narrative of a film.

To consider this question, let us consider again the various types of emotions that viewers have at the movies. Direct emotions are experienced in association with understanding the story and include anticipation, suspense, surprise, curiosity, interest, fascination, and excitement. Sympathetic and antipathetic emotions arise from the spectator's assessment of a narrative situation primarily in relation to a character's concerns; they include such emotions as happiness, sadness, anger, pity, and fear. While viewers can share these emotions in part through various forms of empathy, the response of the viewer is always differently inflected, typically more sympathetic than empathetic. That is, I may empathize with a character, but my response is never purely and solely empathetic (strictly speaking), for the reason that I perceive the situation from my particular perspective, from the outside rather than "from the inside."

Shame and guilt do not seem to be candidates for direct emotions of the sort typically experienced by film viewers. The only condition in which I can imagine that a spectator might be ashamed of or made guilty about the way a story unfolds is if the spectator feels in some way responsible for the film, for example, if the spectator is the film's director or screenwriter, or a close relative of the director or screenwriter. In the typical case, however, shame and guilt cannot be direct emotions in response to a movie.

The case of the sympathetic emotions is more interesting, although here again I will argue that shame and guilt are not sympathetic emotions. I can feel shame and guilt in response to the behavior of another person if the person is closely enough associated with me that I see their behavior as a reflection on me. For example, a family member who behaves boorishly at a wedding celebration may make me ashamed because I am so closely associated with him. We might also consider the case of collective responsibility and guilt, a case in which the viewer feels some kind of ethnic, national, or other affiliation with a fictional or character who commits an act worthy of condemnation. A former Nazi watching *Jud Süss* (1940) or *Open City* (1945), an American watching the Vietnam documentary *Hearts and Minds* (1974) or *Syriana* (2006), a diamond owner while watching *Blood Diamond* (2006)—all might experience a kind of collective shame or guilt. Yet even in these cases we must be careful to distinguish collective from individual guilt and to differentiate between the various objects of guilt. We hear anecdotes about women removing and hiding their diamond rings after screenings of *Blood Diamond*, but the guilt or shame here is directed toward their own sense of complicity in the bloody diamond trade. Their guilt or shame is thus directed at themselves, not at the film's characters.

Collective guilt and shame certainly exists, in and outside the movie theater. Yet in viewing fictional movies, I would argue, it is somewhat rare, and occurs only in relation to films that bear a strong relationship to actual historical events. Guilt and shame are most typically elicited when a person perceives that *she* or *he* has violated some standard of morality or respectable conduct. It is primarily a self-directed emotion that may in some cases be elicited by one's membership in a larger social or ethnic group. But the possibility of collective guilt and shame is attenuated when the movie is fictional and tells a story that is not meant to bear a relationship to actual historical events. The psychic relationship between a character and a viewer is not such that the viewer typically feels responsible for the behavior of a fictional character or tainted by guilt or disrespectability by the behavior or desires of a character. The spectator may have compassion for or experience suspense in relation to the guilt or shame of a character, but he or she typically will not experience guilt or shame merely in response to the behavior, motives, or desires of that character.

SHAME AND GUILT AS META-EMOTIONS

In relation to shame and guilt, we have not yet discussed *meta-emotions*, a very important class of emotional responses to narratives. The spectator may well respond to elements of her or his own experience and behavior as a spectator. For example, I may become disgusted with myself for responding emotionally to a sentimental scene or for missing an obvious clue that is needed to understand a narrative development. The question I will ask now is this: given that these sorts of meta-emotions are possible at the movies, can the spectator experience shame and guilt as meta-emotions? Can a Hitchcock film cause the spectator to feel guilt or shame for having wishes or desires of certain types while viewing a film? Might not spectators come to experience shame or guilt in relation to their own responses?

Consider film scholar Robin Wood's claim that Hitchcock's films "penetrate and undermine our complacency and set notions, and bring about a consequent readjustment in our attitude to life."[23] For Wood, two aspects of Hitchcock's films produce this effect. First, the films exhibit a "complex and disconcerting moral sense,"[24] insisting on the complexity of good and evil and on the presence of evil impulses in all of humanity. Second, the films have an ability to make spectators aware of the "impurity" of their desires. In other words, Hitchcock's films are antidotes to self-righteousness and smug superiority. They challenge the idealization of the self, and thus promote the virtues of humility and self-awareness.

For Wood, Hitchcock's films have therapeutic value in the way that they manage spectator identification. This psychic management is a two-step process. First, the films confront a character with her or his worst fears or obsessions, then cure the character by forcing her or him to squarely confront them. Second, this "therapy" is extended to the spectator by means of what Wood calls "identification." When the spectator identifies with a protagonist, the spectator's own motives, impulses, and responses are involved, not merely those of the character. Thus, Wood implies, spectators are provided with a powerful lesson through a protagonist who serves as their surrogate.

Strangers on a Train (1951) provides a good example of how this process ostensibly works. In this film, Guy, a professional tennis player in a bad marriage, has a chance meeting and conversation on a train with Bruno. Little does Guy know that Bruno is mentally disturbed, and that in Bruno's mind, Guy and Bruno's conversation has resulted in a deal. Bruno will kill Guy's estranged wife Miriam, and Guy will reciprocate by murdering Bruno's hated father. Hitchcock clearly shows that Guy hates Miriam and at times wishes her dead, but he has no plans to kill her. Thus, when Miriam is murdered, Guy shares in Bruno's guilt, despite having had no inkling of Bruno's plans. Wood writes that the spectator, at some level, also is made to have contempt for Miriam and even take some satisfaction in her death. At the same time, spectators are ashamed of that response. "It is this conflict within the spectator," Wood writes, "that is the essence of the ensuing suspense: we, as well as Guy, are implicated in Miriam's murder."[25] Notice that Wood's claim here corroborates my contention that suspense in a Hitchcock film is complex and may involve self-conscious emotions. The main point is that for Wood, certain key scenes of *Strangers on a Train* are therapeutic in that they show spectators how easy it would be for them to share the kinds of motives and desires of which (presumably) they normally would not approve.

In my opinion, Robin Wood operates with an overly expansive notion of character identification in that he too simply aligns the spectator's desires and responses with those of the protagonist. But despite my reservations, I think he is right that spectators may, in some instances, be induced to share some of the desires of, or to have parallel desires with, characters in a film. Thus, for example, it is possible that if spectators of *Strangers on a Train* desire Miriam's murder (as the protagonist does), they may be made to experience shame and/or guilt for having so desired her murder. The spectator of *Henry: Portrait of a Serial Killer* (1986) may be both interested in and ashamed of wanting to see the murders on the killer's videotape. The spectator of *Blue Velvet* (1986) may be both aroused and ashamed of being aroused in relation to the hitting scenes that occur in Dorothy Vallens's apartment. And if the spectator is later encouraged by the narration to reflect on her or his previous desires, it is certainly possible that the spectator may experience guilt and/or shame for having had them. Thus, shame and guilt may be elicited in film not as direct or sympathetic emotions but as meta-emotions.

SHAME/GUILT SCENARIOS AND SYNESTHETIC AFFECT

I still have not fully answered the questions I set out to answer, however. There are cases in the films of Alfred Hitchcock in which the spectator is made to feel something like shame or guilt not in response to the spectator's own thoughts or desires as objects of meta-emotion, but rather in response to narrative events. Yet at the same time, these are not sympathetic emotions, and perhaps not even recognizable emotions at all, strictly speaking. These are what I call synesthetic affects.

Strangers on a Train presents a paradigm scenario for guilt or shame, strongly suggesting that the protagonist is likely to have these emotions. Hitchcock also uses various techniques in an attempt to elicit affect congruent with or expressive of the experience of guilt and shame—for the spectator. In one scene, Guy returns to his apartment at night. As he climbs the steps, Hitchcock gives us two canted angles, suggesting imbalance. On the soundtrack we hear the almost funereal tolling of church bells, further setting a dark mood and sense of foreboding. Then a voice calls out quietly

10.   If *Strangers on a Train* (1951) does not elicit actual guilt or shame in the spectator, it at least elicits affects that are synesthetically fitting to the experience of guilt or shame.

from across the street, almost as though it is a voice from Guy's subconscious: "Guy . . . over here, Guy." It is Bruno, standing in the shadows, who has come to tell Guy that he has killed Miriam. As Guy approaches Bruno, the discordant notes of the program music become eerie and disarming. Bruno insists that Guy is also guilty of the murder, since, he says, they planned it together, "crisscross." As Bruno and Guy speak, Hitchcock takes advantage of proxemics by having the actors stand very close together and filming in a series of shot/reverse shots in close-up, increasing the sense of unwanted intimacy that the scene suggests. The two characters are being linked at the level of feeling. After the police arrive, Guy moves to Bruno's position behind the bars of a wrought iron fence as they both hide from the police, furthering their similarity. The low-key lighting and deep shadows across their faces suggest that Guy shares Bruno's guilt and that like it or not, the two men are aligned. This is a matter of affect and not merely an abstract expression. The lighting creates a mood fitting to the experience. The positions of the actors associate both with action tendencies typical of guilt or shame, such as hiding or escaping detection. The close physical proximity of Guy and Bruno suggests, in felt bodily terms, a strange sort of intimacy.

Guy's fiancée, her sister, and her U.S. Senator father, suspect that Guy may have actually committed the murder. At the party scene, Hitchcock carefully frames their doubtful gazes as they observe Guy and his suspicious association with the madman Bruno. Guy's reactions are not as powerfully affecting as they could be given Farley Granger's limitations as an actor, yet his responses suggest recognition that he is strongly suspected by those he cares about the most. As a direct and bodily sort of communication, the viewer's response to the body on the screen may be one of contagion or synchrony, leading to a contagion that elicits some of the physiological characteristics of shame or guilt, perhaps that knotted feeling in the stomach or increased respiration. These shot compositions, the editing to reaction shots to reveal Guy's sense of guilt, the dark and somber mood created through lighting and music—all are associated with feelings of guilt or shame. In short, *Strangers on a Train* may not elicit guilt or shame directly, as a construal that the spectator has violated some standard. Nonetheless, it may elicit a synesthetic experience that approximates some of the elements of paradigmatic shame and guilt.

Synesthetic affect is very common at the movies, an experience in which the spectator cannot be said to share the same emotions as the characters, but nonetheless experiences powerful elements of the affective experience, such that the spectator might be said to have an approximation of those emotions that is affectively similar (in "feeling tone" or physiological manifestation) and congruent (that is, sharing the same general orientation toward the narrative situation). The spectator may experience the "feeling tone" of shame and guilt without actually being ashamed or guilty. We might also say that a good film like *Strangers on a Train* can give the spectator an excellent sense of what it might be like to *be* ashamed or guilty, without actually eliciting paradigmatic shame and guilt. The multiple channels of information the film presents elicit synesthetic affect with marked cross-modal similarities to the experience of shame and guilt by arousing cognitive and automatic processing, physiological effects, and also spectator desires and wishes, which correspond to what we might call, broadly, the guilt and/or shame experience.

FOUR PARAMETERS OF AFFECTIVE TRAJECTORIES

The intended affective trajectory of a film, then, is governed by the film's narration, which is focused to provide a concern-based construal of the represented events, organized primarily by narrational point of view, narrative paradigm scenarios, sympathies and antipathies for characters, and various film techniques designed to contribute to the overall affective experience. Affective trajectories must be described first and foremost in relation to types of narrative scenarios and degrees of sympathy and antipathy for various characters. Yet we can describe such trajectories in accordance with other, more useful parameters as well. I conclude this chapter by highlighting four of these parameters: kind, strength, valence, and value.

Affective trajectories should first be described by the *kinds* of emotions and affects that are intended. Here, of course, it is important to distinguish between the presumed emotions and affects of characters and those of viewers. Paradigm scenarios for jealousy or anger or vengeance or shame will not necessarily elicit such emotions in the audience. An emphasis on kinds of emotions will inevitably lead to the study of film genres in relation to their particular affective appeals. Studies of melodrama and horror have begun to explore affect and emotion in those genres. The most ambitious attempt to chart the appeals of various genres from a broadly cognitive perspective is found in Torben Grodal's *Moving Pictures: A New Theory of Film Genres, Feelings, and Cognition*,[26] which offers a theory of emotion elicitation somewhat different than mine. A good deal of work remains to be done in investigating the affective arc of various genres.

We can also chart affect in a film according to trajectories of strength. The classical Hollywood film is said to feature rising action building to a climactic point that presumably features the strongest affect. After the climax, suspense and fear are dissolved and replaced in the epilogue by a relief that gradually dissipates affect. Yet other schemas for strength of affect are possible. The contemporary action film, for example, might be thought to begin immediately with a high pitch of affect and alternate between high affect and relative calm throughout the narrative.[27]

"Valence" refers to the pleasure or displeasure associated with particular affects. Affective responses are typically seen as negative or positive in relation to the construals that lead to them. Events perceived as positive for the subject typically lead to positive emotions, while events judged as negative to the subject lead to negative emotions. The question of whether or how emotions thought to be negative may cause pleasure is an essential one for scholars of media emotion. Not only do certain genres such as horror centrally feature such emotions, but all narratives, to a certain extent, *must* elicit some negative emotions. The issue of negative emotions is dealt with in the next chapter.

Finally, one can discuss affective trajectory in relation to the value it represents for the spectator. To assess the value of a film in these terms leads one to questions of uses and gratifications and whether narratives, in the affective experiences they offer, move beyond mere entertainment and have therapeutic or instructional value of some sort. This very difficult question is also touched on in the next chapter.

6. Negative Emotions and Sympathetic Narratives

James Cameron, the director of the 1997 *Titanic*, describes his Hollywood blockbuster as a "canvas offering the full spectral range of human emotion."[1] Cameron assumes that experiencing this full spectral range is inherently enjoyable, something to be strived for. Certainly all audiences want to be excited, exhilarated, curious, awed, delighted, etc. Yet the spectrum of emotions elicited by *Titanic* includes a sort typically thought to be distinctly unpleasant. The ship Titanic sinks, causing terror and death for thousands of passengers; this is presented in powerful and horrifying detail. Among those who die is Jack (Leonardo DiCaprio), the film's lead male character, to whom the audience is encouraged to develop strong allegiance. The sympathetic heroine Rose (Kate Winslet) manages to escape with her life, but suffers the loss of Jack, the man she calls her "savior." Many spectators viewing the film will feel fear, sadness, and pity. Many weep copiously. Why would viewers expose themselves to these negative emotions and their effects? Is the elicitation of negative emotions essential to the pleasure taken in some films? How does the negative, painful element of film viewing figure into viewer pleasure?

This chapter discusses the phenomenon of negative emotions in mass market narratives, using *Titanic* as a means of examining the "working through" and "replacement" of negative emotions with the positive, such that a potentially disagreeable viewing experience becomes instead enjoyable and/or therapeutic. I first distinguish between sympathetic and distanced narratives, arguing that the former typically attempt to elicit strong negative emotions. My claim is that such negative emotions are genuinely painful, but that in successful sympathetic narratives, various techniques are used both to control the pain and transform it into pleasure. First the elicited painful emotions are attenuated and mixed with

11.   Rose cries in grief after Jack's death in *Titanic* (1997).

positive emotions. Second, the painful emotions are eventually replaced by pleasurable emotions through various textual designs that are essential in constituting the story as a fantasy. I conclude the chapter with a discussion of the ideological significance of sympathetic narratives.

SYMPATHETIC AND DISTANCED NARRATIVES

We can distinguish between emotions that are pleasurable (typically positive in valence) and those that are painful (negative in valence). Positive emotions sometimes have to do with the attainment of desires. I am happy and relieved after I learn that my child's injury is minor. I am surprised and exhilarated when the narrative of a film takes an unexpected and fascinating turn. Positive emotions such as curiosity and fascination are also associated with orientation and discovery; this has obvious implications for the pleasures of film viewing, as I discussed in Chapter 1. Negative emotions, on the other hand, are associated with pain and unpleasantness. I grieve over the death of a loved one. I am sad because a film character for whom I have deep sympathy tragically dies. I am bored by a predictable story. It is usually thought that persons avoid the experience of negative emotions, just as they would avoid the objects that elicit them.

There are two dominant kinds of narrative discourse in Hollywood film (and television) that I call *sympathetic* and *distanced* narratives. Sympathetic narratives encourage "closeness" to central characters *and* put those characters into unpleasant and sometimes catastrophic situations. The spectator is typically invited to respond to favored characters with sympathy, and when such characters experience unhappy events or even catastrophe, this elicits negative emotions. Thus, all sympathetic narratives lead to the experience of at least some negative emotions, however mild; some are capable of eliciting very powerful negative emotions that quite literally move spectators to shuddering, tears and/or sobbing.

Distanced narratives avoid such psychic "closeness" to characters. It might be thought that sympathetic narratives are the norm in Hollywood. Yet the distanced narrative is pervasive in Hollywood, as it is in the "art" cinema. The distanced mode rejects the evocation of strong sympathies for characters—sympathies that are sometimes dismissed altogether as sentimentality—in favor of a more distanced, critical, sometimes humorous, and occasionally cynical perspective. *The Hunt for Red October* (1990), for example, is content to generate the direct emotions of suspense, anticipation, interest, and curiosity, and although the audience is directed to form allegiances with the two protagonists, Russian submarine captain Marko Ramius (Sean Connery) and CIA analyst Jack Ryan (Alec Baldwin), the sympathetic emotions are downplayed. Neither man dies or loses a loved one; neither is humiliated or confronted with failure; neither earns the audience's pity, only its admiration, and even that is muted. It is as though a story about gallant military men in dangerous situations requires a masculine stoicism, and pity and sympathy have little place here. Such is the implicit assumption of many (but by no means all) action/adventure films. Think of *Mission Impossible III* (2006), *Indiana Jones and the Temple of Doom* (1984), *Star Wars* (1977), or *Gunga Din* (1939),for other examples.

The same distanced perspective can be found in other genres of film. Ironic comedies such as *Raising Arizona* (1987), *Dumb & Dumber* (1994), *Wayne's World* (1992), and *Austin Powers: International Man of Mystery* (1997) put their characters into embarrassing and fearful situations, but dispel their potential sympathetic force through comedy and irony. The famous screwball comedies such as *His Girl Friday* (1940), *Bringing Up Baby* (1938), and *The Miracle of Morgan's Creek* (1944) maintain a breakneck comic speed that allows for few negative emotions of any strength. Some puzzle films such as *Memento* (2000), *House of Games* (1987), or *The Usual Suspects* (1995) depend on the spectator's interest in deciphering the contours of a fictional world made obscure by various narrational strategies, but these films do not elicit strong negative emotions. (*Eternal Sunshine of the Spotless Mind* [2004] is the exception here, combining such "puzzle film" tactics with melodrama and strong sympathies). American films of the ironic mode would also include various independent productions such as Jim Jarmusch's *Down by Law* (1986) and *Coffee and Cigarettes* (2003), as well as narrative documentaries such as Michael Moore's *Roger & Me* (1989) and Errol Morris's *Gates of Heaven* (1978).[2]

The central feature of a sympathetic narrative, on the other hand, is the elicitation of sympathetic emotions such as pity, sadness, compassion, and admiration. Examples would include *Casablanca* (1942), *The Searchers* (1956), *Blade Runner* (1982), *Tender Mercies* (1983), *Rain Man* (1988), and *Schindler's List* (1993), and more recently, *Mystic River* (2003), *Million Dollar Baby* (2004), *North Country* (2005), and *Babel* (2006). Notice that such films not only encourage strong sympathies but also feature stories in which the major characters undergo catastrophic loss and/or severe emotional upset. In *Casablanca,* Rick drowns his sorrows with whiskey when he sees Ilsa, the love of his life, married to another man. Roy Batty, the replicant of *Blade Runner,* faces his own death after witnessing the death of his beloved Pris. Mac Sledge in *Tender Mercies* fights alcoholism and suffers the death of his daughter in an auto accident.

The sympathetic mode has long played a central role in Hollywood films. Its chief representative is the melodrama, but it extends beyond melodrama narrowly considered. If we refer to sympathetic and distanced narratives as kinds or types, we should also note that many films lie at the blurred boundaries of these categories, mixing ironic distance with sympathetic emotion. An example would be *The Royal Tenenbaums* (2001), in which a reflexive knowingness asserts itself in exaggerated characterizations, eccentric production design, and offbeat dialogue—all of which encourages a certain ironic distance while the film simultaneously encourages strong sympathies for the characters. Many films attempt to strike a balance between sympathetic and distanced character engagement for the purpose of moving the spectator without descending into a sentimentality that will alienate some viewers.

THE PARADOX OF NEGATIVE EMOTIONS

Sympathetic narratives, as we have seen, tend to elicit negative emotions. Why would mass audiences subject themselves to the representation of traumatic events such as those they see in sympathetic narratives like *Titanic,* and furthermore, given the negative emotions elicited for many audiences, how did this film become so popular with mass audiences all over the world?[3] There have been many attempts to account for the popularity of *Titanic,* variously holding, for example, that nostalgia or Leonardo DiCaprio's star power or the film's appeal to both male and female audiences were responsible for its box office success.[4] I suspect that the appeal of the film stems from many varied and intermeshed factors, and that many of these diverse theories have merit. Yet one central element of the film's success has been insufficiently examined: the means by which *Titanic* manages its representation of traumatic events in such a way that it attempts to turn the experience of pain into pleasure and to exchange a representation of irrevocable loss for a quasireligious, ritual affirmation of the proposed transformative power and transcendence of romantic love and self-sacrifice. One can find similar psychological manipulations at the end of many Steven Spielberg films, for example, *E.T.: The Extraterrestrial* (1982), *Schindler's List* (1993), and *Saving Private Ryan* (1998), and indeed, in many of the most popular sympathetic movies emerging from Hollywood. One might call this "catharsis," "transformation," or "working through," but whatever kind of psychological experience it is, it is worth exploring here because it has implications for understanding the spectator's experience of all sympathetic narratives.

Aristotle and others have written of the nature of tragedy, asking what benefits tragedy, with its elicitation of pity and fear, might bring to the reader or spectator. Noël Carroll has written of the paradox of horror, wondering why spectators and readers subject themselves to the fear and disgust he finds to be characteristic of the horror genre.[5] Since I will discuss these issues in relation to *Titanic*, we might speak of the "paradox of melodrama" or the "paradox of melodramatic/disaster genre hybrids." It would be better, however, to recognize that this paradox extends to any film or film genre that elicits strong negative emotions. Thus, I shall call the problem the "paradox of negative emotion."

One way to dissolve the paradox would be to claim that audiences are masochistic, as some psychoanalytic film theorists have done. On this theory, masochism is often equated with passivity or lack of control and sometimes associated with female audiences or feminine viewing positions within a patriarchal viewing system. So the word "masochism" in film studies is used more broadly than I use it in relation to the paradox of negative emotion. Taking up a passive "subject position" is not masochism in the same sense that taking pleasure in physical or psychological pain is masochistic. The latter is what I am interested in here.

One who advocates a theory of the masochistic spectator might claim that audiences derive pleasure from pain and that the movies dole out the pain in the right context and quantity to maximize the pleasure given. I find this claim to be problematic, however. Of course, if one rejects the psychoanalytic framework from which these claims are derived, then there is little evidence that would lead one to accept them. Moreover, it seems that such terms as sadism/sadist and masochism/masochist, while useful in describing various specific conditions of individuals, do not function well as a general theory of spectatorship.[6] The terms function best to describe abnormal or unusual behavior. In the absence of any strong evidence, why give up the firm intuition that most people do not find pleasure in pain, but in fact court pleasure and avoid pain, or at most are willing to abide mild pain when it leads to an eventual strong pleasure? Such an assumption fits the human propensity for individuals to engage in adaptive behavior for maximum flourishing, to avoid harm and court benefits.

My assumption is that mass market narratives, at their heart, are vehicles of pleasure and wish-fulfillment. I use these terms not in the technical senses developed in psychoanalytic film theory, but rather more closely resembling their meanings in folk psychology. As I argue, the negative or painful emotions are not *themselves* the source of audience pleasure, even if their presence is necessary to allow for the deepest pleasures of such films. The problem can be simply stated as follows: mass narratives provide pleasure, excitement, vicarious empowerment, affirmation, and so on. If this is so, why do so many mass narratives seek to elicit painful emotional experiences?

HUME ON THE PARADOX OF TRAGEDY

The paradox of tragedy, or more broadly, the purpose and effect of negative emotions in poetry, has been under scholarly scrutiny for thousands of years, and is a good entry point to the broader "paradox of negative emotions." Aristotle famously suggests that catharsis is one of the benefits of tragedy, while contemporary aestheticians have suggested that the presence of meta-emotions or of some form of psychological control or coping may account for our willingness to entertain and indeed derive pleasure from fantasy. These theories are discussed further below. I wish to begin, however, with the British philosopher David Hume, because my theory is most closely related to his, though it differs in some respects. Hume famously asks the following question in his essay "Of Tragedy," in which he attempts to dissolve the so-called "paradox of tragedy": if tragedy elicits fear and pity, and if fear and pity are fundamentally painful, then why is it that people seem to take pleasure in tragedies and seek them out?[7] Hume first rejects two possible answers to the question—the "excitement" and the "fiction" positions. The "excitement" position holds that people prefer excitement to boredom, even if the excitement involves some negative affect. Thus, readers or viewers of tragedy accept painful emotions because they are exciting, and any excitement is better than boredom. Hume rejects this answer as too broad and diffuse to be of much help. Given the wealth of entertainment opportunities available, why should audiences choose those that involve pain? Certainly, exciting amusements exist that do not elicit negative emotions. Why think that negative emotions are necessary to excitement? In any case, Hume notes, tragedies that occur in the actual world are exciting but do not elicit pleasure, and the "excitement" position does not explain why fictional tragedies *are* often pleasurable. The second position Hume rejects, the "fiction" position, holds that we take pleasure in fictional tragedy because we know it is fictional. But this is an unsatisfactory position as well. Surely *some* fictional representations cause genuine pain and are distinctly unpleasant even though they are fictional; why should the fictional representation of tragedy be pleasurable? From whence stems the pleasure?

Hume's solution to the paradox of tragedy is twofold. First, he argues that negative emotional responses are directed at *what is depicted* in a tragedy, while the pleasure of tragedy stems from the *manner of depiction*. Thus, the pleasures derived from the manner in which the tragedy is represented predominate over feelings of distress caused by what is depicted. The pleasure Hume refers to is in the artfulness, mastery, judgment, and eloquence of the artist as reflected in the work of art. (Typical emotional responses to such eloquence or mastery, we might surmise, would be artifact emotions such as admiration, awe, and gratitude.)

Second, Hume claims that the tragedy will also convert whatever negative emotional responses are elicited into pleasurable emotions and feelings. The pain of what is depicted becomes harnessed to the predominant feeling, which is pleasure in the eloquence and artfulness of the "well-written" tragedy. As Hume writes, "the uneasiness of the melancholy passions is not only overpowered and effaced by something stronger of an opposite kind, but the whole impulse of those passions is converted into pleasure, and swells the delight which the eloquence raises in us." The "impulse of vehemence" deriving from the negative emotions is redirected to "the sentiments of beauty." These sentiments "seize the whole mind" and "tincture" the negative emotions "so strongly as totally to alter their nature." The reader or viewer is at the same time "roused by passion and charmed by eloquence," a feeling, Hume notes, "which is altogether delightful."[8]

In response, we might say that Hume's solution is suggestive if not sufficiently developed. He suggests that the pleasures of tragedy derive from a mixture of emotions, a combination of the pleasures of artifact emotions that take as their object the work of art itself and somehow derive their particular nature *and* power from the negative emotions that stem from the portrayal of tragic events. For Hume, it is the mixture of the passion of the negative emotions and the pleasure of the artifact emotions that produces a powerful and gratifying response.

As evidence for his theory, Hume cites several examples, none of which do the work he wants them to do. Hume first mentions the delights of novelty and suspense that rouse the mind and attach their force to "any passion belonging to the object."[9] Hume also notes that difficulties of various sorts may strengthen passion. Parents commonly love most the child whose illness elicits their sympathies. Our love for a friend is enlarged by her death. Jealousy can increase the force and vehemence of romantic love. Difficulties that elicit negative emotions seem also to strengthen the positive emotions.

These examples seem true enough, yet none of them supports Hume's theory. It is true that suspense rouses the mind, as Hume says, but suspense is a direct and not an artifact emotion. Suspense takes as its object a possible narrative outcome rather than the eloquence or beauty of the work of the play, novel, or film. The delight of novelty may be either an artifact or a direct emotion. Hume is right to claim, however, that suspense and delight in novelty mix with and strengthen other emotions. Moreover, it is true that negative emotions caused by difficulties can strengthen and enlarge positive emotions including all sorts of love (affection, parental love, romantic love). Yet again, this is not a case of the sentiments aroused by beauty or eloquence, as Hume's theory would predict. These examples do demonstrate, however, that particular mixtures of emotions can prove to be more powerful than individual emotions experienced in isolation. Hume may also be right in his implication that the presence of negative emotions serves to make certain positive emotions more powerful. Hume, then, fails to demonstrate that the negative emotions of tragedy are harnessed to and transformed by the eloquence and beauty of the tragedy, although I suspect that Hume is correct in saying that positive artifact emotions (as well as positive direct emotions and meta-emotions) may in fact compensate for negative emotions.

My position here is that Hume's two-part solution to the paradox of tragedy is useful to approach what might generally be called the paradox of negative emotion in narrative fiction. Hume's theory, I claim, provides a good starting point but fails to adequately account for the "conversion" or "transformation" of negative emotions into positive emotions. Hume is right to reject the "excitement" and "fiction" positions if either is taken to be sufficiently explanatory in itself, but it would be wrong not to take these into account as components of any solution to the paradox of negative emotion. Hume's two-part solution needs to be fleshed out and its implications thoroughly vetted.

CATHARSIS?

As we have seen, Hume writes of the conversion or transformation of negative emotional responses into those that are pleasurable, but he provides an unsatisfactory account of how such a conversion or transformation occurs. To get at the contours of the process, we must discuss catharsis. Catharsis is Aristotle's term for the experience of audiences at the end of a tragedy—overwhelming feelings of sorrow, pity, or other strong emotions caused by the representation of tragic and piteous events. Aristotle is somewhat vague about the exact nature of catharsis in the *Poetics* and elsewhere, leaving literary theorists, philosophers, and psychologists to mull over the problem for hundreds of years. Some claim that Aristotle uses the term in relation to Hippocratic medicine, where health was thought to consist in the proper blending or balance of the bodily liquids or humors. Such a discharge of emotions can be seen as promoting emotional health and stability by a purgation of excess or unhealthy emotion. Others claim that catharsis should be considered as a form of cleansing or purification of emotion. Aristotle and most of his commentators agree that tragic catharsis, whatever it is, occurs to the beneficial effect of the audience.[10]

To explore the role of catharsis in narrative fiction is central because, whether the theorist ultimately rejects the idea or not, the discussion will touch on the deeper issues of affect elicitation in the movies and in art generally, including its possible therapeutic, cultural, quasireligious, and ideological effects. Discussions of catharsis raise issues that deserve further exploration, having to do with the central dilemmas identified but never sufficiently resolved by Aristotle: the function and very presence of negative emotions in spectatorship and the nature and possibility of emotional "purgation," "purification," and "clarification." Currently, the debate about catharsis centers on some of the most vital questions we want to ask about the reader and spectator.

I have so far written of Hume's claims for the transformation or conversion of negative into positive emotions. But many of those who write of catharsis hold that it has a therapeutic effect that arises from the *purging* rather than the conversion of negative emotions. Are negative emotions elicited and then purged in viewing a melodrama or horror film? What would that mean to say that such emotions are purged? What would be the therapeutic effect?

Advocates of catharsis as purgation often hold what might be called a "hydraulic" view of the emotions. Thomas J. Scheff, for example, proposes a neo-Freudian view of catharsis when he argues that not only dramatic literature and art but thrill-seeking of all kinds "is an attempt to relive, and therefore resolve, earlier painful experiences which were unfinished."[11] Readers who cry over the fate of Romeo and Juliet, he says, relive their own experiences of overwhelming loss. A well-designed drama, which should also provide a proper emotional distance, will elicit cathartic crying, laughing, and other emotional processes. As Scheff writes, "The repeated emotional discharge of fear, grief, anger, and so on, during a properly distanced re-experiencing of a traumatic scene" leads to a catharsis which purges the self of emotional tensions.[12] The hydraulic conception of the emotions, by which emotions are seen as "filling up" the body, causing pressure that can lead to emotional problems, and requiring "venting," is quite common. We speak colloquially of "letting off steam" and "boiling with anger."

Yet there exist significant problems for such a view. The hydraulic model would predict that the expression of emotions, including negative emotions, would be followed by a diminishment or attenuation of the emotion, but this isn't necessarily the case. Expressions of anger often lead to increased anger, and expressions of joy do not diminish the joy. Contemporary psychology tends to dismiss this version of catharsis theory for this reason, and psychologist Robert Epstein numbers "catharsis" among contemporary psychology's "top 10" misguided ideas.[13] Epstein notes that some time ago, therapies that encouraged the extreme expression of emotion for therapeutic reasons (primal scream therapy, for example) or goaded patients into near panic (implosive therapy) became mainstream. Their assumption was that it was therapeutic to enable people to "let go" of harmful emotions or tensions by expressing them. But in the 1970s and 1980s, psychologists such as Eliot Aronson and Brad Bushman engaged in studies that demonstrated that expressing anger can make one more rather than less angry.[14]

We can preserve the notion of catharsis if we alter it somewhat. What is missing from many catharsis theories is the cognitive component of purgation. It is not the mere expression of negative emotions that purges them from the self, but a "working through" and resolution that must occur, in part, on the level of cognition. Thus what causes relief and exhilaration for many spectators at the end of *Titanic* is not merely crying (although the crying may be pleasurable as the natural expression of emotion), but also the cognitive reframing of the narrative scenario that elicited the crying initially, with such reframing in turn leading to new emotions. Like many psychologists, then, I reject the notion of catharsis as the "purgation" of negative emotions (leaving open the question of whether catharsis in some other sense can be a useful term in aesthetics). The process of dealing with negative emotions in film, I argue, is not purgation but a "working through," a "dealing with," a "reconceptualization"—in short, the development of a construal that takes into account the negative circumstances of the narrative and frames them in such a way that their overall impact is both cognitively and emotionally satisfying, comforting, and pleasurable.

MANAGING THE NEGATIVE EMOTIONS

We now turn to an analysis of the elicitation of negative emotions in *Titanic* with a view to demonstrating the means by which filmmakers manage negative emotions, such that their initial experience is bearable, and replace such negative emotions with positive ones. For those few readers unfamiliar with the story of *Titanic*, Jack and Rose meet on the maiden, cross-Atlantic voyage of the enormous passenger ship Titanic and fall in love, against the wishes of Rose's family and her jealous and violent fiancé, Cal Hockley. Jack and Rose form a romantic bond nonetheless, but just after the consummation of their bond, the ship strikes an iceberg and begins to sink. From that point on, Jack and Rose, like the thousands of others on board, must struggle for survival. Jack loses his life in the cold Atlantic Ocean, but he saves Rose. Rose and Jack's story is told in flashback, as years later Rose relates the events of that day to the crew of an expedition ship exploring the wreck of the Titanic.

The experience of viewing *Titanic* is a temporal process; to gauge the overall emotional effect of a film means, on the one hand, to consider the emotions elicited at specific points as the film progresses, and on the other, to estimate the film's overall emotional appeal after the film has ended. I will first consider the spectator's experience at the moment of one of the most traumatic events in the film—Jack Dawson's death in the icy waters of the Atlantic, after the ship has sunk.

What is the intended emotional effect for audiences at the moment of Jack's death, and how does the narration attempt to manage spectator emotion at this particular moment? Immediately preceding this point in the narrative, predominant emotional responses have been fear and suspense in relation to the safety of Rose and Jack. At this point in the film, after

Jack's death, many spectators experience strong sadness and pity, not only for Jack and the rest of the dead, but also for Rose and the other survivors who have lost loved ones. (Viewers will differ in the degree of response, of course, based in part on differential dispositions toward the experience of empathy, idiosyncratic associations and memories, and individual reactions to the film as an artifact.)

The first question we might ask is whether emotions such as fear, pity, and sadness are pleasurable in themselves, or whether they are merely endured as the cost of the greater pleasures that lie elsewhere. Remember Hume's claim that our pleasure in tragedy stems not from the tragic events themselves, but from their manner of presentation. Assuming that Hume's theory of tragedy applies to *Titanic* at least in part, Hume's answer would be that the pleasure we take in this scene stems from its presentation of Jack's death rather than the death itself, and that such pleasure "predominates" over the pain caused by seeing Jack die. And it is true that the filmmakers exercise great care in showing Jack's demise. After Rose awakes from her stupor and finds that Jack has died, she releases Jack's dead hand from her grip. A high-angle point-of-view shot shows his body descending silently into the blue, gradually disappearing into the deep as his face points upward and his arm stretches out above him, as though he salutes Rose or waves his final good-bye. Viewers may find delight in the visual eloquence of the staging and cinematography of this scene, or in the overall beauty or appropriateness with which Jack's death is presented. (They may also find it to be overblown and sentimental.)

Hume's theory is related to Noël Carroll's claims about the paradox of horror, which is thus worth examining briefly here. If, as Carroll argues, the monster of the horror film elicits a combination of fear and repulsion or disgust, then why do audiences subject themselves to horror films? What could be the pleasure in experiencing fear and disgust? Carroll's answer is that the monster, and the repulsion and fear that it raises, are not the source of the pleasure we take in horror. Instead, it is the narrative itself that holds our interest and provides pleasure by eliciting and satisfying a direct emotion, that is, a curiosity about the nature of a seemingly impossible and unknown being, the monster. Thus, for Carroll, disgust and fear are the price spectators are willing to pay for the experience of a particularly intense form of curiosity. (Hume might add here that the intensity of the disgust and fear elicited by the monster are transformed by the spectator's curiosity into a delightful mixed emotion.)

For Hume, it is the manner of representation that elicits pleasing artifact emotions and transforms and predominates over the pain caused by what is represented. For Carroll, it is a direct emotion, a curiosity about the nature of the monster. My argument, in brief, is that Hume and Carroll are basically right that the negative emotions are actually painful to spectators, and for that reason the film must offer some affective compensation. The sadness and pity elicited by *Titanic*, similarly, are indeed negative emotions that cause mental anguish and other unpleasant affective experiences for many spectators. Thus, the pleasure associated with this sequence, if any, must be attributable to some other cause, such as the artifact emotions elicited by the film's presentation (as Hume would claim) or the direct emotions such as curiosity and anticipation elicited by the narrative (as Carroll would claim). I suspect that this scene elicits artifact more than direct emotions, since for all of its weaknesses (some clichéd and sentimental dialogue, for example), the presentation of Jack's death in the context of the disaster is both visually and aurally remarkable.

But at this point we might ask two other questions. Is the pain elicited by Jack's death a mild or strong pain? And the second: is this pain mixed with pleasurable emotions and affects? The phenomenological quality of the pity and sadness of this scene, I argue, is attenuated and inflected by various contextual factors, and furthermore, the pity and sadness are accompanied by other emotions that in fact are pleasurable. The experience of this scene for many spectators is a classic case of mixed emotions. These mixed emotions stem from varied sources, not merely, as Hume and Carroll seem to claim, solely from the artifact emotions (in Hume's case) or direct emotions (in Carroll's).

On the first point, what contextual factors influence the quality of the negative emotions such as pity and fear as they are experienced while viewing *Titanic*? Here the "fiction" and "excitement" solutions to the paradox of tragedy must be invoked as important elements in the solution to the paradox of negative emotion. The primary contextual factor here is the conventional, institutional nature of mainstream fiction film viewing, which would lead one to predict that most viewers will approach the experience of *Titanic* with a set of expectations or schemas, independent of what might be experienced at any particular moment of the film.[15] The spectator understands first that the story and its characters are rooted in a fictionalized historical event. This historical remoteness and fictionality temper the sadness and pity to some extent. Moreover, any viewer familiar with the most basic conventions of mainstream Hollywood storytelling will also expect that any negative emotions in a melodrama will be in the end recuperated and/or transformed into a pleasurable or otherwise rewarding experience. Thus, the painful emotions are tempered by the strong expectation that the film will provide subsequent emotional compensations. *Titanic* does not fail to meet expectations in this regard, as I show below.

In addition to this attenuation of unpleasant emotions, the pity, fear, and sadness are accompanied by decidedly pleasurable emotions. One of the motivations for audiences to attend any movie, I have argued, is an inherent drive to experience something—any stimulus, cognitive or visceral, that excites the spectator. For those who respond sympathetically to the movie, sadness and pity are accompanied by excitement and exhilaration. For such spectators, negative sympathetic emotions are accompanied by positive direct emotions—not merely excitement about the monumental events depicted, but also curiosity and interest about how the film's protagonist, Rose, will respond to the death of her lover. Add awe to the mix. Awe is experienced in relation to the sublime; we feel awe when confronted with greatness or vast magnitude, and often in relation to nature. Thus the scene of Jack's death, occurring against the backdrop of a universe of stars and the vast depths of the ocean, all carefully displayed by the filmmaker's art, inspires awe. Add to this the nearly incomprehensible forces at work in the sinking of this giant ship and the enormity of the human suffering and death suggested by the hundreds of bodies seen floating in the cold Atlantic, and the opportunities for the experience of awe and the experience of sublimity are plentiful (at least on the big screen).

The mixture of emotions also includes meta-emotions, that is, the spectator's second-order emotions rooted in prior emotional or cognitive responses. As Susan Feagin claims in regard to tragedy (and her claims here would also apply to melodrama), the spectator's initial sympathetic response, a direct response to the plight of the characters, may be followed by a meta-emotion that we might call a species of pride, in which the spectator self-satisfyingly judges him or herself to be the kind of person who responds negatively to villainy or injustice, or in this case, responds with sympathy to the terrifying fate of Jack and the other victims.[16] Communication researcher Mary Beth Oliver finds that among those viewers who show a preference for "tearjerkers," there is a correlation between sadness and the enjoyment of the film. She argues that especially among women, sympathetic sadness is pleasurable in part because it leads to self-enhancing emotions, meta-emotions that are rooted in gender socialization about proper female behavior and response.[17] For many women, sympathetic sadness, when experienced, is self-enhancing because it is just the sort of emotion a woman *should feel* in relation to such events.

To this mixture of positive direct and meta-emotions, we might also add positive sympathetic emotions such as admiration and elevation as both direct and second-order responses. Elevation, you will remember, was introduced in Chapter 3. It is a positive emotion, the opposite of social disgust, which takes as its object the witnessing of acts of human beauty or virtue. Perhaps we could say that elevation is a species of admiration. We can admire someone for many reasons, including their personality and accomplishments, but elevation occurs in response to what is perceived to be their morally superior actions or words. As discussed below, admiration is thought to be one of the important emotions elicited by melodramas generally. The elicitation of the more particular emotion of elevation—rooted as it is in the positive estimation of virtuous action, might be closer to what melodramas are after.

The spectator might feel elevation in response to Jack's self-sacrifice and selfless love, since (in a rather melodramatic fashion) despite what he must now recognize as his impending death as he freezes in the cold waters of the North Atlantic, he says to Rose that winning the ticket that allowed him to embark on the Titanic was "the best thing that ever happened to me" because "it brought me to you." In addition, Jack's actions never fail to put Rose's safety before his own, leading to his allowing Rose to climb aboard the giant hunk of wood that has room for one only, enabling her to escape the freezing waters that take Jack's life.

Another second-order response for some spectators might be the artifact emotions of which Hume writes, a fascination with the tremendous cost of the production, admiration for what is taken to be the skill and/or sensitivity with which the filmmakers have presented the details of the ship's sinking, the rescue efforts, and Jack's death—for example, the shot from Rose's point of view of the dead Jack as his body descends into the ocean's depths. Thus, Hume's claim that spectators take pleasure in the manner of representation is fundamentally correct, but it is merely one of the pleasures so taken. Spectator pleasures during this tragic scene in *Titanic* may include direct emotions, such as curiosity, expectation, and awe; meta-emotions, such as pride and other forms of self-satisfaction; and artifact emotions that take as their object the eloquence, beauty, or (who knows?) sublimity of the film as a constructed artifact.

My argument has been that the spectator's experience at the most traumatic point in the narrative may indeed be characterized as partly negative, and in fact may lead to negative emotions such as pity, fear, and sadness. Yet the affective experience at these traumatic points in the narrative is not only attenuated in its painful aspects, as I have shown, but is likely to be mixed in its emotional valence—a mixture of positive and negative, pleasure and pain.

THE SPILLOVER EFFECT

A brief summary is in order before proceeding. Influenced by the first part of Hume's two-part solution to the paradox of tragedy, I have suggested that the painful aspects of sympathetic narratives are on the one hand attenuated, and on the other, mixed with various pleasures. The second aspect of Hume's solution, you will remember, was to claim that tragedy *converts* feelings of pain into feelings of pleasure. Hume fails to adequately describe how such conversion occurs, and thus I have mentioned the concept of catharsis as a possible aid. Catharsis invokes ideas of purgation, purification, or clarification of emotion. I have rejected the idea of catharsis as the purgation of emotion. By the end of *Titanic*, those spectators who have responded positively to the film are often exhilarated and relieved, and many cry copious tears of sadness mixed with pleasure. It is certainly correct to say that positive emotions, to some extent, *replace* negative emotions and that the negative emotions gradually die away while positive emotions increase. But in what sense are negative emotions *converted* into positive emotions? The word "conversion" implies a relationship not of simple replacement but of dependency, as though there were a sense in which the positive emotions depend on the negative.

Some forms of catharsis theory treat emotions as though they were merely forces divorced from cognition and perception, as though emotions were energies that needed to be released without regard to their genesis in ways of thinking and perceiving. In what follows I agree that something is not so much released as channeled or harnessed. However, it isn't emotion that is so channeled but something else. In its last episodes, which I concentrate on here, *Titanic* offers a quasireligious, virtual ritual of commemoration and celebration. In relation to the spectator's response, the two relevant terms are not the purgation of emotion but the *relief* from strong negative emotions, which are *replaced* by pleasurable emotions that depend for their strength on the arousal caused by physiological spillover remaining from the prior negative emotions. What is channeled is the physiological residue of the painful emotions, which through emotional "spillover" increases the strength of the positive emotions at the film's end. I call this the "spillover effect."

How does this process work? First, the narrative of *Titanic*, for the sympathetic spectator at least, takes this mixture of pleasure and pain of which

I have spoken, and in gradual fashion, increases the pleasure and decreases the pain through a ritual of commemoration that marks the end of the film. The commemoration occurs in a kind of impromptu funeral ritual, as old Rose takes the invaluable blue diamond, the "Heart of the Ocean," and drops it into the ocean, where it descends into the darkness much like Jack's body did earlier in the film. (The diamond has come to signify Jack's life and also the love of Rose and Jack.)

A funeral service functions to celebrate the lives of the dead, offer solace to the living, and facilitate the grieving process, and this scene, similarly, works to memorialize both Jack and the "Great Love" of Rose and Jack. The usual Hollywood narrative is hypercoherent, that is, it compresses life events by leaving out the dull bits and including only those that are most dramatic and/or meaningful. In a similar fashion, the conventions of Hollywood narrative call for the experience of emotions in rapid succession, which audiences find to be pleasurable and possibly therapeutic. This scene serves some of the functions that actual memorial rituals serve, but condensed and perfected by the careful deliberation of the filmmaker. It does so by demonstrating the importance and effectiveness of Jack's sacrifice, thus assuring the spectator that it had a purpose; we see that Rose has led a happy and fulfilled life. It also lays Jack to rest, so to speak, and by having old Rose drop the stone into the deep, releases the spectator from further need to pity, as though the memorial act absolves one of serious further concern and symbolically restores a sense of order. The dropping of Jack's memorial stone into the ocean becomes a kind of sacrifice-in-kind, its value mirroring the value of Jack's life, just as the high-angle shot of the stone descending into the ocean mirrors the descent of Jack's body into the deep.

But the scene also elicits the emotions of elevation and admiration. Rose's action in dropping the expensive diamond into the ocean is not only a ritual commemoration of Jack's life, but also morally virtuous in that she recognizes that the Heart of the Ocean is valuable not for its monetary worth, but primarily because it represents the life of the sacrificial hero, and through him, the lives of those who perished when the Titanic sank. As a kind of memorial stone, it belongs deep in the ocean, where Jack had vanished years before, and Rose is admired for realizing this and acting on it, despite the stone's great monetary value. (The filmmakers also suggest elements of the sublime here, prominently displaying the countless stars above Rose and the infinitude of space in relation to the vast depths of the ocean.)

Near the end of the narrative comes what might be called a scene of transcendence, which adds hope and elation to the mixture of relief, admiration, and elevation that the commemoration scene elicits. After Rose drops the diamond into the sea, the scene dissolves to old Rose's cabin on the research ship, where old Rose lies in bed. The shot dissolves to a tracking shot with a rapid approach to the sunken Titanic deep beneath the ocean's surface, as though Rose's soul or mind is approaching the ship.

As the camera tracks deeper into the sunken ship, the ship becomes the new Titanic once more, the corroded surfaces turning polished and gleaming and the dark of the ocean becoming light. The camera tracks into the ship, and there is the Grand Staircase, gleaming, new, brilliantly lit, with many of the people we know to have died now alive and welcoming Rose. Finally, we see Jack, standing above on the landing.

He turns to look downward, extending his hand to welcome young Rose (whom we now see), and they kiss passionately as the other Titanic passengers smile and applaud. The camera has been tracking elegantly throughout, and it now moves beyond the embracing couple above them to the source of light, where it fades to white. Whether the spectator sees this scene as a wish, a dream, or a vision of heaven, it not only celebrates and commemorates Jack and Rose's "Great Love" but expresses a hope for or perhaps a belief in the transcendence of love, a hope that love can survive death, loss, and separation. The film offers the hope or wish or dream of a connection with loved ones who have died. In this, it is similar to several other relatively recent films offering a vague hope in transcendence, including *Ghost* (1990), *Always* (1989), and perhaps, one could argue, *The Sixth Sense* (1999). (*Places in the Heart* [1984] differs from these in putting its affirmation of transcendence into an explicitly Christian framework, in which the dead are actually seen partaking of Holy Communion together). The success of this scene in *Titanic* depends to an extent on its lack of clear reality status. That is, that the scene is interpretable in so many ways makes it more likely that it will be effective for a diversity of audiences, as in fact it seems to have been.

The sadness, fear, and pity characteristic of the earlier scenes are replaced, for many audiences, by positive emotions—elevation, admiration, hope, and exhilaration—through a ritual commemoration of Jack (and all he stands for) and an affirmation of transcendence. But what remains of the negative emotions is a physiological residue that provides strength for the positive emotions that replace them; this is the spillover effect. The emotions have a marked physiological component, such that the physiological effects of preceding emotions can transfer to the experience of later emotions, because physiological effects recede slowly. Thus, psychologist Dolf Zillman's "Excitation Transfer Theory" would postulate that the spectator's response to a later scene can be affected by the residual physiological effects of an earlier scene that elicited emotion, by increasing the likelihood and/or strength of subsequent emotion.[18] If strong negative emotions are accompanied by physiological arousal, this arousal may contribute to the strength of the positive emotions experienced in the last fifteen minutes of the film. (Interestingly, this theory would predict that arousal may influence cognition, just as cognition influences arousal. This is the basis of the rhetorical strength of emotion, the topic of the next chapter.)

Although I speak of replacement rather than Hume's "conversion," there is another sense, in addition to the spillover effect, in which the latter emotions are influenced by the former. The concern-based construals that constitute the positive emotions at the film's end incorporate what has come before. That is, the construals that lead to admiration, relief, and exhilaration take into account the terrifying and piteous events that preceded them. The positive emotions gain strength from the negative emotions that were endured earlier.

In sum, for many spectators, the overall affective experience is pleasurable despite the painful negative emotions that are elicited near the film's climactic point. This is true because of three things. First, as I have shown, at the point of the film's most traumatic moments, painful affect is both attenuated in its effect *and* mixed with pleasurable affect. Second, through the scenes of commemoration and transcendence, negative emotions are gradually replaced by positive emotions. And finally, such positive emotions gain their strength through the spillover effect. By the film's end, the overall experience for many spectators is intensely pleasurable.

I would argue that this two-step solution, which Hume initially developed in response to the paradox of tragedy, can be generalized to the paradox of negative emotion in fiction generally. What Hume failed to do in the second step of his solution was to sufficiently explain the nature of the transformation from painful to pleasurable emotion. I have argued here that the negative emotions are better described as replaced by positive emotions rather than converted or transformed into them. But the nature of this replacement is not easily glossed over. It is complex and fascinating, having to do with ritual, fantasy, and the very function of the popular arts as palliatives and/or inspirations in the psychic economy of spectators and entire cultures. A sympathetic narrative film that both arouses strong negative emotions *and* succeeds in connecting with audiences, I would claim, must also provide the kind of ritual therapeutic function of the sort I have outlined in *Titanic*.[19]

FANTASIES OF ASSURANCE AND CONTROL

How can we make cultural sense of this therapeutic function of mass market sympathetic narratives such as *Titanic*? To consider this question, let us think of *Titanic*, for the moment, as a melodrama. The film features many of the elements of melodrama—the sympathetic heroine, obstructed love, generational conflict, the problem of female independence within a rigid patriarchal structure, the "pathetic" nobility of self-sacrifice, an exaggerated portrayal of good versus evil, and a dastardly villain—in this case, Rose's jealous, arrogant, controlling, and violent fiancé, Cal Hockley.[20]

Titanic was explicitly designed to strongly move its audience. Director James Cameron writes that his aim in making *Titanic* was to "convey the emotion of that night [of the ship's sinking] rather than the fact of it."[21] It elicits the emotions participants in that disaster must have had, such as fear and sadness, but also those emotions characteristic of the spectator of melodrama, namely pity and admiration.[22] The audience pities the protagonists for the calamities that strike them, yet admires them for their virtuous actions. If we take pity and admiration as characteristics of melodrama, one might legitimately claim that melodrama is less accurately characterized as a genre of Hollywood filmmaking than as one of Hollywood's dominant modes, extending across many genres. The admixture of pity or pathos and admiration extends beyond the so-called women's films such as *An Affair to Remember* (1957) and *Stella Dallas* (1937) to action/adventure films generally thought to appeal more to males, for example, *Braveheart* (1995), *Gladiator* (2000), *Spartacus* (1960), and *Sands of Iwo Jima* (1949). The latter film, for example, features John Wayne as Sergeant Stryker, whose men at first resent him for his tough discipline and harsh words, but then come to admire him when they see him in action at Iwo Jima and discover the benefits of his training regimen for their survival, especially when he takes a bullet and dies. This sort of romantic celebration of virtue and triumph over tribulation and suffering is not limited to either "male" or "female" genres, but encompasses both.[23]

According to Peter Brooks, melodrama is "the principle mode for uncovering, demonstrating, and making operative the essential moral universe in a post-sacred era."[24] Thus, for Brooks, melodrama is a fictional system for making sense of existence, a making sense that is expressed in the moral experience of intimate human relationships. In part, then, one can see *Titanic* as a work of mass art that functions to regulate morality and to make its moral system persuasively attractive through the invited pleasures and wish fulfillments of the text. Brooks is right if we take "moral" in its broadest possible sense. A film like *Titanic* offers not only moral lessons (strictly considered) but also a way of thinking and valuing generally—a worldview if taken to be unified, a mixed bag of possibly contradictory implications if not. For example, in its romantic fantasy, the film promotes an idealized and misleading view of romantic love, implying that romantic love transcends class and family ties, that it is the greatest possible good, and that one who finds it should well expect in their lovers the kind of Christ-like sacrifice embodied in Jack. On a more positive note, *Titanic* lambasts pride and smug arrogance and advocates the traditional virtues of humility, self-sacrifice, love, courage, and loyalty. The film critiques class-based privilege and presumption, and advocates the dissolution of class differences. Melodramas like *Titanic* formulate a moral and metaphysical universe not merely as a set of ideas, but as embodied narratives that are experienced most intensely through feeling. If mass market narratives such as *Titanic* serve in part to regulate morality and ideology, it is primarily through the persuasiveness of their emotional impact. Whatever ideas they embody become salient and attractive to audiences in large part because they are affectively powerful to many spectators.

It should be obvious, however, that Peter Brooks is too quick to claim that we live in a post-sacred era. A quick look around confirms that religion is a pervasive and powerful force in the contemporary world, and that rumors of its demise are greatly exaggerated. And as a melodrama, *Titanic* not only represents a fictional system for the regulation of morality, but it also attempts to make sense of existence in quasireligious terms that extend beyond interpersonal relationships and into the realm of transcendence and the sublime.

Above, I rejected the notion of catharsis as the purgation of emotion, but I bracketed interpretations of catharsis as the clarification or purification of emotion. Such theories of catharsis often assume that the effect of classical tragedy, at least, will be beneficial. But I suspect that such thinking is sanguine. In extending our discussion to popular movies, it would certainly be folly to assume that all works that arouse and then "work through" negative emotions necessarily lead the spectator to a clarification or purification of emotion. It would be more apt to say that such works offer spectators a renewed sense of control by offering a ritualized fantasy of pain and recovery, of hope and assurance. In a tragedy, it might be a grim resignation rather than control that is granted to the spectator. Yet a film such as *Titanic,* through the apotheosis of Jack, offers the saving grace of romantic love and the conquering of death itself through an ill-defined transcendence. This is a fantasy of mastery, not of resignation.

The words "coping" and "control" are apt in this context. Jenefer Robinson writes that formal devices in literature can be construed as coping devices, as means of manipulating or directing reader response in such a way as to manage the emotional experience of the work in question.[25] I have no argument with this, but there is a sense in which the work itself, in its totality, is a coping device. It offers a sense of mastery and control. It displays the world's miseries and demonstrates that they are manageable, that they can ultimately be controlled, that there is an ultimate moral and spiritual order to the universe. A successful movie of this sort reinforces its claims or implications in a way more powerful than mere assertion. It functions through powerful emotions such that the control that is asserted is also felt as relief and exhilaration. Melodramas are not merely about the establishment of morality, as Brooks implies; as the case of *Titanic* demonstrates, they have more profound function in establishing worldviews through the ritual staging of fantasies of control and assurance.

IDEOLOGY IN SYMPATHETIC AND DISTANCED NARRATIVES

Although the term is remarkably ambiguous and loaded with unintended connotations that manifest themselves in diverse ways, I here raise the specter of "ideology." In an orthodox Marxist sense, ideology is "false consciousness," while by a broader definition, "ideology" refers to any system of belief and valuation. The ideological effects of movies can lead to false consciousness, but my use of the term "ideology" assumes the latter definition and the broader context. Thus, a set of true beliefs and ways of valuing is an ideology, just as false beliefs and false consciousness are. Thus, I make no assumptions that ideological persuasion or reinforcement necessarily leads to false consciousness. They may or may not, depending on the film and the context. I will use the term ideology in a neutral sense, as a set of values, beliefs, and assumptions.

The most powerful ideological effects of any film—its capacity to persuade, change, or reinforce belief and value—will be bound up with the particular way in which it elicits emotion, for it is the emotions that have the potential to forge a place for the film in human memory and have the capacity to strengthen or alter ways of thinking and valuing. In *On*

Rhetoric, Aristotle defines an emotion as a kind of feeling caused by a kind of thinking. A skilled rhetorician, Aristotle says, can reverse the direction of this causality and can alter the audience's ways of thinking by causing them to feel a certain way.[26] When we speak of a film as manipulative, we often mean that the mechanisms by which the film elicits emotion have become too transparent and/or that we are uncomfortable and resistant to its appeals. When a film arouses no such metacognitions and meta-emotions, its appeals will go largely unnoticed, but they are still at work. The elicitation of emotion is not merely about feelings; it is also about ways of thinking and valuing that are encouraged by the text and precede and/or accompany emotional response. For these reasons, spectator emotion always raises ideological and ethical issues.[27]

In this section, I offer some observations about the cultural implications of sympathetic and distanced narratives, using the example of *Titanic* as an occasional touchstone. Although the next few paragraphs address sympathetic and distanced narratives as easily distinguished categories, this is a simplification designed for the purposes of illustration. Elements of distanced and sympathetic narratives often coexist in the same film, and some films cannot be clearly identified as one type or the other. Hayden White notes that narratives cast in the ironic mode, the mode that characterizes many narratives that I have called distanced, "are often regarded as *intrinsically* sophisticated and realistic." Unlike romantic narratives, they "appear to signal the ascent of thought in a given area of inquiry to a level of self-consciousness on which a genuinely 'enlightened'—that is to say, self-critical—conceptualization of the world and its processes has become possible."[28] Thus, when a film ostensibly subverts the conventional melodrama, it is often thought to be critical or sophisticated. Like many film scholars, Thomas Elsaesser writes favorably of Douglas Sirk melodramas like *Written on the Wind* (1957) and *Imitation of Life* (1959) because he sees them as reflexively critical of the "incurably naïve moral and emotional idealism in the American psyche."[29] Thus, the sympathetic appeals of melodrama in *Titanic,* with its rejection of the knowing irony that is its rival, is clearly open to moral question on Elsaesser's formulation, since far from being reflexive, it could be seen to embrace the kind of self-deceptions and illusions often thought to be characteristic of melodrama.

Distanced narratives can be thought to enable, and sympathetic narratives to disable, critical thought. Such thinking can typically be traced to Bertolt Brecht's writing about theater and the elicitation of emotion. I have argued elsewhere that Brecht's arguments in this regard are questionable.[30] Many sympathetic narratives are indeed naïve or uncritical, but there is nothing in the elicitation of strong sympathetic emotions that prima facie could be said to disable critical thought. Sympathetic emotions may also encourage critical thought about social and political conditions. *El Norte* (1983), for example, details the troubles of a Guatemalan brother and sister who are persecuted in their homeland and immigrate to the United States. The film elicits strong sympathy for the protagonists, and such sympathy fundamentally depends on the spectator's recognition and understanding of their situation and the sociopolitical factors that cause it. In such a case, both compassion and sociopolitical judgment are simultaneous and mutually dependent.

While distanced narratives do often encourage critical judgment, their detached, nonparticipatory stance can be seen as problematic (were one given to broad judgments of this sort). If emotional detachment encourages judgment, it discourages involvement. If it is desperate to avoid a naïve sentimentality, it is prone to a smug sense of superiority. At its worst, the distanced narrative stance is one that remains off to the side, considering itself above the fray in which the foolish and softhearted participate. Distanced narratives rarely elicit strong negative emotions; the "working through" or replacement of negative emotions with positive ones is too easily construed as naïve. Strong negative emotions would also remove the comfortable distance, and are therefore avoided. If emotion is a concern-based construal, and if distance removes the concern, then emotional response will not be strong. Instead, the distanced narrative is likely to disarm concern through irony and/or humor.

In contrast, sympathetic narratives are more likely to attempt to elicit strong negative emotions and to encourage the spectator to experience compassion, sadness, and the discomfort that occurs when a sympathetic protagonist meets hard times. The potential danger of the sympathetic narrative, however, is naïve idealization and sentimentality. The word "sentiment" is inherently ambiguous. I consider a sentimental emotion to be any emotion that is typically or often accompanied by crying. Thus, grief or sadness, intense elevation and admiration, awe, and even happiness and joy can be sentimental emotions in certain contexts. In their discussion of sentimental emotion in film, Ed Tan and Nico Frijda claim that crying results from the perceiver's felt inability to influence a situation (such as the loss or separation from a loved one), or when the perceiver is released from concern and the necessity of action (when relief is granted after negative emotions and one feels happiness or joy, for example). Sentimental emotions, Tan and Frijda claim, involve yielding to the overwhelming and are often caused by three narrative scenarios: separation and reunion, justice in jeopardy, and "awe-inspiration."[31] As we have seen, *Titanic* incorporates all three of these scenarios.

The wholesale denigration of sentimental emotions is an expression of masculine bravado at best and of rampant sexism at worst. To denigrate the emotions caused by sentiment's concerns is to denigrate the concerns themselves. Molly Haskell, for instance, argues that contempt for the women's film stems from the devaluation of the kinds of narrative concerns they embody: family relationships, romance, and separation and reunion scenarios.[32] Other film scholars such as Christine Gledhill and Linda Williams have also come to the defense of melodrama, arguing that the association of melodrama with excessive or mindless pathos is faulty.[33] In philosophy, one of the prominent defenders of sympathetic narratives, or melodrama, has been Stanley Cavell, who through close analyses of films such as *Letter from an Unknown Woman* (1948) and *Now, Voyager* (1942) shows that such films embody serious and worthwhile contemplations on a range of philosophical issues.[34] Likewise, Flo Liebowitz defends the women's film and the melodrama, claiming that the pleasures of the imagination they offer should be described not as a kind of sickness or trivial wish-fulfillment but as a response to inherently important concerns and a pleasure in the imaginative discovery "of the meanings of certain families of value-laden concepts."[35] For Liebowitz, then, part of the pleasure of the sentimental emotions in film is cognitive, deriving from the spectator's coming to critically understand the nature of love or forgiveness or self-sacrifice, for example.

Sentimental responses and emotions, all things being equal, are laudable in appropriate circumstances, but some argue that *sentimentality* is not. Here is where the language becomes tricky. Sentimentality may be characterized as a false or "unearned" emotional response. Sentimentality, in this sense, is held to be not only distasteful but also ideologically and ethically questionable. It may result from a distorted concern-based construal that is either willfully or unknowingly allowed for the sake of indulging the sentimental emotions,[36] and thus may contribute to self-deception and self-righteousness by promoting an illusory image of the self as compassionate or just.[37] Sentimentality is said to be ideologically and ethically suspect because it willfully obscures the actual nature of its object, becoming a kind of self-deception that, in the case of people, idealizes some and vilifies others. Mark Jefferson writes that sentimentality is not only grounded in a "fiction of innocence" emphasizing the sweetness, littleness, or vulnerability of that which is deemed good, but is also implicated in brutality for its "moral caricature of something unambiguously worthy of hatred."[38] In short, one of the hallmarks of sentimentality is exaggeration: idealization of the good and a deceptive vilification of the bad.

When discussing sentimentality in mass market narratives like *Titanic*, such considerations must be tempered by two characteristics of the fiction film experience. In the realm of fiction, the immorality of sentimentality may be less an issue than its irrationality. The entities in sentimental narratives are fictional characters rather than actual people, so the ideological import of sentimentality in fiction takes on a different flavor. Sentimentality in fiction does not misrepresent actual persons, but may be thought instead to promote irrational habits of thought and response. Sentimentality promotes uncomplicated dichotomies between good and bad, since it simplifies and exaggerates good and evil and encourages self-righteousness when it elicits allegiance for idealized characters. Thus, if we characterize sentimentality as self-deception, it is not self-deception with regard to actual persons or events, but rather self-deception in its assumptions about how the world is in general, leading to habits of mind and tendencies of response that simplify the world for the sake of self-indulgent emotions.

Second, if sentimentality is defined in part as an idealized misrepresentation of the Familiar Good Object and a vilification of the Bad Object or the Other, the claim can be made that this melodramatic way of viewing the world is characteristic of many Hollywood films, as discussed above. This is not necessarily to say that all Hollywood melodramas, whether "women's films" or action-adventure thrillers, are therefore ideologically damnable. To make that claim, one would have to show that all exaggeration and idealization in fiction is ideologically suspect. And it is here that I would disagree with the harshest critics of sentimentality. Should all Hollywood films strictly adhere to the critic's standards of realism or verisimilitude? Is idealization always wrong? Is a strict adherence to some standard of realism always preferable? For all three questions, my answer would be "No."

While the questions raised here deserve a book unto themselves, one observation will suffice for now. I would agree that the simplistic vilification of the Other and exaggerated and simplistic divisions between good and evil are likely to be harmful. So some forms of sentimentality are bound to be wrong. Yet in other cases, presenting idealized representations may encourage and invigorate the spectator toward positive action even while the fiction misrepresents the actual world. Consider some real-world examples. Actor Christopher Reeve's hope that he could overcome his

12. *Titanic* is sentimental in its idealization of romantic love.

quadriplegia may have been unrealistic and ill-founded (and thus sentimental), but it provided him with a life goal and a purpose. One's idealized
belief in the goodness or attractiveness of a spouse may extend beyond
all objectivity but nonetheless contribute to a healthy relationship. The
same might be true of sentimentality in fictions, in which depictions of
virtue or political action may be idealized but nonetheless serve as worthy
goals for emulation. Realism and truth are not necessarily or obviously the
highest good. Perhaps human flourishing, in some cases, trumps epistemic
realism. Although I am inclined to be suspicious of all sentimentality, I
would argue that it should not be dismissed *tout court* as ideologically
pernicious or cognitively unhealthy; its effects must be gauged on a case-
by-case basis.

Titanic, however, is clearly sentimental in a negative way in some of the
respects just discussed. The film plies idealized notions of good and evil,
presenting Jack as a sacrificial hero willing to give his life for a woman he
has only just met, and Cal as a villainous would-be murderer, emotionally
and physically abusive boyfriend, and oppressive control freak. It might
be said that this is not only a lapse in taste but also ethically problematic,
since in its eagerness to provide a pleasurable fantasy, the film may encourage ways of thinking that exaggerate self/other and good/bad differences.
The film also promotes an idealized faith in the transformative powers of
romantic love, suggesting that such love transcends time and space and
all plausibility; Jack becomes a secular savior, whose sacrifice of his life
and being is not for all of humanity but solely for Rose herself. Thus,

Titanic can be seen as promoting a sentimental and narcissistic fantasy of romantic love.

In other respects, however, the film may be seen to escape the charge of sentimentality, or at least to offer it in its less harmful manifestations. *Titanic* refuses to soften the effects of death for the viewer and presents the horrific sinking in all of its terrible detail. Instead of sparing all sympathetic protagonists, as many narratives do, Jack himself dies along with many others. It might be argued that the transcendent scenes on the Grand Staircase embody the sort of wish fulfillment characteristic of sentimentality. Yet this scene does not specify the reality status of this vision, signaling merely a hope that somehow, in some way, love can transcend and survive death. Perhaps some would argue that merely entertaining and promoting such a hope or wish is itself harmful. If so, this demonstrates the degree to which judgments of the benefits or drawbacks of various beliefs may well depend on deeply ingrained worldviews.

What I have attempted to do here is provide some of the terms and concepts by which we can judge cultural and ethical significance of a film in relation to the affective experience it offers, an affective experience which has a strong rhetorical function that I will explore more fully in the next chapter. I will end with a few observations. Like many Hollywood films, *Titanic* values romantic love above all else, and in fact implies that romantic love—"Great Love"—is the highest form of love and is, in some ill-defined way, transcendent. Most important with regard to negative emotions, *Titanic* also serves a therapeutic function for many audiences by affirming the transcendence of love in the face of death. Such affirmation takes root only after a powerful evocation of the horror and reality of death. Thus, negative emotions in this case are essential for the therapeutic function of the overall narrative, which is to elicit, work through, and then dissipate sympathetic responses to the death of a sacrificial protagonist, and then deny the permanence and finality of this death and affirm the value and durability of love. This function is performed through the apotheosis of Jack, a secular savior whose devotion to Rose is wholly selfless, who sacrifices his own life for hers, and whose love transcends all limitations, even death. For the audience members who reportedly viewed the film repeatedly, it functions as a ritual affirmation of a secular redemption fantasy with obvious roots in the Christian story of sacrifice and redemption. A film such as *Titanic*, then, serves not merely to regulate morality, as Peter Brooks would have it, but functions as a powerful ritual with transcendent themes—a quasireligious ritual.

This chapter has also been about the means by which sympathetic narratives manage responses to the horrific and pitiful events that occur in the lives of their protagonists. My claim is that sympathetic narratives always elicit negative emotions, but they manage such elicitation by attenuating the force of negative emotions; mixing negative with positive emotions, such that the painful is mixed with the pleasurable; and enabling a cognitive and emotional process of "working through" the painful experiences represented, such that negative emotions are replaced with positive emotions that gain their force in part from the power of the previously felt negative emotions. This "working through," I would argue, comes in many forms or types of fantasies; among the most prominent of these are "fantasies of assurance and control."

7. The Rhetoric of Emotion

Disgust and Beyond

THE AFFECTIVE RHETORIC OF FILM

In their attempts to gauge the rhetorical and ideological effects of movies on spectators, film scholars have sometimes veered between two extremes, neither of which is entirely satisfactory. The first is deterministic, while the second emphasizes the spectator's freedom. The first insists on the ideological power of films, while the latter cedes seemingly limitless freedom to spectators to use films for their own purposes. The psycho-semiotic theory of the 1970s and 1980s claimed that mainstream films had a deterministic effect on an entity called "the subject" or "the spectator." The "subject," taken as a position or role that the flesh-and-blood viewer might occupy, was thought to be positioned as a capitalist subject, lured by textual pleasure and processes of infantile regression into unconscious submission to dominant ideology. If theorists often disavowed talk of actual people in favor of this abstract entity, the unspoken assumption was that real people often occupied the role of the subject. Were this not the case, then observations about spectator positioning would have been purely academic and would have had little relevance to culture or to film viewing. The "consciousness industry" would not have been deemed significant in its ideological effects were it not assumed that films had effects on actual viewers.

In more current film and media theory, however, the power of the film over the spectator is not only much more likely to be downplayed, but the viewer has been granted a self-conscious agency and a wholesale freedom to use the text as he or she pleases. Various subcultures and individuals are thought to use films for specific cultural and psychological purposes, uses that are often thought to be emancipatory. The film has little power over the spectators, but rather serves as a site of negotiated and oppositional viewings in which the spectator takes what he or she needs and leaves the rest. Such reception theories insist that all textual effects depend not on textual characteristics but on historical, social, and individual contexts of reception, such that *Titanic* (1997) might be found to affect one audience one way and another in a wholly different manner. To take some hypothetical examples, "Elenora" and her friends might sob uncontrollably at the film's end and be strongly moved to accept the film's vision of transcendent romantic love; "Aidan" might find the film to be terminally boring and its clichéd dialogue quite annoying; "Harper" might be excited by the sinking scenes but completely unmoved by the romantic plot; "Kate" might think that Cal Hockley is cute and wonder how Rose could turn down his money; "Francois" might be anxious for the film to end so that he can eat a hamburger. Given such varied possible responses, how can we pronounce that one and only one overall ideological or rhetorical effect holds for all viewers? We cannot. But who would suggest such a thing? The effects of a film, and the workings of ideology, are more complex than this, and the most cogent theories of ideological effect will be found between the two extremes of spectator determinism and absolute freedom.

The word "ideology" has many possible senses, but here I will concentrate on two of its central meanings. First, we might think of ideology in the Marxist sense as false consciousness. A belief or way of responding is ideological when it meets two conditions. First, it is a social construction that is to some extent arbitrary, that is, the belief or way of understanding is not inevitable or natural but rather contingent—one of many that could have been adopted in similar circumstances in another time or culture. Alternative beliefs are equally plausible, and other ways of responding equally possible, natural, or appropriate. Second, this belief or way of responding becomes accepted as natural, taken as a given, or unexamined and automatic, such that it is assumed to be the superior or natural belief or way of responding. Under this conception, what is ideological is often a false belief or an inappropriate or misguided way of responding that is unthinkingly assumed. Racism is an example of such false consciousness. Yet beliefs need not be false or practices harmful or misguided to be ideological. What is false about these is often the unexamined assumption of naturalness or appropriateness and the implicit rejection of alternatives as unnatural or inappropriate. For example, the belief that it is natural or "a given" that a man should provide a woman an expensive diamond ring upon their engagement is false consciousness only in the sense that it is accepted unthinkingly and its social consequences unexamined. I will call this kind of ideology "false consciousness."

In the second, more neutral sense, ideology is not necessarily false consciousness, but can be seen simply as a way of thinking about, valuing, and understanding the world—something like a worldview, but not limited to a set of beliefs. It is a worldview plus ways of valuing and responding. It is something like a way of life or a way of experiencing the world. We can speak about ideology in this second sense without the assumption of critique. Although the term is limiting, let us call this "ideology as worldview."

Although there is clearly more to be said here, it is not my purpose to sort through the complex issues in the theory of ideology. My point is that under either definition of ideology, movies are manifestly ideological because they can both confirm and alter the spectator's beliefs and ways of responding, whether this is seen as a contribution to "false consciousness" or simply the persuasive support for a worldview or way of being in the world. Films are ideological because films are rhetorical constructs, persuasive in their effects on audiences. And this persuasion relies in large part on the emotional and affective qualities of the film text and the experience it affords.

In considering the rhetorical force of a movie, the design of the text is especially salient, given the frequency of preferred, congruent, and partly negotiated viewings that generate at least in part the kinds of responses "built into" or intended by the film's makers. In fact, congruent responses are likely to be the most prevalent among spectators. Just as grocery shoppers choose the foods they like best (within the parameters of what is available to them), moviegoers with choices choose the available films that most closely fit the kind of experience they desire, basing their choices on genre, director, stars, nationality, language, and so on. And if the experience is, to some extent at least, chosen, then what is the motivation to resist such an experience? If congruent responses to film are common, the examination of film rhetoric is not only legitimate but *vital* to an understanding of the effect of the movies on beliefs, values, and ways of thinking.

In this chapter, I concentrate on the rhetoric of emotion in film. How does the elicitation of emotion in movies contribute to their rhetorical persuasiveness? A basic assumption of this book has been that affects, emotions, and cognition are often firmly entwined in the experience of movie viewing. In what is thought to be one of the earliest systematic treatments of psychology in existence—Aristotle's *On Rhetoric*[1]—Aristotle writes that when a speaker can arouse certain types of emotions, she or he can more easily facilitate a judgment sought in the listener. If I am a trial attorney, for example, and am arguing that a convicted felon deserves severe punishment, my ability to arouse the anger and vengefulness of the judge or jury will make them more likely to judge against him. If I argue a case for leniency in the sentencing of a convicted criminal, I may attempt to arouse pity or even admiration for his character or situation, thus winning a lighter sentence. The essential ingredient in the persuasiveness of the emotions is the fact that people often turn to their emotions when making judgments and will sometimes (often?) accept their personal emotional responses without question. As novelist Milan Kundera puts it, "When the heart speaks, the mind finds it indecent to object."[2] Moreover, the skilled rhetorician can manipulate the emotions of an audience for the purposes of modifying their judgment.

How might this apply to film and the other arts? Fiction films are about fictional characters, so the fact that movies persuade audiences to respond emotionally to characters and thus judge them might be thought to be irrelevant to responses to actual people or events. After all, if in viewing *Stella Dallas* (1937), I come to think that Stella Dallas has behaved admirably in sacrificing herself for her daughter, what has this to do with my responses to actual women or actual mothers? As a fiction, *Stella Dallas* is recognized by the spectator as a fantasy. One might argue that the division between fiction and fact is so strong and clear that emotional responses within the confines of movie viewing have no effect on responses or beliefs in other contexts.

This would be a hasty conclusion. It seems far more likely that in many ways as yet poorly understood, fictional stories play an important role in fashioning our real-world beliefs and responses. The long-term concern among film critics about stereotyping, for example, suggests that a view that sharply distinguishes the world of fantasy from reality may be simplistic. The fundamental assumption of those who insist on the cultural importance of stereotypes is that audiences often see individual characters not only as individuals but as actual social types, and that such ways of seeing or responding to those types have implications outside of the movie theater. When character traits congeal into bundles that are repeated over and again—the sacrificial mother, the *femme fatale*, the bitchy mother-in-law—a stereotype is born that resonates in the way we see actual people. It may become a template by which we slot actual persons into superficial categories consisting of assumptions and expectations about character and behavior. None of this is new. What I am adding to stereotype theory is an important bit about emotional responses to characters. In some cases, the responses elicited by films are to character types that are unthinkingly assumed to be actual types of persons. Such responses are rhetorically powerful and can themselves become conventional. That is, Hollywood creates not merely stereotypes but also characteristic ways of responding to them.

Movies also embody conventional ways of responding not only to individuals but to situations, formulaic "concern-based construals." The Western genre typically employs a violent confrontation between the hero and his nemesis to resolve conflicts. The romantic comedy elicits a strong desire for the romantic union of two characters, then builds suspense until the union is achieved and the story ends. Movies may generate stereotyped characters, narrative scenarios, and emotional responses; such patterns of experience have important implications beyond the experience of fiction.

Aside from such particular responses, it could be that movies participate in the general sentimental education of spectators. Martha Nussbaum claims that in reading literature, the reader becomes something like a judge or juror, and the construction of the text is designed to facilitate judgments about the various characters presented. Nussbaum doesn't mean by this that the spectator's only activity is moral criticism. By judgment, she means something more subtle, far-reaching, and above all, sympathetic. Drawing on Adam Smith's idea of the "judicious spectator,"[3] Nussbaum argues that some kinds of literature can lead us "in a pleasing natural way to an attitude that befits a good citizen and judge."[4] The literary or filmic spectator is not a skeptic, at least not when immersed in a work and accepting of its parameters, but relishes engagement with characters, most often sympathetic engagement with the characters who undergo the most dramatic conflict or trials. Good literature, she claims, fosters sympathy; a desire for equality, intimacy, and impartiality; and a comprehension in the realm of the imagination of "the richness and complexity of each citizen's inner world."[5]

Perhaps good literature and film, by Nussbaum's definition, can enlarge understanding and sympathy for characters whose lives and experiences extend far beyond our own experience, and thus enhance our sentimental education. It is not the spectator's attitude toward particular persons or events that are at issue here, but the general training of perception and judgment of which Nussbaum writes. But it must be said that most movies and literature are not of the quality and sophistication of the works she discusses. And many movies and novels, far from enlarging sympathies, elicit strong antipathies for hated or feared characters, perhaps even contempt and (as I argue below) disgust. Since the movies are so widespread in their consumption and intense in their effect, we might also want to entertain the possibility that in their emotional appeals, bad movies and literature can narrow our horizons, confuse us morally, encourage the superficial stereotyping of persons, enhance our taste for trivia, spectacle, and simplistic solutions to difficult problems, and generally and unthinkingly support the status quo. I think it prudent to consider the rhetorical implications of films on a case-by-case basis, rather than assume a particular effect for any type of literature or film. But we must not rule out the possibility that movies do offer a sentimental education that is decidedly bad.

In movie spectatorship as in the rest of life, the repetition of elicited emotions and judgments may solidify ways of thinking and feeling. It is through the elicitation of emotion in relation to moral and ideological judgment that a film may have its most significant ideological force. The marriage of thought and emotion creates a synergy that has been exploited for millennia not only by demagogues and propagandists but also by artists and entertainers.

THE CASE OF DISGUST

So far, this is all quite abstract. What is required is the examination of how this rhetoric of the emotions functions with regard to particular emotions in particular films. And so, before generalizing about the rhetoric of emotion in film at the end of the chapter, I present here a detailed case study.

Any examination of the rhetoric of emotion and affect in a film or films must begin with the clearest possible understanding of the emotion or affect in question, whether it be suspense, compassion, anger, or vengefulness. If an emotion is a concern-based construal, as I have argued, this requires an examination of the particular sort of concern and construal that in part constitutes a particular emotion. After this, the rhetorical functions of such emotions will come into focus.[6]

In this chapter, the particular emotion I explore is disgust, primarily in mainstream films within the American cultural context. But I concentrate on one particular aspect of film-elicited disgust that I find to be particularly interesting, that is, the relationship between what I will call "physical" disgust and "sociomoral" disgust. I will argue that the elicitation of disgust in the cinema establishes a clear connection between bodily reactions and ideology, and that the study of film-elicited disgust may well provide a template for establishing the cultural significance of other film-elicited emotions.

Disgust has been a topic of discussion among Western thinkers for hundreds of years—in German philosophy and aesthetics, in the thought of Freud, Nietzsche, and Sartre, and most recently, in several extended studies dealing exclusively with the emotion of disgust and its implications.[7] As we shall see, disgust is squarely implicated in issues of morality and ideology, and this implication raises some of the most intriguing questions regarding the uses of disgust in movies.

When considering disgust in American movies, what initially came to my mind was the body humor that has become a staple of contemporary Hollywood comedy, perhaps best represented by the Farrelly brothers in their films *Dumb & Dumber* (1994), *There's Something about Mary* (1998), and *Shallow Hal* (2001).[8] Some of the films of Baltimore filmmaker John Waters, whose work is discussed later in the chapter, also come to mind. These films, with their obsessive interest in the body and bodily products (whether noises, smells, wastes, or fluids), gleefully exploit the disgusting aspects of bodily existence to offer viewers pleasure in a kind of adolescent rebellion against the norms of polite society, albeit a rebellion that remains firmly regulated within the institutions of mainstream entertainment. The uses of disgust in film, however, extend far beyond this to the horror genre, to the work and obsessions of directors such as David Lynch and David Cronenberg, and to the prominent place of disgust in films such as Peter Greenaway's *The Cook, the Thief, His Wife, & Her Lover* (1989) and Roman Polanski's *Repulsion* (1965).[9]

DISGUST DEFINED

Most researchers agree that disgust has a universal component; visual, tactile, or olfactory contact with rats, cockroaches, urine, feces, and vomit has a similar effect on people across cultures. In the 1870s, Charles Darwin considered disgust to be an evolved response to things that might harm human prospects for survival. This view is shared by British researcher Val Curtis, who says that disgust "is a form of evasive action to protect us against signs of threat, such as disease." The biological determinants of disgust, she argues, clearly influence who experiences disgust and to what extent. For example, women tend to be more prone to the experience of disgust than men, because they "need to have a higher level of sensitivity to infection or disease, because they are the main carriers of infants." And as Curtis further notes, "as reproductive ability declines with age, so does disgust."[10]

Yet what initially might seem to be a relatively simple instinctive reaction firmly rooted in biological necessity turns out, on closer inspection, to be a complex emotion that is very difficult to define. Psychologists and philosophers disagree about how to conceptualize disgust, in part because disgust often has a marked social component. Take food, for example. Haggis is a delicacy in Scotland, but it turns the stomachs of most Americans and English. Orthodox Jews find the eating of pork to be disgusting, while Hindus have similar reactions to the eating of beef. Of all of the palatable mammals, insects, and birds in any given geographical area, particular human cultures tend to choose a few select species for ingestion, and consider the eating of other palatable species to be disgusting.

The social components of disgust can perhaps be best seen in the way that physical disgust quickly shades into sociomoral disgust. This division between physical and sociomoral disgust stems in part from the work of Jonathan Haidt and his colleagues, who conceive of disgust as a trifaceted emotion, consisting of what they call (1) "core," (2) "animal-reminder," and (3) "sociomoral" disgust.

Core disgust, they write, "is a food-related emotion that makes us cautious about what we touch or put into our mouths."[11] Thus, it has its roots in our sense of taste. But disgust is also elicited by encounters with violations of the body envelope (including amputations, sores, and injuries), diseases and vermin, and certain kinds of sexual phenomena. Haidt and colleagues call this second type of disgust "animal-reminder" disgust, because such phenomena remind us or our animal origins. At its heart, they claim, animal-reminder disgust (in the United States, at least) is rooted in the belief that the body is a kind of "temple" which houses our souls, our spirits, or our essences as persons. Animal-reminder disgust, then, can be regarded as a kind of guardian of the temple of the body or protector of a kind of self-image people have—an assumption that personhood is not in essence physical, but rather spiritual or transcendental.

The biological manifestations of disgust give way very quickly to "sociomoral disgust." Haidt notes that in the United States, the discussion of moral and political issues in disgust terms is extremely common. We often hear about someone finding another's behavior to be disgusting, or we think of certain sorts of activities as morally "contaminating." Neither physical nor sociomoral disgust is merely biological, then; they also encompass cultural patterns of feeling and behavior. In contemporary America, Haidt argues, the social functions of disgust may well be more important to human society than the biological functions.

To summarize, Haidt and colleagues write that disgust begins as a guardian of the mouth, extends to the protection of the "temple of the body," and finally becomes the guardian "of human dignity in the social order."[12] For the sake of simplicity, I will use the term "physical disgust" to refer to Haidt's core and animal-reminder disgust. We might next ask an intriguing question: how are physical and sociomoral disgust linked? In other words, how does such a simple biological emotion become harnessed to psychological, social, and ideological concerns?

To answer this question, Haidt and his colleagues turn to George Lakoff's and Mark Johnson's "experiential realism," a theory in which human cognition is thought to be tied to bodily experience.[13] In short, experiential realism holds that cognitive schemata are largely derived from our bodily existence, and that categories of abstract thought are metaphorical distillations of our biological being. Thus, metaphors of the body have been extended throughout human history to the domain of the social and the moral.

We can see this clearly in the case of disgust. A recent biography of the eighteenth-century American theologian and Calvinist minister Jonathan Edwards features a passage that well illustrates how physical disgust is mobilized into the realm of morality. Edwards, who is famously known for his sermon, "Sinners in the Hands of an Angry God," is here, in another sermon, attempting to frighten his congregation into imitating Christ's holiness. Edwards says that God is not only angry but disgusted at his disobedient creatures:

> There is no expressing the hatefulness and how hateful you are rendered by [your sin] in the sight of God. The odiousness of this filth is beyond all account because 'tis infinitely odious. You have seen the filthiness of toads and serpents and filthy vermin and creatures that you have loathed and of putrefied flesh . . . but there was but a finite deformity or odious-ness in this. . . . 'Tis but a shadow. Your filthiness is not the filthiness of toads and serpents or poisonous vermin, but of devils which is a thousand times worse. 'Tis impossible to express or conceive or measure how greatly God detests such defilement.[14]

This is one of many examples of such a movement or slippage between physical and sociomoral disgust. In many cultures, physical and sociomoral disgust are linked metaphorically; this seems to be a more or less universal quality of the emotion. Yet cultures differ markedly in what they take to be morally disgusting, or in other words, in their means of mapping physical onto sociomoral disgust.

Disgust has an important political dimension. It is interesting to note that Rozin and colleagues claim that in the United States, as in the West generally, sociomoral disgust is marshaled primarily to protect a sense of individual human dignity in the face of a looming suspicion of meaningless in life, and as a means of enforcing strong feelings against cruelty. In Japan, on the other hand, the threat of failing to find a proper fit within the social system is more often described in terms of disgust.

Disgust, then, can function to regulate social norms. Disgust is also used to maintain social hierarchies and even to demonize certain groups. The caste system in India (which designates the lowest caste as "untouchables"),[15] the recent genocide in Rwanda (during which the Tutsi were referred to as "cockroaches"), the Nazi vilification of the Jews (which construed Jews as rats), and various manifestations of homophobia in the United States—all of these demonstrate how physical and sociomoral disgust can be fused to marginalize, stigmatize, and even justify the murder of members of a society.[16]

Haidt and colleagues write of sociomoral disgust as an adaptation of the older core disgust—an adaptation designed to take advantage "of the schemata of core disgust in constructing . . . moral and social lives, and in socializing . . . children about what to avoid."[17] Sociomoral disgust, then, is largely a matter of social construction. But physical disgust is also in part culturally determined, influenced by cultural assumptions and by what cultures find to be sociomorally disgusting in particular historical periods. Disgust is not wholly a social construction, however. As William Ian Miller writes, the social construction of disgust does have limits: "Cultures . . . have much more leeway in admitting things or actions to the realm of the disgusting than in excluding certain ones from it."[18]

THE RISE OF MOVIE DISGUST

With a basic understanding of physical and sociomoral disgust, we now turn to the functions of disgust elicitation in the movies. We might begin by noting the trend in American movies toward the increased prevalence of disgusting subject matter. One could attribute this to a general coarsening of popular culture, but it is also part of a larger movement in which, as Winfried Menninghaus puts it, the vulgar, low-minded, and perverse have enjoyed an epidemic and generally affirmative treatment in the arts, literature, and humanities.[19] The centuries-long trend has been toward the increased acceptance of, and in some cases, the promotion of what has traditionally been thought to be disgusting. In the eighteenth century, physical disgust was thought to do a healthy job in protecting humanity and civilization. In the nineteenth and early twentieth centuries, writers begin to see the costs of overextended disgust and the forbidden attraction of its objects. By the end of the twentieth century, Menninghaus writes, art-

ists were revaluating disgust in artistic and academic work, perhaps even
cultivating it. In the contemporary visual arts, Bill Viola, Sarah Lucas,
Melanie Manchot, and Hermann Nitsch all confront us with conventionally disgusting subject matter.

In the United States, representations of physical disgust in the popular arts such as movies were rare and sporadic before the 1970s. For the
authors of the Motion Picture Production Code of 1930, or Hays Code,
the very possibility that a filmmaker might want to display the physically
disgusting was scarcely entertained. It is as though such a thing had never
occurred to the code's writers. Why would anyone do that? Any explicit
treatment in the Code of the disgusting, revolting, or vulgar is limited
to prohibitions on vulgar language, with the exception of some sexual
matters. The Code prohibits, for no stated reason, the representation of
potentially repugnant sexuality: sexual "perversion," miscegenation,
sexual hygiene, and venereal diseases (all examples of animal-reminder
disgust). It should be noted that the prohibitions on the representation of
miscegenation embody the worst sort of racist presumption and highlights
the association of disgust with ideas of "impurity," for the assumption
seems to have been that the mixing of the races threatens the "purity" of
the races—most likely that of the white race.

Although it does not mention them explicitly, the Hays Code does presume the categories of contamination and purity, using such language in
its discussions of "unclean art" and "pure" and "impure" love. Thus, we
can see that the Code metaphorically extended the language of physical
disgust into the arena of morality, or to put it differently, it presumed a
kind of equivalence between physical and sociomoral contamination. Thus,
the Motion Picture Production Code of 1930 well illustrates the broader
social phenomenon of the conflation of physical and sociomoral disgust.

The elicitation of sociomoral disgust directed toward evil acts, unlike
the elicitation of physical disgust, was not prohibited by the Code, but
neither was it sanctioned. The Code merely held that evil should not be
shown as attractive or beneficial, either morally or practically. Many years
earlier, English literary critic and author Samuel Johnson had gone further
than this when he wrote of vice in fiction:

> Vice, for vice is necessary to be shewn, should always disgust; nor
> should the graces of gaiety, or the dignity of courage, be so united with
> it, as to reconcile it to the mind. Wherever it appears, it should raise
> hatred by the malignity of its practices, and contempt by the meanness
> of its stratagems; for while it is supported by either parts or spirit, it
> will be seldom heartily abhorred.[20]

After the fall of the Production Code, the turn to increasingly graphic representations of sex and violence was accompanied by an increased freedom to explore all types of uncomfortable, shocking, disgusting, and formerly taboo subject matter on the screen. Today, representations of the conventionally disgusting figure prominently in the body humor of adolescent comedies and in the contemporary horror film and its hybrids, and more intermittently in a wide variety of films. A recent example of the increasing centrality of the disgusting in mainstream American film is *Along Came Polly* (2004), in which the protagonist (Ben Stiller) is portrayed to be highly fastidious, in part to exaggerate the affective power of his encounters with the disgusting in the form of a hairy, sweaty man rubbing his torso against his face (in slow motion), a plugged toilet in the apartment of his girlfriend (Jennifer Aniston), the discomfort of public urination in close proximity to others, being touched by those with dirty hands, and his friend (Philip Seymour Hoffman) accidentally defecating in his pants at a party. This type of subject matter is very common in contemporary Hollywood comedies.

Some less mainstream directors seem to specialize in the foregrounding of conventionally disgusting subject matter. Here Canadian David Cronenberg and Americans David Lynch and John Waters come to mind. John Waters's *Polyester* (1981) is discussed below. Although I do not have the space to do so here, an extended critical explication of Cronenberg's and Lynch's films that takes into account the aesthetic and ideological implications of their elicitation of disgust would be very illuminating. Various scholars and critics have begun to explore these issues, although most who explore the psychological implications of the films take a psychoanalytic perspective and show little familiarity with more contemporary discussions of the psychology of disgust.[21]

THE NATURE OF MOVIE DISGUST

The emotions elicited by film, as I have argued, can be roughly divided into those that are primarily *sympathetic* in nature—that is, experienced through or in response to the subjective experience of a character—and those that are *direct,* experienced by the viewer directly rather than primarily in response to the plight of a fictional character. The sympathetic emotions are what Andrew Ortony calls "fortunes-of-others" emotions.[22] Sympathetic emotions in fiction—for example, compassion, pity, and fear—always differ from their counterparts in our everyday lives, because our concern takes into account the fictional nature of the situation to which we respond.

In the case of direct emotions and affiliated affects, on the other hand, the viewer responds to her or his direct concerns. One example is suspense, which can occur independent of character engagement. Two more examples are startle and erotic desire. Psychologists disagree about whether these should be characterized as emotions, strictly speaking. But whether they are conceived of as emotions or more broadly as a type of affect, they are also direct. The viewer will respond to an attractive character if the viewer finds the character to be alluring, and it may matter little whether the protagonist or some other fictional character finds her or him to be alluring. Similarly, a sudden loud noise may elicit startle in the spectator independent of the protagonist's reactions.

Disgust is also a direct and not a sympathetic emotion, since it depends on the viewer's direct exposure to its stimulus. It is among the most visceral of the emotions. As William Ian Miller writes, disgust demands reference to the senses: "Disgust cannot dispense with direct reference to the sensory processing of its elicitors. All emotions are launched by some perception; only disgust makes that process of perceiving the core of its enterprise."[23] In other words, to feel disgust means to feel what it is like to see something, smell something, or be put in the presence of something disgusting. An excellent writer may be able to elicit disgust through vivid description, calling into play the imaginative faculties of the reader. The moving image media are more directly sensual and can afford a direct sensual representation of the disgusting object, apprehended through sight and hearing.

Core disgust is primarily invoked through taste and smell, and the moving image media may invoke this sort of disgust by eliciting the imagination of tastes and smells though the evocative presentation of sights and sounds. In the case of animal-reminder disgust—disgust at violations of the body envelope and various sorts of sexual phenomena—hearing and especially seeing are central. And it is the representation of this sort of disgusting object that has captured the attention of many filmmakers.

Disgust in the movies results from the sensory stimulus put directly before the spectator. Disgust in the movies is not an aesthetic emotion, in which the spectator is distanced by the knowledge of the fictional status of what is seen. The strength of the disgust reaction may be attenuated in movies, since the film medium typically emits no smells and since there is no threat of bodily contact with the disgusting entity. Yet seeing (and hearing) the disgusting object causes aversive tendencies that are identical to those we might experience outside the movie theater. While fearing an actual monster is much different than fearing a fictional one, our reactions to actual and photographically represented disgusting objects is one of degree, not of kind. Both cases could result in similar aversive action, such as closing one's eyes, averting one's gaze, crinkling up the face in the characteristic facial expression, and in strong cases, vomiting or moving away from the object of disgust (for example, walking out of the theater or stopping the DVD).

That disgust is a particularly visceral, direct emotion means that it is unlikely that we will experience physical disgust merely in sympathy with a character. It is an emotion that is by nature nonsympathetic.[24] This does not imply, however, that the viewer's response is never influenced or manipulated in relation to the response of a character in the fiction. Although disgust is direct, the audience may still take its cue for response from a character, restraining the effect or allowing it to take its full force depending on character cues. The reactions of a favored protagonist are often used to cue spectators about the desired response to various stimuli in the film. An example of what we might call "mimetic cueing" is in David Lynch's *Blue Velvet* (1986), in which the young Jeffrey Beaumont (Kyle MacLachlan) comes upon a severed human ear in a field near his home. Lynch gives us an extreme close-up of the ear, and we see that dozens of ants are crawling in and out of the ear canal (perhaps in a reference to the ant-ridden hole in the hand in *Un chien andalou* [1929]). Jeffrey is neither frightened, disgusted, nor horrified. Nor does he make a "disgust face." Instead, he touches the ear, calmly picking it up (albeit with as little contact with his fingers as possible), depositing it in a paper bag, and delivering it to the police. Thus, the audience is cued to take a calm, curious approach to Lynch's explorations of the seamy underside of suburban American life, where viewers will come into contact with a diverse array of conventionally disgusting objects, practices, and persons. The spectator is asked to suppress feelings of disgust to allow for the satisfaction of solving the mystery of the origins of the ear, and to engage in this filmic journey into the impure, unclean, and contaminated areas of American life. In a process that I described in the preceding chapter, disgust, as a negative emotion, is both attenuated and mixed with the positive emotions of fascination and anticipation.

Within the context of film viewing, disgust tends to be a short-term emotion. Unlike suspense or anticipation, which may extend through long periods of the film and build to climactic levels, the elicitation of disgust tends to be only intermittent. Its elicitation can be repeated, however, as it is in many of the films of David Lynch, becoming a motif or even an essential element of a worldview and outlook.

Disgust also has a distinct phenomenological feel and associated action tendencies. It is an unpleasant emotion, causing aversion to its object. When disgusted, people tend to want to distance themselves by moving away from, removing from their presence, spitting or vomiting out, or avoiding and censoring that which elicits disgust. A characteristic movement is to reject the disgusting object, person, or event. The experience of both physical and sociomoral disgust encourages persons to flee, avoid, ignore, suppress, and otherwise shun that which is unclean or contaminated. Yet in the realm of art, at least, the disgusting may also attract the viewer, creating a push and pull between curiosity and fascination on the one hand and aversion and repulsion on the other.

THE RHETORIC OF MOVIE DISGUST

The disgusting in film can be used as an "attraction," that is, as a device designed to create a momentary sensation with few global or narrative functions. Yet it often takes on more complex functions, becoming a thematic motif, figuring into structures of sympathy and antipathy, and promoting the film's ideological perspective. As such, the elicitation of disgust is often used to manipulate the spectator's stance toward characters and narrative events, playing a central role in a film's poetic and rhetorical system.

Of particular interest here is the melding of physical and sociomoral disgust. Since disgust is by nature an emotion that moves toward rejection, it is hardly surprising to find that physical disgust is used to create—whether explicitly or implicitly—moral or ideological antipathy toward certain characters and their actions and to promote their condemnation. Conventional physical disgust may be elicited by any number of bodily deformities, mutilations, and injuries; by body piercings or tattoos; and by the mixing of genders. If anthropologist Mary Douglas is correct, any categorical mixing that might be considered to be "impure" or "dangerous" is likely to elicit disgust.[25] One can see this in the history of the representation of race, homosexuality, and disability in the movies, where in many cases the minority, homosexual, or disabled person is shown to be both physically and morally repulsive by conventional standards.

Many James Bond films, for example, feature a criminal mastermind and lesser evil associates whose physical deformities, disabilities, and otherwise unusual physical attributes become metaphors for their malevolence. Many Bond villains are foreigners, by the way, and they also feature, for example, amputated hands that have been replaced by metal ones

(Dr. No); pronounced scars, a dead eye, and being bound to a wheelchair (Ernst Blofield); enormous height, a mouth full of metal teeth, and muteness (Jaws); or diminutive smallness (Nick Nack). These traits are in distinction from the smooth and sophisticated Bond, a man who is seemingly incapable of arousing the least wave of disgust or repugnance, and whose fastidious appearance and clean, flawless body often serve to soften the viewer's possible repugnance toward his libertarian sexual behavior.

In vengeance narratives, physical disgust is often used to make dispatch of the criminal an act that functions to ritually purify society of an unwanted contaminant. Thus physical disgust becomes wedded to sociomoral disgust, and this disgust is so exaggerated that it is meant to contribute to the justification of murder or execution in the name of a larger social good. We can see this tendency in many Western films, for example, or in the *Lethal Weapon* films with Danny Glover and Mel Gibson. A fine example of this is *Dirty Harry* (1971), the Clint Eastwood vigilante story in which Harry, the renegade cop, faces down his nemesis, the killer Scorpio. The sadistic serial killer Scorpio is the classic example of a character who is both morally depraved and physically repulsive. His sniveling demeanor, putrid-looking skin and complexion (as though his face is partially decayed), and sadomasochism all make his murder at the end of Harry's .44 Magnum seem not merely welcome and justifiable at the film's end, but positively necessary and pleasurable (to those that allow the film to do its rhetorical work). Not only does Harry rid the world of an evil criminal, but of a biological being who is represented as a kind of vermin. During Harry's confrontation with Scorpio in the football stadium, Harry steps on Scorpio's injured leg and twists his foot as though he were squishing a bug. The camera reveals the look of disgust on Harry's face, then moves quickly away from Harry in a rapidly retreating crane shot. The action tendency of disgust is either to remove the physically disgusting object from one's presence, or to remove oneself from *its* presence. This camera movement, rushing the spectator away from the disgusting Scorpio, is a filmic equivalent.

The whole weight of human history and biology predisposes filmmakers to use disgust as an aversive emotion, as a means to create audience antipathy for characters, events, or objects. It is much rarer, but not unheard of, for a film to deliberately minimize the elicitation of disgust in its representation of conventionally disgusting objects, usually to encourage the audience to look behind physical deformities or grotesqueries in order to celebrate the common humanity or spirituality of a character. Such films differentiate and attempt to decouple the relationship between

13.   Mrs. Kendal (Anne Bancroft) overcomes her disgust and kisses the hideous Merrick (John Hurt) on the cheek, thus affirming his humanity. From *The Elephant Man* (1980).

physical and sociomoral disgust, implying that the former need not, and indeed should not, imply the latter. Among such films we might include *The Elephant Man* (1980) and *Mask* (1985).

Both of these films elicit strong sympathy for characters with severely deformed, and thus conventionally disgusting, bodies. *Mask* sympathetically portrays the travails of a young boy afflicted with elephantiasis. Here I will give more attention to David Lynch's *The Elephant Man*, which develops a similar rhetorical project. Set in the nineteenth century, *The Elephant Man* gives an account of John Merrick, who suffered from Proteus Syndrome, which horribly deformed his whole body such that, as is said in the film, "nervous persons fly in horror from the sight of him." Although the body of the Elephant Man is conventionally repulsive, the film's overarching intention is to cause us to look beyond appearances to his essential humanity, to his extraordinary refinement in personality and demeanor, and to his desire "to be good" that he might be loved.

Many of the characters in the film must overcome their initial disgust at Merrick's appearance, including Dr. Frederick Treves (Anthony Hopkins), his wife Anne, and various nurses and acquaintances. People who are conventionally repulsive or grotesque are more so when we imagine them sexually, or in some sort of intimacy with us or with others. Thus it is a powerful moment in the film when the elegant society woman, Mrs. Kendal (Anne Bancroft), leans forward and kisses the hideous Merrick on his misshapen cheek. This is another mimetic cue for the audience, show-ing the viewer that just as Mrs. Kendal is able to overcome her disgust in recognizing Merrick's humanity, dignity, and inner beauty, so should the viewer respond.

POLYESTER AND IRONIC DISGUST

The elicitation of disgust functions in diverse other ways in fiction films, but for now I note one other such use, which occurs in John Waters's "cult" film *Polyester*. We might call this "ironic" and "reflexive" disgust. *Polyester* details the travails of Francine, a suburban Baltimore house-wife whose life is falling apart. Francine's travails are legion. Her cheating husband runs a pornographic film theater, which leads her neighbors to picket in front of the family house; her son is the infamous serial "foot stomper," who heavily stamps on the feet of unsuspecting women at malls and grocery stores; her nymphomaniac daughter socializes with drug-addicted ex-cons; and her hateful mother is scheming to steal Francine's house. This film is the Jerry Springer of melodrama, or like the work of a drunken, teenaged Douglas Sirk, an over-the-top parody of suburban domestic troubles.

What interests me in relation to disgust is this. Francine is played by Divine, an obese transvestite. The very choice of Divine for this role marks the film as counter-cultural parody. A gay man, director John Waters is clearly interested in poking fun at conventional middle-class life and mores. If the suburban housewife is thought to be the primary guardian of bourgeois morality, then casting a transvestite in that role takes on a clear subversive function. (John Waters also parodies the conventional image of the suburban housewife in his film *Serial Mom* [1994], in which Kathleen Turner is willing to defend family values to the point of becoming a serial killer.)

By having an obese transvestite play the lead role here, and by subject-ing Francine to such a series of trials and humiliations, Waters is doing a curious thing. The director seems to relish the ways he makes Francine the object of exaggerated disgust. This goes far beyond Francine's trans-vestism and obesity. It even extends beyond Waters's showing Francine on the toilet. Waters seems to be interested in the ritual humiliation of Francine. After reaching the depth of her troubles, she drinks so much that it becomes repulsive. At her nadir, we see her unable to stand, crawling on the floor of her house on hands and knees, drunk, sweating profusely, her mascara running down her cheeks. She is helpless and simpering. Later

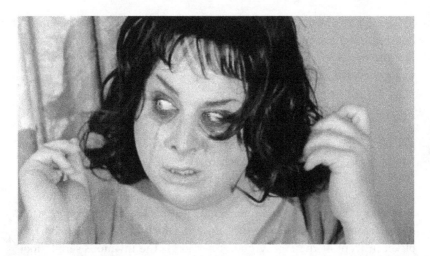

14. The transvestite Francine (Divine), drunk and simpering in *Polyester* (1981).

that day, suffering from a hangover, a friend takes her shopping, where she vomits into her purse at the clothing store.

Waters could be taken to be more interested in humiliating Francine and eliciting the audience's disgust than he is in eliciting its sympathy. Francine triumphs in the end, in a kind of tacked-on parody of a happy ending. The images and experience of her travails, her appearance, and her behavior—all of which make her conventionally disgusting—are much more powerful and convincing than her eventual triumph. Waters does not encourage the audience to overcome its disgust, as Lynch does in *The Elephant Man*, but expects them to revel in it, enjoy it, and find it amusing.

Waters's irony extends to many different levels. Erving Goffman writes that a trait that stigmatizes an individual, whether it be homosexuality, race, disability, or deformity, "assumedly taints every aspect of the person, pervasively spoiling social identity."[26] Sociomoral disgust draws lines of behavior, and those who cross them are called disgusting. The Zimbabwean dictator Robert Mugabe compares homosexuals to dirty animals, once saying that they "are worse than dogs and pigs."[27] In the United States, some groups identify homosexuality as disgusting, treating it as a disease that can be "cured." Martha Nussbaum claims that "the central locus of disgust in today's United States . . . [is] male loathing of the male homosexual."[28]

Goffman notes that those stigmatized may be likely to internalize the disgust and opprobrium of which they have become the target. One could argue that the film gives evidence of Waters's internalization of the stigmatization of transvestism and homosexuality, for rather than defending

Francine against the audience's potential disgust, John Waters exaggerates that disgust and asks the viewer to wallow in it.

Such an interpretation would be wrong, in my opinion, because in *Polyester*, Waters also encourages delight in his reflexive parody of the disgust response itself. Waters asks his audience to laugh at themselves being disgusted (and thus to ironically dispel the force of the disgust). As a "cult film," *Polyester* will attract an audience that is informed about the "rules" for spectatorship that a John Waters film demands. The savvy spectator of *Polyester* will recognize the film as a parody not only of the melodrama but also of the very conditions for the elicitation of disgust found in conventional melodrama and perhaps also in middle-class culture. These conditions could be characterized as a fastidious attachment to cleanliness and a rigid social order. Thus, the film is parody that functions in part through the gross exaggeration of disgusting behavior and objects.[29] In this way, the film encourages laughter at the sociomoral disgust that serves as a kind of gatekeeper emotion, functioning as it can to stigmatize and ostracize various members of society. *Polyester* laughingly mocks the entire system that subtends the disgust response in relation to various forms of transgressive sexuality, such as transvestism and homosexuality.

Any wholesale rejection of sociomoral or physical disgust on the grounds that it enforces some hated "bourgeois" or "repressive" morality would be simplistic indeed, although this has not stopped some observers from promoting such a rejection. Like many other emotions, the elicitation and experience of disgust can only be evaluated in relation to particular moral and social systems. When disgust is marshaled against miscegenation or against homosexuals, it is clearly being misused. Yet to entirely reject sociomoral disgust would also be to reject all boundaries between the beautiful and the repugnant, between the morally good, indifferent, and reprehensible. It would constitute a blanket denial of the usefulness of emotion in enforcing any sort of social or moral norms, or the proscription of abominations such as cruelty and torture. As I argued about the ideological effect of film in general at the chapter's beginning, so would I argue about the sociomoral functions of disgust in the movies. Each must be evaluated in particular contexts and in particular films.

THE RHETORIC OF EMOTION IN FILM

Cognitive film theory is sometimes thought to be unable or unwilling to consider questions of ideology and is thought to assume only, or merely, the universal viewing strategies rooted in the unchanging human mind. This is a caricature, but it is true that cognitive film theorists could do more to demonstrate the link between universal human capacities, culturally specific variation, and ideological concerns in the viewing and reception of films.

The study of film-elicited emotion from a cognitive-perceptual perspective promises to offer just such a link, integrating a consideration of the human body, cognitive capacities, and cultural differences into an approach to film poetics, film rhetoric, audience response, and issues of ideology. The movies are a sensual art form able to strongly affect audiences in a variety of ways. This elicitation of affect and emotion is strongly related to the moral judgment of spectators because, as I have claimed, people look to their emotions when making judgments about characters, events, or ideas, and often fail to question those emotional responses, accepting them as a given. Thus, if a filmmaker is able to elicit disgust directed toward Scorpio, the spectator may more likely accept and perhaps enjoy the righteous vengeance enacted by Dirty Harry. In some cases, the spectator may more likely accept as natural or legitimate such ways of responding to criminality or generally to people thought to be disgusting, whether sociomorally or physically. In this way, films may alter or reinforce patterns of thinking and feeling through their emotional appeals.

Disgust might be a particularly telling emotion through which to discover the means by which film-elicited affect moves from the biological to the ideological and vice versa. This is because disgust, like the emotions of guilt, shame, and embarrassment, is a primary means for the internalization of cultural prohibitions, and thus for socialization. In discovering the links between physical and sociomoral disgust in film-elicited emotion, we may work toward a general understanding of film response in its biological, cognitive, and cultural components.

But the relationship between emotion and persuasion extends far beyond disgust. Consider other sorts of emotions in relation to their intended rhetorical effects. Sympathetic responses to characters—pity and compassion, for example—may lead spectators to form generalized beliefs about types of people in types of situations, extending responses of film viewing to extra-filmic reality. Such might be argued in the case of *El Norte* (1983), a film that elicits pity and compassion for Rosa and Enrique, Guatemalan refugees who are led to escape persecution by immigrating illegally to the United States. Consider admiration: if a film manages to elicit admiration for a character, it can reinforce or alter the spectator's perception of what kinds of attributes are worthy of such admiration generally. Thus, if a spectator is led to admire Clarice Starling in *The Silence of the Lambs* (1991), it may lead her or him to admire the persistence and courage of women in career positions typically dominated by men (in this case, the FBI). In *Legends of the Fall* (1994), Brad Pitt plays Tristan, the wild son of a Montana farmer. Tristan is a child of nature who fights with grizzly bears and cannot be contained by conventional society; his inclinations are represented as natural and outside the bounds of conventional, imposed, or artificial morality. The audience, arguably, is asked to forgive Tristan when he is unable to remain faithful to his wife, when he sleeps with his brother's wife, or when he murders his enemies, because he is an untamed child of nature. At the film's end, when Tristan's wildness is explicitly compared to that of the grizzly bear, it is also linked to the expansive natural beauty of Montana (and of course to the attractiveness of Brad Pitt as a star). Some might argue that we are led to admire Tristan and thus excuse, if not celebrate, the kinds of actions he undertakes; through various cinematic techniques, the spectator is led to have various sympathetic emotions in response to his actions and in relation to the attractiveness of his persona.

What about the ironic or distanced responses found in John Waters's *Polyester*; can we find similar instances in other films and in relation to other emotions? What is most important about ironic responses is that they self-consciously oppose what is taken to be the conventional or "appropriate" response. In such instances, spectators are encouraged to take a critical stance toward either the conventional response that is implicitly critiqued or the response of an unsympathetic character.

In *The Picture of Dorian Grey*, Oscar Wilde writes: "The advantage of the emotions is that they lead us astray, and the advantage of science is that it is not emotional." Here he is espousing a variation on the familiar reason versus emotion dichotomy that I have opposed elsewhere in this book. Yet although reason and emotions are not *necessarily* opposed (and science is certainly not free of emotion), the use of the emotions in rhetorical persuasion might *often* be opposed to the kind of persuasion that occurs through reasoned evidence and argument. It is clear that our emotions can influence our judgments, and those emotions may be rooted in construals and concerns that are false, exaggerated, misleading, or in some other fashion antithetical to any conception of what a rational response might appear to be. I am convinced that a wide range of emotions elicited in film have a strong persuasive impact, even if the nature and causality of that impact is as yet poorly understood.

The study of the rhetoric of human emotions and affects in relation to film viewing is clearly an enormous topic and certainly in its infancy. A scholar wishing to investigate the topic further could approach it from the perspective of film genres, individual films, or as I have done here, by focusing on a particular kind of human emotion as it is elicited in certain mainstream American films. There is obviously much left to explore, since the functions of many other emotions have not been examined in film viewing. With the exception of horror and melodrama, neither have film scholars explored the particular affective appeals that various genres make to audiences. It would also be important to examine the rhetoric of affect elicitation in film traditions outside of the United States. Researchers could also approach affective response by focusing on the text in relation to particular audiences and contexts, since those audiences and contexts will reveal much about the tendencies toward the formation of concerns and construals that may alter or inflect emotional response. Even at this early stage of research, however, it is clear that careful attention to emotion elicitation in film promises to enable further understanding not only of the aesthetic and phenomenological experience films offer, but also of their rhetorical and ideological functions, and ultimately of the place films occupy in culture.

Conclusion

Moving Viewers

One reaction I received to this project at an early stage in its writing left an indelible impression on me. "Hasn't the topic of film and affect already been written about?" this person inquired. "Why explore such well-trodden territory?" The sentiments behind this question seem quite naïve, for two reasons. First, the study of affect in relation to film and the other media is in its infancy, at least in the disciplines of film and media studies.[1] In part, this is due to the former dominance of psychoanalysis as a model of spectator psychology. Psychoanalytic film theory has little to say about cognition or emotion as I have discussed them in this book, and it assumes a model of the unconscious mind in which I am not confident. It is only in the past few decades, in my opinion, that viable and plausible alternatives to psychoanalysis in film studies have emerged.

Second, the study of affect in response to film and media is a project too large, complex, and important for anyone to assume that scholars have discovered all there is to know or have settled on such solid and powerful theories that all relevant debates have ended. One could not plausibly conclude that further scrutiny of the human brain should cease, simply because brain researchers have already written about it. Emotional response, like the brain, is as yet only poorly and/or partially understood. Emotion and affect lie at the heart of spectator psychology and the aesthetic, rhetorical, and cultural importance of the media. To my mind, the explorations of this fascinating field of study have just begun. My hope is that *Moving Viewers: American Film and the Spectator's Experience* goes some way in facilitating further research in affect in one of the most influential modes of media of the past century, Hollywood movies, and beyond that contributes to a theory of affect in the media generally. To conclude the book, I offer some summarizing thoughts and direct the reader's attention to areas of research that demand further investigation.

A fair question to ask is why anyone should be interested in the ways that films elicit emotion. Is the purpose to develop a poetics of affect in film, or something else? A poetics of film might incorporate various elements. Some might conceive of film poetics as the study of film style and structure. My conception of poetics extends beyond this to how film style and structure function in the overall experience of a film. It asks questions such as the following. How do narration, structure, and style elicit affect? How is affective response incorporated into aesthetic experience, however one defines such an experience? Finally, how does the elicitation of affect contribute to the evaluation of a film's aesthetic excellence? If these are three central questions in a poetics of affect in film, I have concentrated only on the first of these in this book. I have made no attempt to define aesthetic experience or to relate affect elicitation to artistic excellence. The latter two questions are important, but the first—the question of the impact of style and structure in relation to affect—has occupied my attention here because it is vast and complex enough, and because it is in some ways a prolegomenon to the other two.

I ask the question again. Why should we be interested in film and affect? Aside from a poetics of film, perhaps we study affective response in an attempt to understand the place of films in culture, to understand the rhetorical and ideological import of films and their function as mass market fantasies or entertainments. Or perhaps our interest in spectator affect arises from a fascination with the psychology of the viewing experience. As numerous observers have noted (beginning with Hugo Munsterberg in 1916), film viewing in its phenomenal aspects approximates human consciousness to a certain extent. Films are designed to appeal to, or to "fit" the human psyche. What can films, then, teach us about human psychology?

Ultimately, my interests extend to film in relation to poetics, culture, and psychology. I am convinced that an understanding of affective experience at the movies is essential to the study of film in relation to any of these areas. The goal of this book has been to develop a theory of affect elicitation in Hollywood movies and to provide some impetus for future work that examines questions of film poetics and the relationship between movies, culture, and psychology at greater length and in more depth. Thus, I see this book as part of what I hope will remain an ongoing research project.

Within the overarching goal of developing a theory of affect at the movies, *Moving Viewers* has three broad purposes. The first, developed in Chapter 1, is to free the notions of pleasure, desire, and fantasy from the conceptual constraints that are an after-effect of the once-dominant influence of psychoanalytic film theory in film studies. Although psychoanalytic film theory has fallen from favor, its conceptions of pleasure, desires, and fantasy continue to have a powerful hold on the thinking of many film and media scholars. Yet alternative ways of conceiving of emotion and affect demand in turn that we rethink pleasure, desires, and fantasy in relation to the film viewer. Rather than offering fully developed theories of pleasure, desires, and/or fantasy in this book, I argued for and took a first step, which is to conceive of these terms in a much broader and more ecumenical way than psychoanalytic theory has prescribed. It is still necessary to develop a satisfying theory of the place of desires in film spectatorship in relation to emotion and to the kinds of gratifications narrative films offer viewers. Most important from the standpoint of film in relation to culture would be the development of a theory of fantasy rooted in plausible accounts of the psychological and cultural significance of popular narratives in film.

The second purpose of this book, carried out in Chapters 2 to 5, is to develop a cognitive-perceptual theory of spectator affect at the movies. I call the theory "cognitive-perceptual" rather than simply "cognitive" to recognize the role of unconscious processes in the elicitation of emotional and affective response. I described an emotion as a concern-based construal, but insisted that the concerns and construals on the part of the film spectator are not necessarily either the result of conscious deliberation or consciously recognized. Thus, a concern-based construal may be a conscious judgment, but it is often a "way of perceiving" events that has its roots in automatic and unconscious processes. In making a distinction between affect and the emotions, I also want to preserve a place of importance for affective processes that are distinctly noncognitive in their causality.

I see the cognitive-perceptual theory developed here as a beginning; there is much work left to do. First, we need more discussion of spectator difference in relation to the emotional responses cued by films. The effects of various extra-filmic factors, such as gender, ethnicity, race, class, age, and religious affiliation, on the spectator's affective response is an important area of further study. In this book, I discuss spectator difference at various points but develop no general theory of difference in relation to response. I suspect that for some cultural theorists, this will be an issue of contention. Cognitive film theory and cultural studies are often thought to be firmly camped on opposite sides of the nature/nurture debate, with cognitive theory favoring nature and cultural studies nurture. Yet the two approaches need not be opposed. Cognitive film theory is in its infancy, and one direction in which it should mature is in identifying the ways in which differences in individual and social cognition influence spectator response.

In cognitive film theory, Per Persson's *Understanding Cinema* has so far offered the most promising means of discussing individual and cultural differences among spectators. Persson identifies what he calls "dispositions," that is, "the totality of expectations, assumptions, hypotheses, theories, rules, codes, and prejudices that individuals project onto the world." Through such mental entities, Persson claims, "humans are *disposed* to understand the world in a certain preconfigured way, already prepared for some regularities of the world."[2] For Persson, it is unnecessary to choose between nature and nurture; both are at work. The dispositions of which he writes are universally human and/or culturally inflected. In his book, Persson explores such dispositions in relation to the spectator's interaction with and responses to variable framing, fictional characters, and point-of-view editing. Such an approach would be rewarding in relation to the study of emotional response as well.[3]

Another area of further research would be to apply the theory I develop here to various genres of media. The theory of affect here presented is applied only to movies—mainstream Hollywood films. Yet it has implications for all of film viewing and for the media in general. We must ask how art films, experimental films, video games, television serials, television advertising, web sites, and diverse other media elicit affect and emotion.

Also in need of further research are some types of emotions that I have mentioned but not discussed deeply. I concentrate most in this book on what I have called direct and sympathetic emotions, that is, emotions elicited by the content of the film's fictional story. But the artifact emotions, those emotions that take the film's artifactual status as their object, are an important area of further research. This research could examine the ways in which marketing and advertising influence response to films, and how response in relation to extra-fictional factors such as a film's budget, the well-publicized personal life of a star, or the perceived aesthetic excellence or failure of a film, for example, interact with the direct and sympathetic emotions that take as their object the film's fictional story. Meta-emotions, those emotions that arise from the spectator's responses to her or his own previous responses, are also in need of further research. If the emotions spectators experience in relation to films are inherently social and communicative, as some scholars argue, then the gratifications viewers experience while viewing films may depend on what meta-emotions communicate to others and the self. I have touched on these ideas in this book, but more systematic work exists, and more should be done.[4]

The relationship between genre and emotion is also very promising for future scholars. What sort of emotional experiences are offered by specific genres? Scholars have explored this question most fully in relation to horror, comedy, suspense, and melodrama. Yet there is much more to do, both in relation to these genres and to various others for which such questions have not been asked. It would be very useful to examine the typical mixture and ordering of emotions elicited in the various mainstream genres, in part to better understand the aesthetic experience they offer, but also to come to terms with the kind of fantasies and emotional gratifications major genres provide. Such a study could shed light on the psychological and cultural functions of movies and on how such functions are inflected by audience and context.

The third purpose of this book, undertaken in Chapters 6 and 7, is to begin to explore the implications of this cognitive-perceptual theory of film for cultural issues that extend beyond the experience of film viewing and speculate on its broader significance. To this end, Chapter 6 examines some of the psychological and culture implications of sympathetic narratives that elicit strong negative emotions, and Chapter 7 discusses the rhetoric of emotion in fiction film. In my discussion of *Titanic* (1997) in Chapter 6, I attempt to come to terms with the elicitation of negative emotions in mainstream narrative films. But as I mentioned above, a well-developed theory of fantasy in mainstream film would perhaps lead to a better understanding of the cultural and psychological functions of such narratives. What is the psychological process by which such narratives therapeutically "work through" the trauma of terrible events? I claimed that in the case of *Titanic*, for example, what is worked through is not hidden or unconscious residue from childhood trauma, but rather the explicit issues dealt with in the story, such as romantic love in relation to death and the wish for transcendence. However, this merely scratches the surface of the topic of mass narratives as therapeutic fantasies. In Chapter 7, I showed how the elicitation of disgust plays a role in the promotion of beliefs and attitudes toward characters or events that stand in for or represent ideas or types in the actual world. Yet the rhetorical role of many other emotions, and especially those such as guilt, shame, and fear used to enforce social prohibitions and conventions, remains to be examined.

Popular narratives have a communal function, the significance of which can easily be undervalued. In embodying virtual solutions to traumatic problems, they play a role in the development of what might be called distributed or social cognition. Cognitive scientist Merlin Donald suggests that the arts play a central role in culture "as a collective vehicle for self-reflection and as a shared source of cultural identity."[5] For Donald, as for other cognitive theorists, the arts are bound up with metacognition, which should not be considered solely as an individual activity but as an element of "distributed cognitive networks." Mimetic expressions of all types, Donald argues, are fundamental to much of what we do as humans, helping to synchronize our cognitive systems and facilitate learning and socialization. Movies and the other arts, according to Donald's theory, are not merely imitative or reflective but also creative and conventional interventions that form culture and influence both individual and social identity. This idea—both fascinating and suggestive—holds that mimetic expressions such as movies are constitutive of "distributed cognitive networks," which in turn partly constitute individual minds. You are what you see.

Add to this the growing consensus in cognitive science and related fields that thinking cannot be so easily separated from the body and from feeling, and that in fact thinking depends on the body and on metaphors that arise from the bodily experience of humans. Mark Johnson argues that all aspects of meaning-making in humans are fundamentally aesthetic, incorporating bodily and affective experience—sensual and proprioceptive experience—into abstract thought. If this is so, then studying the aesthetic dimensions of our experience could be crucial in discovering the bodily sources of meaning.[6]

The affective nature of the experience of movies and the media demands further examination. There is much left to discover and much that can be better understood. What is clear is that this affective experience is firmly implicated in questions of the aesthetics, psychology, and cultural impact of movies, and indeed, of all entertainment and artistic media.

Notes

INTRODUCTION

1. *Film* (London: Penguin Books, 1950).

2. V. F. Perkins, *Film as Film: Understanding and Judging Movies* (Harmondsworth, UK: Penguin Books, 1972), 155.

3. *The Film: A Psychological Study, The Silent Photoplay in 1916* (New York: Dover Publications, 1970), 53.

4. For an overview and theory of the affective gratifications offered by the media, see Anne Bartsch, Roland Mangold, Reinhold Viehoff, and Peter Vorderer, "Emotional Gratifications during Media Use—An Integrative Approach," *Communication* 31 (2006): 261–78.

5. See Noël Carroll, *Mystifying Movies: Fads and Fallacies in Contemporary Film Theory* (New York: Columbia University Press, 1988), and David Bordwell and Noël Carroll, eds., *Post-Theory: Reconstructing Film Studies* (Madison: University of Wisconsin Press, 1996).

6. *Film as Film*, 157.

7. Explorations of personal or idiosyncratic responses to films can be found, for example, in Annette Kuhn, *Family Secrets: Acts of Memory and Imagination* (New York: Verso, 1995), and Barbara Klinger, "The Art Film, Affect and the Female Viewer: *The Piano* Revisited," *Screen* 47, no. 1 (Spring 2006): 19–41.

8. "Hitchcock and the Mechanics of Suspense, I," *Movie* 3 (October 1962): 6.

9. Among those critics and filmmakers whose work recognizes the affective components of film viewing are Victor Perkins, Pauline Kael, Raymond Durgnat, Alfred Hitchcock (in his interviews), Robert Warshow, Robin Wood, and in general, the critics who wrote for the film journal *Movie* (some of whom are listed here).

10. In film studies, perhaps the most extensive theoretical justification for such an approach can be found in Janet Staiger, *Interpreting Films: Studies in the Historical Reception of American Cinema* (Princeton, NJ: Princeton Uni-

versity Press, 1992). For recent reception studies, see also Janet Staiger, *Perverse Spectators: The Practices of Film Reception* (New York: New York University Press, 2000); Janet Staiger, *Blockbuster TV: Must-See Sitcoms in the Network Era* (New York: New York University Press, 2000); Richard Maltby and Melvyn Stokes, eds., *Hollywood Spectatorship: Changing Perceptions of Cinema Audiences* (London: British Film Institute, 2001). Reception studies that rely on actual spectator testimony include Annette Kuhn, *Dreaming of Fred and Ginger: Cinema and Cultural Memory* (New York: New York University, 2002), and Tom Stempel, *American Audiences on Movies and Moviegoing* (Lexington: University of Kentucky Press, 2001). For a useful overview of media reception studies, see Janet Staiger, *Media Reception Studies* (New York: New York University Press, 2005).

11. See the introduction to Staiger's *Interpreting Films*.

12. I distinguish between a person's public report of an interior evaluative and emotional response and her or his actual private experience. In other words, self-reports are themselves problematic, because the subject may have many motivations for censoring, altering, or fabricating such a public report.

13. My terms are derived from Stuart Hall's "dominant reading," "negotiated reading," and "resistant reading," as found in "Encoding/Decoding," in Stuart Hall, Dorothy Hobson, Andrew Lowe, and Paul Willis, eds., *Culture, Media, Language* (London: Hutchinson, 1980).

14. My claim here is not that there are no such perverse uses of the media, nor that such uses are unimportant or uninteresting. Staiger has clearly shown that such responses are of great importance in the history of the reception of motion pictures. My argument here is that such "perverse" spectatorship should not be made normative for the typical spectator.

15. Jacqueline Bobo, "*The Color Purple:* Black Women as Cultural Readers," in E. Deirdre Pribram, ed., *Female Spectators: Looking at Film and Television* (London: Verso, 1988), 90–109.

16. Susan Feagin, *Reading with Feeling: The Aesthetics of Appreciation* (Ithaca, NY: Cornell University Press, 1996), 23–41.

17. Psychoanalytic theories have not been clear about when and under what conditions actual viewers occupy the role constructed for the spectator-as-position. See Stephen Prince, "Psychoanalytic Film Theory and the Case of the Missing Spectator," in Bordwell and Carroll, eds., *Post-Theory*, 71–87.

18. For David Bordwell's critique of "subject position theory," see "Contemporary Film Studies and the Vicissitudes of Grand Theory," in Bordwell and Carroll, eds., *Post-Theory*, 3–36.

19. *New Vocabularies in Film Semiotics: Structuralism, Post-Structuralism and Beyond* (London and New York: Routledge, 1992), 147.

20. *Film Theory: An Introduction* (London: Blackwell Publishers, 2000), 231.

21. In a similar way, we can use the word "bird" to refer to an individual bird, as in "The bird is eating a worm," or we can use "bird" to refer to the class of birds, as in "A bird in the hand is worth two in the bush."

CHAPTER 1

1. *Philosophical Investigations,* 3rd ed. (New York: Prentice Hall, 1999), 144.

2. Perkins, *Film as Film,* 157.

3. Gregory Currie, "Cognitivism," in Toby Miller and Robert Stam, eds., *A Companion to Film Theory* (Oxford, UK: Blackwell, 1999), 108.

4. Richard Maltby, "'A Brief Romantic Interlude': Dick and Jane Go to 3-and-One-Half Seconds of the Classical Hollywood Cinema," in Bordwell and Carroll, *Post-Theory,* 436. Maltby may well assume a false competition between economies of pleasure and the aesthetics of organic forms, but he is surely right that when the two do conflict, the provision of easy pleasures will often take precedence.

5. For a survey of apparatus theory, see Teresa de Lauretis and Stephen Heath, eds., *The Cinematic Apparatus* (New York: St. Martin's Press, 1984).

6. My criticisms of screen theory are not meant to apply to psychoanalysis generally. For a critical, yet sympathetic, examination of screen theory in spectatorship, see Judith Mayne's *Cinema Spectatorship* (New York: Routledge, 1993) and E. Ann Kaplan's *Psychoanalysis and Cinema* (New York: Routledge, 1989). Noël Carroll's *Mystifying Movies* is uniformly critical. One of the early critiques of screen theory came from dissenting members of the editorial board of *Screen,* the journal that eventually had much to do with the dissemination of the theory. Their summation of the project of screen theory reveals their deep skepticism: "An ill-defined monolith (sometimes described as classic American cinema, sometimes as mainstream cinema) produces a passive audience, which is also conceived as a monolith and never investigated" (Edward Buscombe, Christopher Gledhill, Alan Lovell, and Christopher Williams, "Statement: Psychoanalysis and Film," *Screen* 16, no. 4 [Winter 1975/1976], 129).

7. One line of defense for screen theory is to claim that it describes spectator "positions," not actual spectators. But this description of spectator positioning, as I argued in the Introduction, is useful only if actual viewers inhabit those positions. At the least, apparatus theory should have explained the relationship between the concept of spectator positions and actual viewers (on this it has remained largely silent). Recent theory derived from the original apparatus theory describes numerous and sometimes contradictory "positions of desire" offered by films. See, for example, Janet Bergstrom and Mary Ann Doane, *Camera Obscura* 20–21 (1989), a special issue on the spectatrix. Also see David Rodowick, *The Difficulty of Difference* (New York: Routledge, 1991). The use of the word "positions," unfortunately, retains some of the deterministic force of original apparatus theory (the subject is positioned) and downplays the ability of the spectator to respond from a standpoint independent of the particular film.

8. Barbara Klinger, "Digressions at the Cinema: Reception and Mass Culture," *Cinema Journal,* 28, no. 4 (Summer 1989), 10.

9. The first three categories of spectator pleasures—cognitive play, visceral

experience, and the sympathy and antipathy of character identification—are in part influenced by Jon Boorstin's account of spectator pleasures in *The Hollywood Eye: What Makes Movies Work* (New York: Harper Collins, 1990). Boorstin describes what he calls the "voyeur's eye," the "vicarious eye," and the "visceral eye." Though I think his fundamental distinction among these types of pleasures is sound, my account of the particulars differs substantially. Boorstin's book and Francois Truffaut's *Hitchcock/Truffaut* (New York: Simon and Schuster, 1983) are two of the most illuminating insider accounts of the spectator pleasures of mainstream film.

10. Morton Hunt, *The Story of Psychology* (New York: Doubleday, 1993), 493–510.

11. Edward Branigan, *Narrative Comprehension and Film* (New York: Routledge, 1992); David Bordwell, *Narration in the Fiction Film* (Madison: University of Wisconsin Press, 1985).

12. *Narration in the Fiction Film*, 40–47.

13. *Narrative Comprehension and Film*, 3.

14. *Mystifying Movies*, 171–81.

15. *Hitchcock/Truffaut*, 73.

16. One could counter my claim by saying that the fact that movies are socially sanctioned captures an important feature of the voyeurism of film viewing. Movies, one could say, offer a socially acceptable means of engaging in voyeurism, much as marriage offers a socially sanctioned means of engaging in sex. In reply, I offer two responses. First, I would agree that movies provide a socially sanctioned form of looking (and listening). However, that looking is varied in its nature and in what is looked at, and is not essentially sexual or voyeuristic. Second, my argument is not that voyeurism has no place in characterizations of film viewing, only that we should not characterize film viewing as essentially voyeuristic.

17. Quoted in David Cook, *A History of Narrative Film*, 3rd ed. (New York: W. W. Norton and Company, 1996), 927.

18. It is also true that with the rise of home theater technology, it is becoming possible to imitate the movie-going experience at home, with wide-screen DVD projection and digital multichannel sound. Add three or four family members or friends, and one also has the crowd experience characteristic of the movie theater. A full exploration of film spectatorship should also consider it as an individual and private activity. Individual spectatorship raises fascinating issues about group versus individual viewing, about choice of experiences under different contexts, differences in response, and so on.

19. On the means by which motion pictures depend on real-world perceptual skills, see Stephen Prince, "The Discourse of Pictures: Iconicity and Film Studies," *Film Quarterly* 47, no. 1 (Fall 1993): 16–28. Also see Paul Messaris, *Visual "Literacy": Image, Mind, and Reality* (Boulder, CO: Westview Press, 1994).

20. *Hitchcock/Truffaut*, 73.

21. *Hitchcock/Truffaut*, 297.

22. Aggressive uses of film technique are explored in Noël Burch, *Theory of Film Practice*, trans. Helen R. Lane (Princeton, NJ: Princeton University Press, 1973), 122–35.

23. Adam Smith, *The Theory of Moral Sentiments* (London: Dover, 2006), 9.

24. *Hitchcock/Truffaut*, 73.

25. For a good account of developments in psychoanalytic film theory, see Barbara Creed, "Film and Psychoanalysis," in John Hill and Pamela Church Gibson, eds., *The Oxford Guide to Film Studies* (Oxford, UK: Oxford University Press, 1998), 77–90.

26. "Film Bodies: Gender, Genre, and Excess," in Leo Braudy and Marshall Cohen, eds., *Film Theory and Criticism: Introductory Readings*, 5th ed. (New York and Oxford, UK: Oxford University Press, 1999), 701–15.

27. Sigmund Freud, *The Interpretation of Dreams* (New York: Avon Books, 1966).

28. Of course, psychoanalysis has a built-in defense against claims of implausibility. Such seeming implausibility is the work of repression, which makes opaque the actual workings of our minds. If one is skeptical of the Freudian conception of repression, however, this defense will not hold water. Moreover, the repression suspiciously renders the theory impervious to any objections, because the defender of psychoanalysis can simply appeal to the impenetrability of the deep recesses of the mind, or to the discovery of these deep recesses in private therapy sessions.

29. See Carroll, *Mystifying Movies*, and Bordwell and Carroll, *Post-Theory*.

30. Therefore the trouble with psychoanalytic film theory was not that it offered a theory of pleasure, but that the theory implicitly claimed to find the essential or vital pleasures at the heart of mainstream film viewing. Thus, it tended toward reductionism.

31. Bordwell, *Narration in the Fiction Film*, 157.

32. Torben Grodal offers an evolutionary approach to the fundamental psychic appeals of romantic melodrama and pornography in his "Love and Desire in the Cinema: An Evolutionary Approach to Romantic Films and Pornography," *Cinema Journal* 43, no. 2 (Winter 2004): 26–46.

33. Bill Nichols describes various types of reflexivity in *Representing Reality* (Bloomington: Indiana University Press, 1991), 69–75.

34. Vachel Lindsay, *The Art of the Moving Picture* (1915) (New York: Liveright, 1970), 224.

35. William Paul, *Laughing, Screaming: Modern Hollywood Horror and Comedy* (New York: Columbia University Press, 1994), 17–18.

36. Dolf Zillman and J. B. Weaver II, "Gender-socialization Theory of Reactions to Horror," in J. B. Weaver II and R. Tamborini, eds., *Horror Films: Current Research on Audience Preferences and Reactions* (Mahwah, NJ: Lawrence Erlbaum Associates, 1996), 81–101.

37. Clifford Geertz, *The Interpretation of Cultures* (New York: Basic Books, 1973).

38. James Hillman, *Emotion* (Evanston, IL: Northwestern University Press, 1997), 55–65.

39. Peter Brooks, *Reading for the Plot: Design and Intention in Narrative* (New York: Alfred A. Knopf, 1984), 37.

40. For an account of psychoanalytic film theory as it relates to affect, see Carl Plantinga and Greg M. Smith, eds., *Passionate Views: Film, Cognition, and Emotion* (Baltimore: Johns Hopkins University Press, 1999), 10–13.

41. "Masochism and the Perverse Pleasures of the Cinema," in Bill Nichols, ed., *Movies and Methods*, Vol. 2 (Berkeley: University of California Press, 1985), 610.

42. "Looking and the Gaze: Lacanian Film Theory and Its Vicissitudes," *Cinema Journal* 42, no. 3 (Spring 2003), 33.

43. See Laura Mulvey, "Visual Pleasure in the Narrative Cinema," in Braudy and Cohen, *Film Theory and Criticism*, 833–44. Williams, "Film Bodies," in Braudy and Cohen, *Film Theory and Criticism*, 712.

44. Peter Brooks, *Body Works: Objects of Desire in Modern Narrative* (Cambridge, MA: Harvard University Press, 1993), 96–99.

45. *Reading for the Plot*, 90–112.

46. Ibid., 46.

47. Carroll, *Mystifying Movies*, 227.

48. Some may take this definition to be tautological. To engage with the philosophical intricacies of "desire" in this context, however, risks distracting the reader from the thread of my argument. It is enough here to work with a simple and intuitive sense of the concept.

49. The dangers of trying on vicarious desires is an issue Gregory Currie addresses in "Narrative Desire," in Plantinga and Smith, *Passionate Views*, 183–99.

50. Thanks to Paisley Livingston for raising this question.

51. A recent and mightily strained argument for the analogy of viewing films and dreaming can be found in Colin McGinn's *The Power of Movies: How Screen and Mind Interact* (New York: Vintage, 2007).

52. Thierry Kuntzel, "The Film-work 2," *Camera Obscura* 5 (1980). Note how the essay's title is a reference to Freud's notion of dream work, the means by which the dream "figures," through various displacements, symbolizations, and condensations, the contents of the unconscious mind.

53. On this see Perkins, *Film as Film*, 140–41. For a critique of Christian Metz on the film/dream analogy, see Carroll, *Mystifying Movies*, 44–48.

54. Perkins, *Film as Film*, 134.

55. After brute perception, of course, the spectator's imaginative capacities are elicited.

56. Roger Odin, "A Semio-Pragmatic Approach to the Documentary Film," in Warren Buckland, ed., *The Film Spectator: From Sign to Mind* (Amsterdam: Amsterdam University Press, 1995), 227.

57. Ibid.

58. *Film Structure and the Emotion System* (Cambridge: Cambridge University Press, 2003).

CHAPTER 2

1. *The Varieties of Religious Experience* (New York: Modern Library, 1994), 150–51.

2. "In the River of Consciousness," *New York Review of Books* LI, no. 1 (January 15, 2004): 41.

3. *The Photoplay.*

4. Quoted in "In the River of Consciousness," 41.

5. *Film as Film,* 133.

6. Gerard O'Brien and Jon Jureidini, "Dispensing with the Dynamic Unconscious," *Philosophy, Psychiatry, and Psychology* 9, no. 2 (June 2002): 143–44.

7. Ibid.: 144–46.

8. John F. Kihlstrom, "The Rediscovery of the Unconscious," in Harold Morowitz and Jerome Singer, eds., *The Mind, the Brain, and Complex Adaptive Systems* (Reading, MA: USAddison Wesley Longman, 1994), 123–43. Also available online at http://ist-socrates.Berkeley.edu/~kihlstrm/rediscovery .htm (accessed November 9, 2004).

9. Quoted in Kihlstrom, "The Rediscovery of the Unconscious," 125.

10. Kihlstrom, "The Rediscovery of the Unconscious."

11. Ibid., 140–41.

12. Charles Darwin and Paul Ekman, *The Expression of Emotions in Man and Animals* (Oxford, UK: Oxford University Press, 2002), 25.

13. John A. Bargh and Tanya L. Chartrand, "The Unbearable Automaticity of Being," *American Psychologist* 54, no. 7 (July 1999): 462–79.

14. Ibid., 473.

15. A good, brief overview of some of these theories can be found in Paul Thomas Young, "Feeling and Emotion," in B. Wolman, ed., *Handbook of General Psychology* (Englewood Cliffs, NJ: Prentice-Hall, 1973). Also see Robert Plutchik, "Emotions: A General Psychoevolutionary Theory," in Klaus R. Sherer and Paul Keman, eds., *Approaches to Emotion* (Hillsdale, NJ: Lawrence Erlbaum, 1984), 197–219.

16. *Emotions: An Essay in Aid of Moral Psychology* (Cambridge: Cambridge University Press, 2003), 189.

17. *The Rationality of Emotion* (Cambridge, MA: MIT Press, 1987), 22.

18. Berys Gaut has argued that "art" is a "cluster concept," that is, a concept definable only by a disjunctively sufficient set of criteria. One could make a similar argument for the concept "emotion." See Gaut's "'Art' as a Cluster Concept," in Noël Carroll, ed., *Theories of Art Today* (Madison: University of Wisconsin Press, 2000), 25–44.

19. The literature on cognition and emotion is voluminous. For a brief

overview, see Hunt, *The Story of Psychology*, 479–510. For a philosopher's perspective, see William Lyons, *Emotion* (Cambridge: Cambridge University Press, 1980).

20. S. Schachter and J. Singer, "Cognitive, Social and Physiological Determinants of Emotional State," *Psychological Review* 69 (1962): 395–96. While this classic experiment has generated considerable controversy, what it shows at minimum—that emotion in some cases is influenced by cognition—is nonetheless commonly accepted by both psychologists and philosophers of emotion. A discussion of the debate surrounding this experiment can be found in Paul E. Griffiths, *What Emotions Really Are* (Chicago: University of Chicago Press, 1997), 24–27.

21. Appraisal of a situation is sometimes considered and volitional, and at other times automatic and involuntary. Psychologists who deny the connection between emotion and cognition usually describe emotion as a hardwired, innate process, emphasizing its automaticity. Those who claim an essential link between cognition and emotion, however, do not claim that emotions all involve conscious deliberation. Richard S. Lazarus, for example, describes both deliberate and involuntary modes of appraising situations. He also discusses preconscious modes of evaluation, and though he does not embrace the Freudian model, he allows for the possibility that sometimes ideas are kept out of awareness as an ego defense. In other words, cognitive appraisal is not always conscious and rational. See "Cognition and Motivation in Emotion," *American Psychologist* 46, no. 4 (April 1991): 352–67.

22. Roberts, *Emotions*, 96, 102.

23. For an influential theory of emotion that rejects the cognitive thesis, see Griffiths, *What Emotions Really Are.*

24. Roberts, *Emotions*, 101.

25. "Low" and "high" in this context refers to the neurological processing of emotion. Processing in the older brain structures such as the "reptilian" amygdala is considered "low," while processing that occurs in the more recently-evolved cortical areas is "high."

26. W.R. Kunst-Wilson and R.B. Zajonc, "Affective Discrimination of Stimuli That Cannot Be Recognized," *Science* 207 (1980): 558. For an overview of Zajonc on human emotion, see Jenefer Robinson, *Deeper Than Reason: Emotion and Its Role in Literature, Music, and Art* (Oxford, UK: Clarendon Press, 2005), 38–44.

27. I make reference here in part to a series of lectures on emotion and the arts given by Jenefer Robinson at the NEH Summer Institute "Art, Mind, and Cognitive Science," University of Maryland, 2002. See Robinson, *Deeper Than Reason*. Also see her essays "Startle," *Journal of Philosophy* 92, no. 2 (February 1995): 53–74, and "L'éducation sentimentale," *Australasian Journal of Philosophy* 73, no. 2 (June 1995): 212–27.

28. Roberts, *Emotions*, 38–45.

29. Nancy L. Stein, Tom Trabasso, and Maria Liwag, "The Representation and Organization of Emotional Experience: Unfolding the Emotion Episode,"

in Michael Lewis and Jeannette M. Haviland, eds., *Handbook of Emotions* (New York: Guilford Press, 1993), 279–300.

30. Roberts, *Emotions*, 80.

31. *The Photoplay.*

32. Benedetto Croce, *The Aesthetic as the Science of Expression and of the Linguistic in General* (1902), trans. Colin Lyas (Cambridge and New York: Cambridge University Press, 1992); R.G. Collingwood, *The Principles of Art* (Oxford, UK: Oxford University Press, 1938). Also see John Spackman, "Expression Theory of Art," in Michael Kelly, ed., *Encyclopedia of Aesthetics,* vol. 2 (New York and Oxford: Oxford University Press, 1998), 139–44. I would argue that emotional experience is *not* separate from conceptual knowledge or cognitive activity, but that perhaps the arts are uniquely able to combine conceptual activity and emotional response.

33. Clive Bell, *Art* (New York: BiblioBazaar, 2007), 46.

34. How do we know the form is significant? We know, Bell says, because it elicits aesthetic emotions. How do we know that these are aesthetic emotions? This we know because such emotions arise from significant form. What is significant form? It is form that enables the experience of aesthetic emotion. And thus this circular argument proceeds.

35. Stephen Prince, "True Lies: Perceptual Realism, Digital Images and Film Theory," *Film Quarterly* 49, no. 3 (Spring 1996): 27–37.

36. *Emotion and the Structure of Narrative Film* (Mahwah, NJ: Lawrence Erlbaum, 1996), 82, 153.

37. "Notes on Audience Response," in Bordwell and Carroll, *Post-Theory,* 396.

38. Gerrig and Prentice recognize that viewers do not believe that they can draw the attention of the characters or affect the narrative outcome, which immediately, to my mind, calls into question their characterization of a film spectator as a "participant." I'm not sure that the analogy between a side participant in a conversation and a film spectator is helpful, there being so many fundamental differences between the two situations. Attending a film is unlike hearing a conversation in many ways. Using human conversation as a model for film viewing is something like using the model of scuba diving to understand snow skiing. It would be better to examine snow skiing itself.

39. See Murray Smith, "Film Spectatorship and the Institution of Fiction," *Journal of Aesthetics and Art Criticism* 53 (1995): 113–27.

40. For a survey of thought on the paradox of fiction, see Robert Yanal, *Paradoxes of Emotion and Fiction* (University Park: Pennsylvania State University Press, 1999). See also Derek Matravers, *Art and Emotion* (Oxford, UK: Clarendon Press, 1998), especially Chapter 3, "Fearing Fictions," on the relationship between emotion and belief in fictions.

41. Colin Radford, "How Can We Be Moved by the Fate of Anna Karenina?" *Proceedings of the Aristotelian Society,* supp. vol. 49 (1975): 67–80.

42. Kendall Walton, *Mimesis as Make-Believe: On the Foundations of the Representational Arts* (Cambridge, MA: Harvard University Press, 1990).

43. For an extended discussion of this issue, see Noël Carroll, *The Philosophy of Horror* (New York and London: Routledge, 1990), 59–88.

44. Ibid., 83.

45. *The Fictive and the Imaginary: Charting Literary Anthropology* (Baltimore: Johns Hopkins University Press, 1993).

46. Odin, "A Semio-Pragmatic Approach," 227.

47. Hitchcock quotes in Truffaut, *Hitchcock/Truffaut*, 72.

48. Ed S. Tan, *Emotion and the Structure of Narrative Film*, 85–120.

49. Carroll E. Izard, ed., *Human Emotions* (New York: Plenum Press, 1977), 211.

50. See Nico Frijda, *The Emotions* (Cambridge: Cambridge University Press, 1986).

51. Andrew Ortony, Gerald L. Clore, and Allan Collins, *The Cognitive Structure of the Emotions* (Cambridge: Cambridge University Press, 1988), 174.

52. Tan writes that interest comes in three varieties—curiosity, suspense, and surprise. I would say that other emotions are involved in maintaining our desire to focus on a film, and that these cannot be subsumed under the rubric of a single emotion.

53. For a debate between Ed Tan and me on taking interest as the overarching emotion in film viewing, see Carl Plantinga and Ed Tan, "Interest and Unity in the Emotional Response to Film," *Journal of Moving Image Studies* 4, no. 1 (2007), www.avila.edu/journal/vol4/Plantinga_Tan_JMIS_def.pdf.

54. Smith, *Film Structure and the Emotion System.* Further references to page numbers of this text in this chapter will be made parenthetically within the text.

55. The long-term, direct emotions, such as suspense, curiosity, anticipation, and interest, are not listed in the index of Smith's book. Although Smith does use the term "anticipation" in his analysis of particular films, he seems not to consider it an emotion. Such long-term emotions, unlike moods, can better be used to account for the forward-looking mental activity required by the viewer's processing of narrative and the kind of affective experience this engenders.

56. Quoted in Stein Haugom Olsen, "Literary Aesthetics," in Michael Kelly, ed., *Encyclopedia of Aesthetics*, vol. 3 (New York and Oxford, UK: Oxford University Press, 1998), 148.

57. For a discussion of compassion as an emotion, see Richard S. Lazarus, *Emotion and Adaptation* (Oxford, UK: Oxford University Press, 1994), 287–92.

58. Tan also distinguishes between fiction and artifact emotions, although in some fundamental ways our terminology differs; see *Emotion and the Structure of Narrative Film*, 65–66.

59. Lazarus, *Emotion and Adaptation*, 293.

60. *The Mind and Its Stories: Narrative Universals and Human Emotion* (Cambridge: Cambridge University Press, 2003), 51–54. Hogan goes on to describe (or perhaps translate) Abhinavagupta's theories into the terms of contemporary cognitive science.

61. Ibid., 53–54.

62. Something similar to this is suggested by W. K. Wimsatt and Monroe Beardsley in "The Affective Fallacy," in Hazard Adams, ed., *Critical Theory since Plato* (New York: Harcourt Brace Jovanovich, 1971), 1030. Wimsatt and Beardsley explicitly assert only that the critic should not confuse the poem with its results, and argue that the results (affective responses) are not the proper study of criticism at all. Rather, the critic ought to at most recognize objective correlatives, or in other words, the objective features of the text—its elicitors—that might be thought to elicit response. Despite my concentration on such elicitors in this book, I think Wimsatt and Beardsley were wrong to deny the importance and interest of the study of conditioners in responses to art.

CHAPTER 3

1. *Film as Film*, 141.

2. Noël Carroll, *A Philosophy of Mass Art* (Oxford, UK: Clarendon Press, 1998), 261–62. See also Carroll's "Film, Emotion and Genre," in Plantinga and Smith, *Passionate Views*, 21–47.

3. Carroll calls this "criterial prefocusing," since, on his claim, all emotions have criteria. See *A Philosophy of Mass Art*, 264.

4. I reject the claim, common to many expression theories of art, that the work of art is an expression of the emotions of the artist. On my theory, this is not necessarily the case. A film might be the expression of an emotional experience no actual person has ever had.

5. "I Feel, Therefore I Am—I Think," in Paul Ekman and Richard J. Davidson, eds., *The Nature of Emotion* (Oxford, UK: Oxford University Press, 1994), 385.

6. *The Rationality of Emotion*, xvi.

7. *The Rationality of Emotion*, 182. De Sousa's information on childhood development and paradigm scenarios comes from Daniel Stern, *The First Relationship: Infant and Mother* (Cambridge, MA: Harvard University Press, 2002).

8. See also Naomi Scheman, "Anger and the Politics of Naming," in Sally McConnell-Ginet, Ruth Borker, and Nelly Furman, eds., *Women and Language in Literature and Society* (New York: Praeger, 1980).

9. *Emotions* (New York: The Ronald Press Company, 1939), 113–14.

10. Plutchik, "Emotions," 202.

11. One exception to this tendency is J. R. Averill, who downplays the role of biology and argues that all emotions are essentially socially constructed. See *Anger and Aggression: An Essay on Emotion* (New York: Springer-Verlag,

1982). Most theorists contend that a limited number of the basic emotions have evolved due to their adaptive significance. See Darwin and Ekman, *The Expression of Emotions in Man and Animals;* Izard, *Human Emotions;* and Silvan Tomkins, *Exploring Affect: The Selected Writings of Silvan S. Tomkins,* ed. E. Virginia Damos (Cambridge: Cambridge University Press, 1995).

12. *Counter-Statement* (Berkeley: University of California Press, 1968), 124.

13. David Bordwell, Janet Staiger, and Kristin Thompson, *The Classical Hollywood Cinema: Film Style and Mode of Production to 1960* (New York: Columbia University Press, 1985), 157.

14. See Tom Gunning, "The Cinema of Attraction: Early Film, Its Spectator, and the Avant-Garde," in Robert Stam and Toby Miller, eds., *Film Theory: An Anthology* (Oxford, UK: Blackwell Publishers, 2000), 229–35.

15. Eleanor Burgess, "Denby Sez: Hollywood Alive, but Barely Conscious," *The Yale Herald,* www.yaleherald.com/article.php?Article=2638 (accessed December 15, 2003).

16. Jon Lewis, "The End of Cinema as We Know It and I Feel . . . ," in Jon Lewis, ed., *The End of Cinema as We Know It: American Film in the Nineties* (New York: New York University Press, 2001), 1–8.

17. Tino Balio, "'A Major Presence in All of the World's Important Markets': The Globalization of Hollywood in the 1990s," in Steve Neale and Murray Smith, eds., *Contemporary Hollywood Cinema* (London and New York: Routledge, 1998), 60.

18. *High Concept: Movies and Marketing in Hollywood* (Austin: University of Texas Press, 1994), 8.

19. "End of Story: The Collapse of Myth in Postmodern Narrative Film," in Jon Lewis, *The End of Cinema as We Know It,* 320.

20. "Post-classical Hollywood," in John Hill and Pamela Church Gibson, eds., *American Cinema and Hollywood: Critical Approaches* (Oxford, UK: Oxford University Press, 2000), 80.

21. Kristin Thompson, *Storytelling in the New Hollywood: Understanding Classical Narrative Technique* (Cambridge, MA: Harvard University Press, 1999), x.

22. See Bordwell, Staiger, and Thompson, *The Classical Hollywood Cinema;* Bordwell, *Narration in the Fiction Film;* Thompson, *Storytelling in the New Hollywood;* David Bordwell, *The Way Hollywood Tells It: Story and Style in the Movies* (Berkeley: University of California Press, 2006).

23. Carl Plantinga, "Spectacles of Death: Clint Eastwood and Violence in *Unforgiven,*" *Cinema Journal* 37, no. 2 (Winter 1998): 65–83.

24. For an excellent examination of Hollywood story structure, see Thompson's *Storytelling in the New Hollywood.*

25. "The Positive Emotion of Elevation," *Prevention and Treatment* 3 (March 2000), http://journals.apa.org/prevention/volume3/pre0030003c.html (accessed September 2, 2004).

26. See, for example, Fritz Heider and Marianne Simmel, "An Experimen-

tal Study of Apparent Behavior," *American Journal of Psychology* 57 (1944): 243–59.

27. For more on this phenomenon, see Tan, *Emotion and the Structure of Narrative Film*, 160–63.

28. *The Theory of Moral Sentiments*, 9.

29. For a clear and succinct account of this history, see Mark H. Davis, *Empathy: A Social Psychological Approach* (Boulder, CO: Westview Press, 1996), 1–9.

30. Truffaut, *Hitchcock/Truffaut*, 145.

31. See, for example, Alex Neil, "Empathy and (Film) Fiction," in Bordwell and Carroll, *Post-Theory*, 175–194; Murray Smith, *Engaging Characters: Fiction, Emotion, and the Cinema* (Oxford, UK: Clarendon Press, 1995), 94, 102–6.

32. "Empathic Engagement with Narrative Fictions," *Journal of Aesthetics and Art Criticism* 62, no. 2 (Spring 2004), 145. For a classic discussion of the psychology of empathy in literature and film, see Hans Kreitler and Shulamith Kreitler, *Psychology of the Arts* (Durham, NC: Duke University Press, 1972), 257–84. For an overview of various theories of empathy, see Dolf Zillman, "Empathy: Affect from Bearing Witness to the Emotions of Others," in Jennings Bryant and Dolf Zillman, eds., *Responding to the Screen: Reception and Reaction Processes* (Hillsdale, NJ: Erlbaum, 1991), 135–41.

33. Carl Plantinga, "The Scene of Empathy and the Human Face on Film," in Plantinga and Smith, *Passionate Views*, 244–47.

34. For example, the first definition of "sympathy" in *The American Heritage Dictionary of the English Language* reads, "A relationship or affinity between persons or things in which whatever affects one correspondingly affects the other." This implies shared feelings in the case of emotional empathy. "Empathy," on the other hand, is in its second definition called "understanding so intimate that the feelings, thoughts, and motives of the one are readily comprehended by the other." Here empathy is conceived of as cognitive and not as shared feeling. William Morris, ed. (Boston: Houghton Mifflin, 1976).

35. For an overview of various theories of empathy, see Zillman, "Empathy," 135–41.

36. Lauren Wispé, *The Psychology of Sympathy* (New York: Plenum Publishing, 1991), 79–80.

37. Jean Beavin Bavelas, Alex Black, Charles R. Lemery, and Jennifer Mullett, "Motor Mimicry as Primitive Empathy," in Nancy Eisenberg and Janet Strayer, eds., *Empathy and Its Development* (Cambridge University Press, 1987), 318.

38. Bordwell, *Narration in the Fiction Film*, 205–33.

39. "Identification and Emotion in Narrative Film," in Plantinga and Smith, *Passionate Views*, 200–216.

40. On this point, see Carroll, *The Philosophy of Horror*, 88–96.

41. (Oxford, UK: Clarendon Press, 1997).

42. For Grodal's critique of Carroll on identification, see *Moving Pictures,* 84–86. A good summary of Grodal's position is found in Smith, *Film Structure and the Emotion System,* 75–81.

43. Grodal, *Moving Pictures,* 84–85.

44. Murray Smith, "Altered States: Character and Emotional Response in the Cinema," *Cinema Journal* 33, no. 4 (Summer 1994): 34–56. See also Smith's *Engaging Characters.*

45. Smith, *Engaging Characters,*143.

46. See Wayne Booth, *The Rhetoric of Fiction* (Chicago: University of Chicago Press, 1961), 245–46.

47. On this point, see Smith's "Gangsters, Cannibals, Aesthetes, or Apparently Perverse Allegiances," in Plantinga and Smith, *Passionate Views,* 217–38.

48. This is a term used by Bordwell in *The Way Hollywood Tells It.*

49. "Visual Pleasure and Narrative Cinema," in Marshall Cohen and Leo Braudy, eds., *Film Theory and Criticism: Introductory Readings,* 5th ed. (New York and Oxford, UK: Oxford University Press, 1999), 833–44.

50. For a thorough examination of gender and subjectivity in Hitchcock's films, see Paula Cohen, *Alfred Hitchcock: The Legacy of Victorianism* (Lexington: University of Kentucky Press, 1995).

51. "Women and Representation: Can We Enjoy Alternative Pleasure?" in Patricia Erens, ed., *Issues in Feminist Film Criticism* (Bloomington: Indiana University Press, 1990), 84.

52. Judith Mayne, *Cinema Spectatorship,* 77–102.

53. See for example, Eisenberg and Strayer, *Empathy and Its Development;* Averill, *Anger and Aggression;* June Crawford et al., *Emotion and Gender* (London: SAGE Publications, 1992); Hazel Markus and Shinobu Kitayama, *Emotion and Culture* (Washington, DC: American Psychological Association, 1994).

CHAPTER 4

1. Some people describe film viewing as passive in relationship to reading, but these same critics would rarely say that listening to music is passive. To turn the argument around, those who promote literature above film do so in part on the basis of the presumed effort involved in reading. Yet supposing that reading requires more effort than viewing, the same kind of mental effort, presumably, is not required when listening to a Mozart violin concerto, and would not be marshaled against taking Mozart's music as equal to fine literature. Whatever it is that makes Mozart's music "great art," then, it cannot be merely difficulty or effort in comprehension, since it does not require such effort.

2. James Monaco, *How to Read a Film* (Oxford, UK: Oxford University Press, 2008).

3. Prince, "True Lies," 27–37. Also see Prince, "The Discourse of Pictures";

Carl Plantinga, *Rhetoric and Representation in Nonfiction Film* (Cambridge: Cambridge University Press, 1997), 40–58. The most thorough treatment is Paul Messaris, *Visual "Literacy."*

4. On indexicality in nonfiction film, see Plantinga, *Rhetoric and Representation in Nonfiction Film,* 59–82.

5. Prince, "True Lies," 30–31.

6. For a fascinating study of Hollywood screen violence, see Stephen Prince, *Classical Film Violence: Designing and Regulating Brutality in Hollywood Cinema, 1930–1968* (New Brunswick, NJ: Rutgers University Press, 2003).

7. Charles Musser, *The Emergence of Cinema: The American Screen to 1907* (Berkeley: University of California Press, 1990), 82, 118.

8. "Film Bodies," 701–15.

9. See Robert Baird, "The Startle Effect: Implications for Spectator Cognition and Media Theory," *Film Quarterly* 53, no. 3 (Spring 2000): 22.

10. *The Address of the Eye: A Phenomenology of Film Experience* (Princeton, NJ: Princeton University Press, 1992), 5.

11. Ibid., 271.

12. Ibid., 9.

13. Ibid., 25. It should be noted that Sobchack's emphasis on the film as a literal body is significantly downplayed in her more recent *Carnal Thoughts: Embodiment and Moving Image Culture* (Berkeley: University of California Press, 2004).

14. In saying this, I agree with David Bordwell that all films have a narration but not all films have a narrator. See his *Narration in the Fiction Film,* 61–62.

15. Benjamin Detenber and Byron Reeves, "A Bio-Informational Theory of Emotion: Motion and Image Size Effects on Viewers," *Journal of Communication* 46, no. 3 (Summer 1996).

16. www.epilepsy.ca/eng/left_menu/news_Update/NU_Photosensitive Seizures.htm (accessed November 16, 2004).

17. Noël Burch writes of "structures of aggression" in *Theory of Film Practice,* 124–25.

18. Jenefer Robinson considers startle to be a central example of an emotion, arguing that as such it strongly challenges what she calls "judgmentalist" theories of emotion that insist on prior cognitive activity in emotional response. Many psychologists think of startle as a reflex or primitive affective response rather than an emotion. I think of startle as an affect rather than a full-fledged emotion. See Robinson, "Startle," 53–74.

19. Baird, "The Startle Effect," 21.

20. "Motion Analysis Overview" (paper delivered at the conference "Narration, Imagination, and Emotion in the Moving Image Media," Grand Rapids, MI, July 2004).

21. See Louis Giannetti, *Understanding Movies,* 7th ed. (Englewood Cliffs, NJ: Prentice Hall, 1996), 95.

22. "Violent Dance in Martial Arts Films," *Jump Cut* 44 (Fall 2001): 1.

23. Aaron Anderson, "Action in Motion: Kinesthesia in Martial Arts Films," *Jump Cut* 42 (1998): 1–11, 83.

24. *The Modern Dance* (New York: A. S. Barnes, 1933), 13.

25. Anderson, "Action in Motion," 5–6.

26. On proxemics, see John R. Aiello, "Human Spatial Behavior," in D. Stokols and I. Altman, eds., *Handbook of Environmental Psychology* (New York: John Wiley & Sons, 1987). The classic book is E. T. Hall, *The Hidden Dimension* (New York: Doubleday, 1966).

27. For evidence for this claim, see Plantinga, *Rhetoric and Representation in Nonfiction Film*, 54–58; Messaris, *Visual "Literacy,"* 60–64. See also Noël Carroll, "The Power of Movies," in *Theorizing the Moving Image* (Cambridge: Cambridge University Press, 1996), 80–83. A good study of the perception of two-dimensional images across cultures can be found in Michael Cole and Sylvia Scribner, *Culture and Thought: A Psychological Introduction* (New York: Wiley, 1974), 61–97.

28. The word "body" is very common in the titles and subject lines of works in film and media studies these days. In this discourse, bodies become not only the actual physical bodies of actors or characters but also persons, stars, and by pun, bodies of films and other objects. My use of the word "body" narrowly refers to the physical bodies of actors or characters.

29. Noël Carroll, "Film, Attention, and Communication: A Naturalistic Account," in *Engaging the Moving Image* (New Haven, CT: Yale University Press, 2003), 45–54.

30. Johannes Riis, "Naturalist and Classical Styles in Early Sound Film Acting," *Cinema Journal* 43, no. 3 (Spring 2004): 3–17.

31. Darwin and Ekman, *The Expression of Emotions in Man and Animals.*

32. Jeffrey Pittam and Klaus R. Scherer, "Vocal Expression and Communication of Emotion," in Michael Lewis and Jeannette M. Haviland, eds., *Handbook of Emotions* (New York and London: Guilford Press, 1993), 190.

33. Davis, *Empathy*, 106.

34. Giacomo Rizzolatti and Laila Craighero, "The Mirror-Neuron System," *Annual Review of Neuroscience* 27 (2004): 169–82; Evelyne Kohler et al., "Hearing Sounds, Understanding Actions: Action Representation in Mirror Neurons," *Science* 297 (August 2, 2002): 846.

35. Rizzolatti and Craighero, "The Mirror-Neuron System," 179.

36. See, for example, G. J. McHugo, J. T. Lanzetta, D. G. Sullivan, R. D. Masters, and B. G. Englis, "Emotional Reactions to a Political Leader's Expressive Displays," *Journal of Personality and Social Psychology* 49 (1985), 1513–29. See also Bavelas, Black, Lemery, and Mullett, "Motor Mimicry as Primitive Empathy," 317–38.

37. On emotional contagion, see Elaine Hatfield, John T. Cacioppo, and Richard L. Rapson, *Emotional Contagion* (Cambridge: Cambridge University Press, 1994).

38. *Theory of Film: Character and Growth of a New Art* (New York: Dover Publications, 1972), 42–44.

39. Readers who wish a more in-depth study should see Plantinga, "The Scene of Empathy and the Human Face on Film," and Smith's *Engaging Characters*, 98–102.

40. *Emotional Contagion*, 48. Also see Cynthia Freeland, "Empiricism and the Philosophy of Film," *Film and Philosophy* 8 (2004): 154–71.

41. C. K. Hsee, E. Hatfield, J. G. Carlson, and C. Chemtob, "The Effect of Power on Susceptibility to Emotional Contagion," *Cognition and Emotion* 4 (1990): 327–40.

42. Marvin Minsky, *The Society of the Mind* (New York: Simon and Schuster, 1988), 308. See also Jerry Fodor, *The Modularity of Mind* (Cambridge, MA: MIT Press, 1983). On the mind as composed of "mental organs," see Steven Pinker, *How the Mind Works* (New York: W. W. Norton and Company, 1997), 27–31.

43. R. O'Toole and R. Dubin, "Baby Feeding and Body Sway: An Experiment in George Herbert Meade's 'Taking the Role of the Other,'" *Journal of Personality and Social Psychology* 10 (1968): 59–65.

44. See David Bordwell, *The Cinema of Eisenstein* (Cambridge, MA: Harvard University Press, 1993), 115–20.

45. "Action in Motion," 12.

46. Pierre Nora, *Realms of Memory: The Construction of the French Past* (New York: Columbia Press, 1996).

47. David Bordwell, *Planet Hong Kong: Popular Cinema and the Art of Entertainment* (Cambridge, MA: Harvard University Press, 2000), 228–47.

48. Fred Karlin, *Listening to the Movies: The Film Lover's Guide to Film Music* (New York: Schirmer Books, 1994), 9–12.

49. Earl Vickers, "Music and Consciousness," www.sfxmachine.com/docs/ musicandconsciousness.html (accessed November 5, 2004). Vickers notes that traditional cultures often use rhythm to induce changes in consciousness. Examples he gives are Australian aboriginal playing of the didgeridoo, Native American drumming and dancing, and the drumming and rhythmic movement of Siberian Shamans and some Northern Tribes. He also notes the use of physiologically compatible rhythms of dance and music in the various dance clubs of contemporary youth culture, which can actually change neurological states. For an experiment on "false heart-rate feedback," see R. M. Stern, R. W. Botto, and C. D. Herrick, "Behavioral and Physiological Effects of False Heart-Rate Feedback: A Replication and Extension," *Psychophysiology* 9 (1972): 21–29.

50. Kathryn Kalinak, *Settling the Score: Music and the Classical Hollywood Film* (Madison: University of Wisconsin Press, 1992), 5.

51. For a more comprehensive account of the effects of music on human physiology, see Robinson, *Deeper Than Reason*, 391–400.

52. Although I disagree with certain elements of Smith's conception of moods, he is very good at describing mood as an orienting state that primes

spectators for certain emotions. See Greg M. Smith, *Film Structure and the Emotion System,* 38–40.

53. For an excellent account of the philosophical debates about emotion expression in music, see Robinson, *Deeper Than Reason,* 293–412.

54. Noël Carroll, "Notes on Movie Music," in *Interpreting the Moving Image* (New York: Cambridge University Press, 1998), 139–45.

55. Carroll, "Notes on Movie Music," 142.

56. Jeff Smith, "Movie Music as Moving Music: Emotion, Cognition, and the Film Score," in Plantinga and Smith, *Passionate Views,* 156–60.

57. See Bordwell, *The Way Hollywood Tells It,* 56.

58. The increased reliance on spectacle does not eclipse narrative, nor does it minimize the importance of narrative, as some observers claim. The typical Hollywood film that relies on spectacle also relies on narrative. The two often operate together, with narrative setting up the pleasure of the spectacle, and spectacle sometimes (though not always) used in part to tell the story. Story and spectacle are not necessarily opposed; even in blockbusters such as *The Rock* (1996) and *The Long Kiss Goodnight* (1996), the pleasures of narrative and spectacle alternate as the narrative unfolds, halts momentarily to allow for the pleasures of spectacle, continues to unfold, and so on.

59. See Geoff King, *Spectacular Narratives: Hollywood in the Age of the Blockbuster* (London and New York: I. B. Tauris Publishers, 2000), 91–116.

60. Ibid., 99.

61. *The Way Hollywood Tells It,* 120.

62. See Noël Carroll, "The Future of an Allusion: Hollywood in the '70s and Beyond," in *Interpreting the Moving Image,* 240–64; Thomas Elsaesser and Warren Buckland, *Studying Contemporary American Film: A Guide to Movie Analysis* (London: Arnold, 2002).

63. See Bordwell, *The Way Hollywood Tells It,* 58–62.

CHAPTER 5

1. *Emotions,* 346.

2. See Sobchack, *The Address of the Eye,* 76. Sobchack foregrounds the eye over the ear in this book, to some extent ignoring hearing at the expense of seeing.

3. *Film Structure and the Emotion System,* 42.

4. Francois Truffaut, *Hitchcock/Truffaut,* rev. ed. (New York: Simon and Schuster, 1983), 73.

5. Smith's theory of emotion elicitation relies on stylistic cues to a greater degree than do the theories of Ed Tan or Torben Grodal, and Smith takes this to be a strength of his theory. Smith, however, could go much further in providing a causal explanation for how stylistic cues elicit emotions and moods. In the absence of directed response in relation to narrative and character, what is the global mechanism that guides the spectator's mental activity and responses?

6. Martin Barker and Kate Brooks, *Knowing Audiences: Judge Dredd, Its Friends, Fans and Foes* (Luton, UK: University of Luton Press, 1998).

7. King, *Spectacular Narratives*, 105.

8. Klinger, "The Art Film, Affect and the Female Viewer," 40.

9. See Bordwell, *Narration in the Fiction Film*, 156–204. For his theory of "erotetic" narrative, see Carroll, *Theorizing the Moving Image*, 88–90.

10. *The Reality of Illusion: An Ecological Approach to Cognitive Film Theory* (Carbondale: Southern Illinois University Press, 1996), 86.

11. "Film, Emotion, and Genre," in Plantinga and Smith, *Passionate Views*, 28.

12. *The Theory of the Moral Sentiments*, 12.

13. Richard Maltby claims that Hollywood films presuppose "multiple viewpoints, at multiple textual levels, for their consuming audience" in "'A Brief Romantic Interlude,'" in Bordwell and Carroll, *Post-Theory*, 434–59. Maltby's point is similar to one that I would make, or one that V. F. Perkins might make. It is more important to audiences that a narrative feel closed than that logical consistency be maintained in the interpretive strategies spectators use to presume that closure.

14. Carroll, *The Philosophy of Horror*, 95–96.

15. I borrow this term from Kristin Thompson and her *Storytelling in the New Hollywood*.

16. Media scholar Kathrin Fahlenbrach has developed the notion of "audiovisual metaphor" to account for similar affective phenomena. Body-based "image schemata," she claims, are "metaphorically projected from one experiential domain to another." See "The Emotional Design of Music Videos: Approaches to Audiovisual Metaphors," *Journal of Moving Image Studies* 3, no. 1 (2005): 22–28.

17. See G. Martino and L. E. Marks, "Synesthesia, Strong and Weak," *Current Directions in Psychological Science* 10 (2001): 61–65.

18. Quoted in Daniel J. Boorstin, *The Creators: A History of Heroes of the Imagination* (New York: Vintage Books, 1992), 376.

19. *Hitchcock/Truffaut*, 269.

20. Ibid., 282–83.

21. For a philosophical examination of shame and guilt, see Roberts, *Emotions*, 222–33.

22. Susan Miller, *The Shame Experience* (Hillsdale, NJ: The Analytic Press, 1985), 44.

23. Robin Wood, *Hitchcock's Films Revisited*, rev. ed. (New York: Columbia University Press, 2002), 67.

24. Ibid.

25. Ibid., 93.

26. Torben Grodal, *Moving Pictures: A New Theory of Film Genres, Feelings, and Cognition* (Oxford, UK: Clarendon Press, 1997).

27. See Geoff King, *New Hollywood Cinema: An Introduction* (New York: Columbia University Press, 2002), 185–93.

CHAPTER 6

1. James Cameron, "Forward," in *James Cameron's Titanic*, by Ed W. Marsh (New York: Harper Perennial, 1997), vi.

2. For a discussion of the implications of irony in *Roger & Me*, see Plantinga "Roger and History and Irony and Me," *Michigan Academician* 24 (1992): 511–20.

3. At the time of this writing, *Titanic* has grossed roughly $1.85 billion in theatrical receipts worldwide, making it the all-time leader in worldwide grosses. See www.boxofficemojo.com/alltime/ (accessed November 18, 2006).

4. See Gaylyn Studlar and Kevin S. Sandler, eds., *Titanic: Anatomy of a Blockbuster* (New Brunswick, NJ: Rutgers University Press, 1999).

5. Carroll, *The Philosophy of Horror*. Also see Cynthia Freeland, *The Naked and the Undead: Evil and the Appeal of Horror* (Boulder, CO: Westview Press, 2000), for a cognitive and feminist perspective on the appeal of the horror film.

6. One all-too-common practice in film theory is to illustrate a general theory of the spectator with a handpicked and unusual film that is hardly illustrative of the usual or typical. For example, Patrick Fuery illustrates this practice in his *New Developments in Film Theory* (New York: St. Martin's Press, 2000), where he provides a theoretical discussion of "masochism" as a general theory of film viewing and illustrates these general points with a discussion of Luis Buñuel's *Belle de Jour* (1967), a unique film that features a protagonist who has overt masochistic fantasies (8–13). Yet to illustrate or prove a general theory of masochism in the cinema, a film that features overtly masochistic characters can hardly count as evidence. Instead, one should show how the typical or usual film—one that has no overt masochistic content—provides evidence for a general theory of masochism in film viewing.

7. David Hume, "Of Tragedy," in John V. Lenz, ed., *Of the Standard of Taste and Other Essays* (Indianapolis and New York: Bobbs-Merrill, 1965), 29–37.

8. Ibid., 32.

9. Ibid., 33.

10. Good introductions to Aristotle's aesthetics and the paradox of tragedy can be found in Nicholas Pappas, "Aristotle," and Alex Neill, "Tragedy," both in Berys Gaut and Dom Lopes, eds., *The Routledge Companion to Aesthetics* (New York: Routledge, 2005). Also see Amelie Oksenberg Rorty, ed., *Essays on Aristotle's Poetics* (Princeton, NJ: Princeton University Press, 1992).

11. Thomas J. Scheff, *Catharsis in Healing, Ritual and Drama* (Berkeley: University of California Press, 1979), 13.

12. Ibid., 79.

13. Robert Epstein, "The Loose Screw Awards," *Psychology Today* (January/February 2005), www.psychologytoday.com/articles/pto-20050119-000004 .htm (accessed July 12, 2005).

14. See, for example, Brad J. Bushman, "Does Venting Anger Feed or Extinguish the Flame? Catharsis, Rumination, Distraction, Anger, and Aggres-

sive Responding," *Personality and Social Psychology Bulletin* 28, no. 6 (June 2002): 724–31.

15. See Smith, "Film Spectatorship and the Institution of Fiction," 113–27.

16. Susan Feagin, "The Pleasures of Tragedy," *American Philosophical Quarterly* 20 (1983): 95–104. Feagin claims that such metaresponses are sufficient to dissolve the paradox of tragedy, but I would say that while their existence is surely pleasurable, they must be put in the context of the attenuation of the painful emotions and the other pleasures I detail.

17. Mary Beth Oliver, "Exploring the Paradox of Sad Films." *Human Communication Research* 19 (1993): 315–42.

18. See Dolf Zillman, "Excitation Transfer in Communication-Mediated Aggressive Behavior," *Journal of Experimental Social Psychology* 7 (1971): 419–34; Dolf Zillman, "Transfer of Excitation in Emotional Behavior," in J. T. Capacioppo and R. E. Petty, eds., *Social Psychology: A Sourcebook* (New York: Guildford Press, 1983), 215–40.

19. *The Exorcist* (1973) exemplifies a film that, for many viewers, elicits negative emotions without sufficient coping mechanisms to both attenuate and work through the emotions. For an account of psychological trauma following screenings of the film, see James C. Bozzuto, "Cinematic Neurosis Following *The Exorcist*," *Journal of Nervous and Mental Disease* 161 (1975): 43–48.

20. A succinct and useful account of the nature of movie melodrama may be found in Ben Singer's *Melodrama and Modernity* (New York: Columbia University Press, 2001), 37–58. Although his theory of emotion elicitation differs in some respects from mine, Torben Grodal's account of affect elicitation in the melodrama deserves a hearing. See his *Moving Pictures*, 253–77. Grodal claims that melodramas enact a passive position for the protagonist and thus, through "identification," elicit particular sorts of affective responses in the spectator that are caused by a vicarious sense of passivity in the face of grand events that cannot be altered.

21. Cameron, "Forward," vi, ix.

22. Carroll, "Film, Emotion, and Genre," in Plantinga and Smith, *Passionate Views*, 21–47.

23. For more on this issue, see Linda Williams, "Melodrama Revisited," in Nick Brown, ed., *Refiguring American Film Genres* (Berkeley: University of California Press, 1998), 42–62.

24. Peter Brooks, *The Melodramatic Imagination: Balzac, Henry James, Melodrama, and the Mode of Excess* (New Haven, CT: Yale University Press, 1995), 15.

25. Robinson, *Deeper Than Reason*, 195–228. For a general theory or the relationship between aesthetic pleasure and "control," see Marcia Eaton, "A Strange Kind of Sadness," *Journal of Aesthetics and Art Criticism* 41 (Autumn 1982): 51–63.

26. George A. Kennedy, trans. (New York: Oxford University Press, 1991), 139.

27. For a more thorough discussion, see Plantinga, "Notes on Spectator Emotion and Ideological Film Criticism," in Richard Allen and Murray Smith, eds., *Film Theory and Philosophy* (Oxford, UK: Clarendon Press, 1997), 372–93.

28. Hayden White, *Metahistory* (Baltimore: Johns Hopkins University Press, 1973), 37.

29. "Tales of Sound and Fury," *Monogram* 4 (1972): 12.

30. See Plantinga, "Notes on Spectator Emotion and Ideological Film Criticism."

31. Ed S. H. Tan and Nico H. Frijda, "Sentiment in Film Viewing," in Plantinga and Smith, *Passionate Views*, 48–64.

32. *From Reverence to Rape: The Treatment of Women in the Movies*, 2nd ed. (Chicago: University of Chicago Press, 1987).

33. Christine Gledhill, *Home Is Where the Heart Is: Studies in Melodrama and the Women's Film* (London: British Film Institute, 1987); Williams, "Melodrama Revisited."

34. *Contesting Tears: The Hollywood Melodrama of the Unknown Woman* (Chicago: University of Chicago Press, 1997).

35. "Apt Feelings, or Why 'Women's Films' Aren't Trivial," in Bordwell and Carroll, *Post-Theory*, 226.

36. See Mary Midgeley, "Brutality and Sentimentality," *Philosophy* 54 (1979): 385.

37. Marcia Muelder Eaton, "Laughing at the Death of Little Nell: Sentimental Art and Sentimental People," *American Philosophical Quarterly* 26, no. 4 (October 1989): 273.

38. "What Is Wrong with Sentimentality?" *Mind* 92 (1983): 524, 527.

CHAPTER 7

1. George A. Kennedy, trans., 119–62.

2. *The Unbearable Lightness of Being* (London: Faber and Faber, 1984), 244.

3. See *The Theory of the Moral Sentiments*.

4. *Poetic Justice: The Literary Imagination and Public Life* (Boston: Beacon Press, 1995), 75.

5. Ibid., 120.

6. Such examinations of the particularity of individuated emotions will also provide a clearer understanding of the phenomenological feel of particular movies, since emotions elicit physiological changes, aversive or attractive or other sorts of action tendencies, facial expressions, gestures, postures, and so on.

7. These are (1) Aurel Kolnai, "Der Ekel," in Edmund Husserl, ed., *Jahrbuch für Philosophie und phänomenologische Forschung*, vol. 10 (Halle and Saale, Germany: Max Niemeyer, 1929); the book *On Disgust* by Aurel Kolnai, Carolyn Korsmeyer, and Barry Smith includes Kolnai's essay (Open Court Publishing, 2003); (2) a series of essays by Paul Rozin and others, for example, "Dis-

gust," Lewis and Haviland, *Handbook of Emotions*, 575–94; (3) William Ian Miller, *The Anatomy of Disgust* (Cambridge, MA: Harvard University Press, 1997); (4) Winfried Menninghaus, *Disgust: Theory and History of a Strong Sensation*, trans. Howard Eiland and Joel Golb (Albany: State University of New York Press, 2003); (5) Robert Rawdon Wilson, *The Hydra's Tale: Imagining Disgust* (Edmonton, Canada: University of Alberta Press, 2002); (6) Susan Miller, *Disgust: The Gatekeeper Emotion* (Hillsdale, NJ: The Analytic Press, 2004); and (7) Martha Nussbaum, *Hiding from Humanity: Disgust, Shame, and the Law* (Princeton, NJ: Princeton University Press, 2004).

8. The Farrelly brothers' upcoming film, *The Three Stooges* [2009], will be an interesting test case, since the original Three Stooges films, while relying on simple slapstick violence and inane behavior for their comedy, did not elicit physical disgust. If the Farrelly brothers introduce physical disgust into their remake, it may fail to capture the particular tone and feel of the original Stooges movies. This would, of course, be a tragedy.

9. Most of what is written about disgust in films is from a psychoanalytic perspective that assumes that disgust reactions result from a return of the repressed. On David Lynch and *Blue Velvet*, for example, the following sources all employ psychoanalytic theory: Tracy Biga, "*Blue Velvet*," *Film Quarterly* 41, no. 4 (1987), 44–49; Lynne Layton, "*Blue Velvet*: A Parable of Male Development," *Screen* 35, no. 4 (Winter 1994), 374–93; Lynda K. Bundtzen, "'Don't Look at Me!': Woman's Body, Woman's Voice in *Blue Velvet*," *Western Humanities Review* 42, no. 3 (1988), 187–203; Laura Mulvey, "The Pre-Oedipal Father: The Gothicism of *Blue Velvet*," in Victor Sage and Allan Lloyd Smith, eds., *Modern Gothic: A Reader* (Manchester, UK: Manchester University Press, 1996), 38–57; Michel Chion, *David Lynch*, trans. Robert Julian (London: British Film Institute, 1995); Sam Ishii-Gonzales, "Mysteries of Love: Lynch's *Blue Velvet*/Freud's Wolf-Man," in Erica Sheen and Annette Davison, eds., *American Dreams/Nightmare Visions* (London: Wallflower Press, 2004); Linda Badley, *Film, Horror, and the Body Fantastic* (Westwood, CT: Greenwood Press, 1995), 117–18. The only broadly cognitive interpretation of the film comes from David Chute, who, apparently unconstrained by disciplinary commitments to psychoanalytic theory, uses the language of disgust in a context similar to mine. See "Out to Lynch," *Film Comment* 22 (September/October 1986): 32.

10. Gaia Vince, "Disgust Is Good for You, Shows Study," www.newscientist .com/news/print.jsp?id=ns99994563 (accessed June 23, 2004).

11. Jonathan Haidt, Paul Rozin, Clark McCauley, and Sumio Imada, "Body, Psyche, and Culture: The Relationship between Disgust and Morality." *Psychology and Developing Societies* 9 (1997): 107–31.

12. Ibid., 121.

13. See, for example, Mark Johnson, *The Body in the Mind* (Chicago: University of Chicago Press, 1987).

14. George Marsden, *Jonathan Edwards: A Life* (New Haven, CT: Yale University Press, 2003), 165.

15. The recent Bollywood hit *Lagaan* (2001) features the Indian superstar Aamir Khan as the leader of a cricket team fighting for his village's honor (and for freedom from taxes) against a British cricket team. From the standpoint of disgust and its implications, it is especially interesting that against the protestations of his team members, Khan welcomes onto the team a member of the lowest caste, an "untouchable," and the film makes very apparent (with close-ups and medium shots) Khan's willingness to touch him, thus counteracting the disgust reactions that have been used to reinforce the caste system.

16. "Anatomy of Disgust," www.channel4.com/culture/microsites/A/anatomy_disgust/t_index.html (accessed June 18, 2004).

17. Haidt et al., "Body, Psyche, and Culture," 124.

18. Miller, *The Anatomy of Disgust*, 16.

19. Menninghaus, *Disgust*, 15.

20. Quoted in Miller, *The Anatomy of Disgust*, 179.

21. For an examination of disgust in relation to taste and gustatory pleasure, see Carolyn Korsmeyer, "Delightful, Delicious, Disgusting," *Journal of Aesthetics and Art Criticism* 60, no. 3 (Summer 2002): 217–25.

22. Ortony, Clore, and Collins, *The Cognitive Structure of Emotions*.

23. Miller, *The Anatomy of Disgust*, 36.

24. Tan, *Emotion and the Structure of Narrative Film*, 83.

25. *Purity and Danger: An Analysis of Concepts of Pollution and Taboo* (New York and Washington: Praeger Publishers, 1966).

26. *Stigma: Notes on the Management of Spoiled Identity* (New York: Touchstone, 1986), 3.

27. Benjamin Cohen, "Mugabe Attacks Gays and Threatens Pro-Gay Clergy with Prison," *Pinknews*, http://pinknews.co.uk/news/articles/2005–608.html (accessed July 14, 2008).

28. *Hiding from Humanity*, 113.

29. Mathew Tinkcom makes a similar point about *Polyester* in his *Working Like a Homosexual: Camp, Capital, Cinema* (Durham, NC: Duke University Press, 2002), 170–72.

CONCLUSION

1. As Greg M. Smith writes in *Film Structure and the Emotion System*, "there is relatively little written by cinema scholars on film and emotion per se" (3). Communications researchers, on the other hand, have explored the relationships between media and affect quite extensively. It is a weakness of this book, and indeed of humanistic approaches to film and affect generally, that the social science research is not sufficiently taken into account. For an overview of this research and an extensive bibliography on media and emotion, see Werner Wirth and Holger Schramm, "Media and Emotions," *Communication and Research Trends* 24, no. 3 (2005): 3–39.

2. *Understanding Cinema: A Psychological Theory of Moving Imagery* (Cambridge: Cambridge University Press, 2003), 13.

3. For more on Persson's work, see Tico Romao, "Spectatorship and Social Cognition," *New Review of Film and Television Studies* 4, no. 1 (April 2006), 53–61; Carl Plantinga, "Cognitive Theory in Film Studies: Three Recent Books," *College Literature* 33, no. 1 (Winter 2006): 215–24.

4. See Anne Bartsch, "Meta-Emotionen und ihre Vermittlung im Film," in Jens Eder, Kathrin Fahlenbrach, and Anne Bartsch, eds., *Audiovisuelle Emotionen* (Cologne, Germany: Halem, 2007). Also see Christoph Jäger and Anne Bartsch, "Meta-Emotions," *Grazer Philosophische Studien* 73 (2006): 136–61.

5. "Art and Cognitive Evolution," in Mark Turner, ed., *The Artful Mind: Cognitive Science and the Riddle of Human Creativity* (New York: Oxford University Press, 2006), 5.

6. See Mark Johnson, *The Meaning of the Body* (Chicago: University of Chicago Press, 2007).

Bibliography

Aiello, John R. "Human Spatial Behavior." In *Handbook of Environmental Psychology*, edited by D. Stokols and I. Altman, 505–31. New York: John Wiley & Sons, 1987.

Anderson, Aaron. "Action in Motion: Kinesthesia in Martial Arts Films." *Jump Cut* 42 (1998): 1–11, 83.

———. "Violent Dance in Martial Arts Films." *Jump Cut* 44 (Fall 2001): 1–17.

Anderson, Joseph D. *The Reality of Illusion: An Ecological Approach to Cognitive Film Theory*. Carbondale: Southern Illinois University Press, 1996.

Aristotle. *On Rhetoric*. Translated by George A. Kennedy. New York: Oxford University Press, 1991.

Averill, James R. *Anger and Aggression: An Essay on Emotion*. New York: Springer-Verlag, 1982.

———. "I Feel, Therefore I Am—I Think." In *The Nature of Emotion*, edited by Paul Ekman and Richard J. Davidson, 379–85. Oxford, UK: Oxford University Press, 1994.

Badley, Linda. *Film, Horror, and the Body Fantastic*. Westwood, CT: Greenwood Press, 1995.

Baird, Robert. "The Startle Effect: Implications for Spectator Cognition and Media Theory." *Film Quarterly* 53, no. 3 (Spring 2000): 12–24.

Balio, Tino. "'A Major Presence in All of the World's Important Markets': The Globalization of Hollywood in the 1990s." In *Contemporary Hollywood Cinema*, edited by Steve Neale and Murray Smith, 58–73. London and New York: Routledge, 1998.

Bargh, John A., and Tanya L. Chartrand. "The Unbearable Automaticity of Being." *American Psychologist* 54, no. 7 (July 1999): 462–79.

Barker, Martin, and Kate Brooks. *Knowing Audiences: Judge Dredd, Its Friends, Fans and Foes*. Luton, UK: University of Luton Press, 1998.

Bartsch, Anne. "Meta-Emotionen und ihre Vermittlung im Film." In *Audio-*

visuelle Emotionen, edited by Jens Eder, Kathrin Fahlenbrach, and Anne Bartsch, 277–96. Cologne: Halem, 2007.

Bartsch, Anne, Roland Mangold, Reinhold Viehoff, and Peter Vorderer. "Emotional Gratifications during Media Use—An Integrative Approach." *Communication* 31 (2006): 261–78.

Bavelas, Janet Beavin, Alex Black, Charles R. Lemery, and Jennifer Mullett. "Motor Mimicry as Primitive Empathy." In *Empathy and Its Development,* edited by Nancy Eisenberg and Janet Strayer, 317–38. Cambridge: Cambridge University Press, 1987.

Belázs, Béla. *Theory of Film: Character and Growth of a New Art.* New York: Dover Publications, 1972.

Bell, Clive. *Art.* New York: BiblioBazaar, 2007.

Bergstrom, Janet, and Mary Ann Doane. Special issue on the spectatrix, *Camera Obscura* 20–21 (1989).

Biga, Tracy. "*Blue Velvet.*" *Film Quarterly* 41, no. 4 (1987): 44–49.

Bobo, Jacqueline. "*The Color Purple:* Black Women as Cultural Readers." In *Female Spectators: Looking at Film and Television,* edited by E. Deirdre Pribram, 90–109. London: Verso, 1988.

Boorstin, Daniel J. *The Creators: A History of Heroes of the Imagination.* New York: Vintage Books, 1992.

Boorstin, John. *The Hollywood Eye: What Makes Movies Work.* New York: Harper Collins, 1990.

Booth, Wayne. *The Rhetoric of Fiction.* Chicago: University of Chicago Press, 1961.

Bordwell, David. *Narration in the Fiction Film.* Madison: University of Wisconsin Press, 1985.

———. *The Cinema of Eisenstein.* Cambridge: Harvard University Press, 1993.

———. "Contemporary Film Studies and the Vicissitudes of Grand Theory." In *Post-Theory: Reconstructing Film Studies,* edited by David Bordwell and Noël Carroll, 3–36. Madison: University of Wisconsin Press, 1996.

———. *Planet Hong Kong: Popular Cinema and the Art of Entertainment.* Cambridge, MA: Harvard University Press, 2000.

———. *The Way Hollywood Tells It: Story and Style in the Movies.* Berkeley: University of California Press, 2006.

Bordwell, David, and Noël Carroll, eds. *Post-Theory: Reconstructing Film Studies.* Madison: University of Wisconsin Press, 1996.

Bordwell, David, Janet Staiger, and Kristin Thompson. *The Classical Hollywood Cinema: Film Style and Mode of Production to 1960.* New York: Columbia University Press, 1985.

Bozzuto, James C. "Cinematic Neurosis Following *The Exorcist.*" *Journal of Nervous and Mental Disease* 161 (1975): 43–48.

Branigan, Edward. *Narrative Comprehension and Film.* New York: Routledge, 1992.

Brooks, Peter. *Reading for the Plot: Design and Intention in Narrative.* New York: Alfred A. Knopf, 1984.

———. *Body Works: Objects of Desire in Modern Narrative.* Cambridge, MA: Harvard University Press, 1993.

———. *The Melodramatic Imagination: Balzac, Henry James, Melodrama, and the Mode of Excess.* New Haven, CT: Yale University Press, 1995.

Bundtzen, Lynda K. "'Don't Look at Me!': Woman's Body, Woman's Voice in *Blue Velvet," Western Humanities Review* 42, no. 3 (1988): 187–203.

Burch, Noël. *Theory of Film Practice.* Translated by Helen R. Lane. Princeton, NJ: Princeton University Press, 1973.

Burgess, Eleanor. "Denby Sez: Hollywood Alive, but Barely Conscious." *The Yale Herald,* November 7, 2003. www.yaleherald.com/article.php ?Article=2638 (accessed December 15, 2003).

Burke, Kenneth. *Counter-Statement.* Berkeley: University of California Press, 1968.

Buscombe, Edward, Christopher Gledhill, Alan Lovell, and Christopher Williams, "Statement: Psychoanalysis and Film." *Screen* 16, no. 4 (Winter 1975/1976): 129.

Bushman, Brad J. "Does Venting Anger Feed or Extinguish the Flame? Catharsis, Rumination, Distraction, Anger, and Aggressive Responding." *Personality and Social Psychology Bulletin* 28, no. 6 (June 2002): 724–31.

Cameron, Evan. "Hitchcock and the Mechanics of Suspense, I." *Movie* 3 (October 1962): 6–8.

Cameron, James. "Forward." In *James Cameron's Titanic,* by Ed W. Marsh, v–xiii. New York: Harper Perennial, 1997.

Carmant, Lionel, and Shashi Seshia. "Photosensitive Seizures." www.epilepsy .ca/eng/left_menu/news_Update/NU_PhotosensitiveSeisures.htm (accessed August 11, 2008).

Carroll, Noël. *Mystifying Movies: Fads and Fallacies in Contemporary Film Theory.* New York: Columbia University Press, 1988.

———. *The Philosophy of Horror.* New York and London: Routledge, 1990.

———. "The Power of Movies." In *Theorizing the Moving Image,* 80–83. Cambridge: Cambridge University Press, 1996.

———. *Theorizing the Moving Image.* Cambridge: Cambridge University Press, 1996.

———. *A Philosophy of Mass Art.* Oxford, UK: Clarendon Press, 1998.

———. *Interpreting the Moving Image.* New York: Cambridge University Press, 1998.

———. "Notes on Movie Music." In *Interpreting the Moving Image,* 139–45. New York: Cambridge University Press, 1998.

———. "The Future of an Allusion: Hollywood in the '70s and Beyond." In *Interpreting the Moving Image,* 240–64. New York: Cambridge University Press, 1998.

———. "Film, Emotion and Genre." In *Passionate Views: Film, Cognition, and Emotion,* edited by Carl Plantinga and Greg M. Smith, 21–47. Baltimore: Johns Hopkins University Press, 1999.

————. *Engaging the Moving Image.* New Haven, CT: Yale University Press, 2003.

————. "Film, Attention, and Communication: A Naturalistic Account." In *Engaging the Moving Image,* 45–54. New Haven, CT: Yale University Press, 2003.

Cavell, Stanley. *Contesting Tears: The Hollywood Melodrama of the Unknown Woman.* Chicago: University of Chicago Press, 1997.

Chion, Michel. *David Lynch,* translated by Robert Julian. London: British Film Institute, 1995.

Chute, David. "Out to Lynch." *Film Comment* 22 (September/October 1986): 32–35.

Cohen, Benjamin. "Mugabe Attacks Gays and Threatens Pro-Gay Clergy with Prison." *Pinknews.* http://pinknews.co.uk/news/articles/2005-608.html (accessed July 14, 2008).

Cohen, Paula. *Alfred Hitchcock: The Legacy of Victorianism.* Lexington: University of Kentucky Press, 1995.

Cole, Michael, and Sylvia Scribner. *Culture and Thought: A Psychological Introduction.* New York: Wiley, 1974.

Cook, David. *A History of Narrative Film.* 3rd ed. New York: W. W. Norton and Company, 1996.

Coplan, Amy. "Empathic Engagement with Narrative Fictions." *Journal of Aesthetics and Art Criticism* 62, no. 2 (Spring 2004): 141–52.

Crawford, June, et al. *Emotion and Gender.* London: SAGE Publications, 1992.

Creed, Barbara. "Film and Psychoanalysis." In *The Oxford Guide to Film Studies,* edited by John Hill and Pamela Church Gibson, 77–90. Oxford, UK: Oxford University Press, 1998.

Croce, Benedetto. *The Aesthetic as the Science of Expression and of the Linguistic in General.* 1902. Translated by Colin Lyas. Cambridge and New York: Cambridge University Press, 1992.

Currie, Gregory. "Cognitivism." In *A Companion to Film Theory,* edited by Toby Miller and Robert Stam, 105–22. Oxford, UK: Blackwell, 1999.

————. "Narrative Desire." In *Passionate Views: Film, Cognition, and Emotion,* edited by Carl Plantinga and Greg M. Smith. Baltimore: Johns Hopkins University Press, 1999.

Darwin, Charles, and Paul Ekman. *The Expression of Emotions in Man and Animals.* Oxford, UK: Oxford University Press, 2002.

Davis, Mark H. *Empathy: A Social Psychological Approach.* Boulder, CO: Westview Press, 1996.

de Lauretis, Teresa, and Stephen Heath, eds. *The Cinematic Apparatus.* New York: St. Martin's Press, 1984.

de Sousa, Ronald. *The Rationality of Emotion.* Cambridge, MA: MIT Press, 1987.

Detenber, Benjamin, and Byron Reeves. "A Bio-Informational Theory of Emotion: Motion and Image Size Effects on Viewers." *Journal of Communication* 46, no. 3 (Summer 1996): 66–84.

Donald, Merlin. "Art and Cognitive Evolution." In *The Artful Mind: Cognitive Science and the Riddle of Human Creativity,* edited by Mark Turner, 3–20. New York: Oxford University Press, 2006.

Douglas, Mary. *Purity and Danger: An Analysis of Concepts of Pollution and Taboo.* New York and Washington: Praeger Publishers, 1966.

Eaton, Marcia. "A Strange Kind of Sadness." *Journal of Aesthetics and Art Criticism* 41 (Autumn 1982): 51–63.

Eaton, Marcia Muelder. "Laughing at the Death of Little Nell: Sentimental Art and Sentimental People." *American Philosophical Quarterly* 26, no. 4 (October 1989): 269–82.

Eisenberg, N., and J. Strayer. *Empathy and Its Development.* New York: Cambridge University Press, 1987.

Elsaesser, Thomas. "Tales of Sound and Fury." *Monogram* 4 (1972): 2–15.

Elsaesser, Thomas, and Warren Buckland. *Studying Contemporary American Film: A Guide to Movie Analysis.* London: Arnold, 2002.

Epstein, Robert. "The Loose Screw Awards." *Psychology Today,* January/February 2005. www.psychologytoday.com/articles/pto-20050119-000004.htm (accessed July 12, 2005).

Fahlenbrach, Kathrin. "The Emotional Design of Music Videos: Approaches to Audiovisual Metaphors." *Journal of Moving Image Studies* 3, no. 1 (2005): 22–28.

Feagin, Susan. "The Pleasures of Tragedy." *American Philosophical Quarterly* 20 (1983): 95–104.

———. *Reading with Feeling: The Aesthetics of Appreciation.* Ithaca, NY: Cornell University Press, 1996.

Fehsenfeld, Lisa. "Motion Analysis Overview." Paper delivered at the conference "Narration, Imagination, and Emotion in the Moving Image Media," Grand Rapids, MI, July 2004.

Fodor, Jerry. *The Modularity of Mind.* Cambridge, MA: MIT Press, 1983.

Freeland, Cynthia. *The Naked and the Undead: Evil and the Appeal of Horror.* Boulder, CO: Westview Press, 2000.

———."Empiricism and the Philosophy of Film." *Film and Philosophy* 8 (2004): 154–71.

Freud, Sigmund. *The Interpretation of Dreams.* New York: Avon Books, 1966.

Frijda, Nico. *The Emotions.* Cambridge: Cambridge University Press, 1986.

Fuery, Patrick. *New Developments in Film Theory.* New York: St. Martin's Press, 2000.

Gaines, Jane. "Women and Representation: Can We Enjoy Alternative Pleasure?" In *Issues in Feminist Film Criticism,* edited by Patricia Erens, 75–93. Bloomington: Indiana University Press, 1990.

Gaut, Berys. "Identification and Emotion in Narrative Film." In *Passionate*

Views: Film, Cognition, and Emotion, edited by Carl Plantinga and Greg M. Smith, 200–216. Baltimore: Johns Hopkins University Press, 1999.

———. "'Art' as a Cluster Concept." In *Theories of Art Today,* edited by Noël Carroll, 25–44. Madison: University of Wisconsin Press, 2000.

Geertz, Clifford. *The Interpretation of Cultures.* New York: Basic Books, 1973.

Gerrig, Richard J., and Deborah A. Prentice. "Notes on Audience Response." In *Post-Theory: Reconstructing Film Studies,* edited by David Bordwell and Noël Carroll, 388–403. Madison: University of Wisconsin Press, 1996.

Giannetti, Louis. *Understanding Movies.* 7th ed. Englewood Cliffs, NJ: Prentice Hall, 1996.

Gledhill, Christine, ed. *Home Is Where the Heart Is: Studies in Melodrama and the Woman's Film.* London: British Film Institute, 1987.

Goffman, Erving. *Stigma: Notes on the Management of Spoiled Identity.* New York: Touchstone, 1986.

Griffiths, Paul E. *What Emotions Really Are.* Chicago: University of Chicago Press, 1997.

Grodal, Torben. *Moving Pictures: A New Theory of Genres, Feelings, and Cognition.* Oxford, UK: Clarendon Press, 1997.

———. "Love and Desire in the Cinema: An Evolutionary Approach to Romantic Films and Pornography." *Cinema Journal* 43, no. 2 (Winter 2004): 26–46.

Gunning, Tom. "The Cinema of Attraction: Early Film, Its Spectator, and the Avant-Garde." In *Film and Theory: An Anthology,* edited by Robert Stam and Toby Miller, 299–335. Oxford, UK: Blackwell Publishers, 2000.

Haidt, Jonathan. "The Positive Emotion of Elevation." *Prevention and Treatment* 3 (March 2000). http://journals.apa.org/pt/prevention/volume3/pre0030003c.html (accessed September 2, 2004).

Haidt, Jonathan, Paul Rozin, Clark McCauley, and Sumio Imada. "Body, Psyche, and Culture: The Relationship between Disgust and Morality." *Psychology and Developing Societies* 9 (1997): 107–31.

Hall, E. T. *The Hidden Dimension.* New York: Doubleday, 1966.

Hall, Stuart. "Encoding/Decoding." In *Culture, Media, Language,* edited by Stuart Hall, Dorothy Hobson, Andrew Lowe, and Paul Willis, 128–38. London: Hutchinson, 1980.

Haskell, Molly. *From Reverence to Rape: The Treatment of Women in the Movies.* 2nd ed. Chicago: University of Chicago Press, 1987.

Hatfield, Elaine, John T. Cacioppo, and Richard L. Rapson. *Emotional Contagion.* Cambridge: Cambridge University Press, 1994.

Heider, Fritz, and Marianne Simmel. "An Experimental Study of Apparent Behavior." *American Journal of Psychology* 57 (1944): 243–59.

Hillman, James. *Emotion.* Evanston, IL: Northwestern University Press, 1997.

Hogan, Patrick Colm. *The Mind and Its Stories: Narrative Universals and Human Emotion.* Cambridge: Cambridge University Press, 2003.

Hsee, C. K., E. Hatfield, J. G. Carlson, and C. Chemtob. "The Effect of Power on Susceptibility to Emotional Contagion." *Cognition and Emotion* 4 (1990): 327–40.

Hume, David. "Of Tragedy." In *Of the Standard of Taste and Other Essays*, edited by John V. Lenz, 29–37. Indianapolis and New York: Bobbs-Merrill, 1965.

Hunt, Morton. *The Story of Psychology.* New York: Doubleday, 1993.

Iser, Wolfgang. *The Fictive and the Imaginary: Charting Literary Anthropology.* Baltimore: Johns Hopkins University Press, 1993.

Ishii-Gonzales, Sam. "Mysteries of Love: Lynch's *Blue Velvet*/Freud's Wolf-Man." In *American Dreams/Nightmare Visions*, edited by Erica Sheen and Annette Davison. London: Wallflower Press, 2004.

Izard, Carroll E., ed. *Human Emotions.* New York: Plenum Press, 1977.

Jäger, Christoph, and Anne Bartsch. "Meta-Emotions." *Grazer Philosophische Studien* 73 (2006): 136–61.

James, William. *The Varieties of Religious Experience.* New York: Modern Library, 1994.

Jefferson, Mark. "What Is Wrong with Sentimentality?" *Mind* 92 (1983): 519–29.

Johnson, Mark. *The Body in the Mind.* Chicago: University of Chicago Press, 1987.

———. *The Meaning of the Body.* Chicago: University of Chicago Press, 2007.

Kalinak, Kathryn. *Settling the Score: Music and the Classical Hollywood Film.* Madison: University of Wisconsin Press, 1992.

Kant, Immanuel. *Critique of Judgment.* Translated by Werner S. Pluhar. Indianapolis, IN: Hackett Publishing, 1987.

Kaplan, E. Ann. *Psychoanalysis and Cinema.* New York: Routledge, 1989.

Karlin, Fred. *Listening to the Movies: The Film Lover's Guide to Film Music.* New York: Schirmer Books, 1994.

Kihlstrom, John F. "The Rediscovery of the Unconscious." In *The Mind, the Brain, and Complex Adaptive Systems*, edited by Harold Morowitz and Jerome Singer, 123–43. Reading, MA: USAddison Wesley Longman, 1994.

King, Geoff. *Spectacular Narratives: Hollywood in the Age of the Blockbuster.* London and New York: I. B. Tauris Publishers, 2000.

———. *New Hollywood Cinema: An Introduction.* New York: Columbia University Press, 2002.

Klinger, Barbara. "Digressions at the Cinema: Reception and Mass Culture." *Cinema Journal* 28, no. 4 (Summer 1989): 3–19.

———. "The Art Film, Affect and the Female Viewer: *The Piano* Revisited." *Screen* 47, no. 1 (Spring 2006): 19–41.

Kohler, Evelyne, et al. "Hearing Sounds, Understanding Actions: Action Representation in Mirror Neurons." *Science* 297 (August 2, 2002): 846–48.

Kolnai, Aurel. "Der Ekel." In *Jahrbuch für Philosophie und phänomenologis-*

che Forschung. Vol. 10, edited by Edmund Husserl. Halle and Saale, Germany: Max Niemeyer, 1929.

Kolnai, Aurel, Carolyn Korsmeyer, and Barry Smith. On Disgust. Chicago: Open Court Publishing, 2003.

Korsmeyer, Carolyn. "Delightful, Delicious, Disgusting." Journal of Aesthetics and Art Criticism 60, no. 3 (Summer 2002): 217–25.

Kramer, Peter. "Post-classical Hollywood." In American Cinema and Hollywood: Critical Approaches, edited by John Hill and Pamela Church Gibson, 63–83. Oxford, UK: Oxford University Press, 2000.

Kreitler, Hans, and Shulamith Kreitler. Psychology of the Arts. Durham, NC: Duke University Press, 1972.

Kuhn, Annette. Family Secrets: Acts of Memory and Imagination. New York: Verso, 1995.

———. Dreaming of Fred and Ginger: Cinema and Cultural Memory. New York: New York University, 2002.

Kundera, Milan. The Unbearable Lightness of Being. London: Faber and Faber, 1984.

Kunst-Wilson, W.R., and R.B. Zajonc. "Affective Discrimination of Stimuli That Cannot Be Recognized." Science 207 (1980): 557–58.

Kuntzel, Thierry. "The Film-work, 2." Camera Obscura 5 (1980): 6–69.

Layton, Lynne. "Blue Velvet: A Parable of Male Development." Screen 35, no. 4 (Winter 1994): 374–93.

Lazarus, Richard S. "Cognition and Motivation in Emotion." American Psychologist 46, no. 4 (April 1991): 352–67.

———. Emotion and Adaptation. Oxford, UK: Oxford University Press, 1994.

Lewis, Jon. "The End of Cinema as We Know It and I Feel . . . " In The End of Cinema as We Know It: American Film in the Nineties, edited by Jon Lewis, 1–10. New York: New York University Press, 2001.

Liebowitz, Flo. "Apt Feelings, or Why 'Women's Films' Aren't Trivial." In Post-Theory: Reconstructing Film Studies, edited by David Bordwell and Noël Carroll, 219–29. Madison: University of Wisconsin Press, 1996.

Lindsay, Vachel. The Art of the Moving Picture. 1915. New York: Liveright, 1970.

Lund, Frederick H. Emotions: Their Psychological and Educative Implications. New York: The Ronald Press Company, 1939.

Lyons, William. Emotion. Cambridge: Cambridge University Press, 1980.

Manvell, Roger. Film. London: Penguin Books, 1950.

Maltby, Richard. "'A Brief Romantic Interlude': Dick and Jane Go to 3-and-One-Half Seconds of the Classical Hollywood Cinema." In Post-Theory: Reconstructing Film Studies, edited by David Bordwell and Noël Carroll, 434–59. Madison: University of Wisconsin Press, 1996.

Maltby, Richard, and Melvyn Stokes, eds. Hollywood Spectatorship: Changing Perceptions of Cinema Audiences. London: British Film Institute, 2001.

Markus, Hazel, and Shinobu Kitayama. *Emotion and Culture.* Washington, DC: American Psychological Association, 1994.

Marsden, George. *Jonathan Edwards: A Life.* New Haven, CT: Yale University Press, 2003.

Martin, John. *The Modern Dance.* New York: A. S. Barnes, 1933.

Martino, G., and L. E. Marks. "Synesthesia, Strong and Weak." *Current Directions in Psychological Science* 10 (2001): 61–65.

Matravers, Derek. *Art and Emotion.* Oxford, UK: Clarendon Press, 1998.

Mayne, Judith. *Cinema Spectatorship.* New York: Routledge, 1993.

McGinn, Colin. *The Power of Movies: How Screen and Mind Interact.* New York: Vintage, 2007.

McGowan, Todd. "Looking for the Gaze: Lacanian Film Theory and Its Vicissitudes." *Cinema Journal* 42, no. 3 (Spring 2003): 27–47.

McHugo, G. J., J. T. Lanzetta, D. G. Sullivan, R. D. Masters, and B. G. Englis. "Emotional Reactions to a Political Leader's Expressive Displays." *Journal of Personality and Social Psychology* 49 (1985): 1513–29.

Menninghaus, Winfried. *Disgust: Theory and History of a Strong Sensation.* Translated by Howard Eiland and Joel Golb. Albany: State University of New York Press, 2003.

Messaris, Paul. *Visual "Literacy": Image, Mind, and Reality.* Boulder, CO: Westview Press, 1994.

Midgeley, Mary. "Brutality and Sentimentality." *Philosophy* 54 (1979): 385–89.

Miller, Susan. *The Shame Experience.* Hillsdale, NJ: The Analytic Press, 1985.

———. *Disgust: The Gatekeeper Emotion.* Hillsdale, NJ: The Analytic Press, 2004.

Miller, William Ian. *The Anatomy of Disgust.* Cambridge, MA: Harvard University Press, 1997.

Minsky, Marvin. *The Society of the Mind.* New York: Simon and Schuster, 1988.

Monaco, James. *How to Read a Film.* Oxford, UK: Oxford University Press, 2008.

Morris, William, ed. *The American Heritage Dictionary of the English Language.* Boston: Houghton Mifflin, 1976.

Mulvey, Laura. "The Pre-Oedipal Father: The Gothicism of *Blue Velvet.*" In *Modern Gothic: A Reader,* edited by Victor Sage and Allan Lloyd Smith, 38–57. Manchester, UK: Manchester University Press, 1996.

———. "Visual Pleasure in the Narrative Cinema." In *Film Theory and Criticism: Introductory Readings,* 5th ed., edited by Marshall Cohen and Leo Braudy, 833–44. New York and Oxford, UK: Oxford University Press, 1999.

Munsterberg, Hugo. *The Photoplay: A Psychological Study.* 1916. Reprinted as *The Film: A Psychological Study, The Silent Photoplay in 1916.* New York: Dover, 1970.

Musser, Charles. *The Emergence of Cinema: The American Screen to 1907*. Berkeley: University of California Press, 1990.

Neill, Alex. "Empathy and (Film) Fiction." In *Post-Theory: Reconstructing Film Studies*, edited by David Bordwell and Noël Carroll, 175–94. Madison: University of Wisconsin Press, 1996.

———. "Tragedy." In *The Routledge Companion to Aesthetics*, edited by Berys Gaut and Dom Lopes, 457–68. New York: Routledge, 2005.

Nichols, Bill. *Representing Reality*. Bloomington: Indiana University Press, 1991.

Nora, Pierre. *Realms of Memory: The Construction of the French Past*. New York: Columbia Press, 1996.

Nussbaum, Martha. *Poetic Justice: The Literary Imagination and Public Life*. Boston: Beacon Press, 1995.

———. *Hiding from Humanity: Disgust, Shame, and the Law*. Princeton, NJ: Princeton University Press, 2004.

O'Brien, Gerard, and Jon Jureidini. "Dispensing with the Dynamic Unconscious." *Philosophy, Psychiatry, and Psychology* 9, no. 2 (June 2002): 141–53.

Odin, Roger. "A Semio-Pragmatic Approach to the Documentary Film." In *The Film Spectator: From Sign to Mind*, edited by Warren Buckland, 227–35. Amsterdam: Amsterdam University Press, 1995.

Oliver, Mary Beth. "Exploring the Paradox of Sad Films." *Human Communication Research* 19 (1993): 315–42.

Olsen, Stein Haugom. "Literature: Literary Aesthetics." In *Encyclopedia of Aesthetics*. Vol. 3, edited by Michael Kelly, 147–55. New York and Oxford, UK: Oxford University Press, 1998.

Ortony, Andrew, Gerald L. Clore, and Allan Collins. *The Cognitive Structure of the Emotions*. Cambridge: Cambridge University Press, 1988.

O'Toole, R., and R. Dubin. "Baby Feeding and Body Sway: An Experiment in George Herbert Meade's 'Taking the Role of the Other.'" *Journal of Personality and Social Psychology* 10 (1968): 59–65.

Pappas, Nicholas. "Aristotle." In *The Routledge Companion to Aesthetics*, edited by Berys Gaut and Dom Lopes, 15–28. New York: Routledge, 2005.

Paul, William. *Laughing, Screaming: Modern Hollywood Horror and Comedy*. New York: Columbia University Press, 1994.

Perkins, V. F. *Film as Film: Understanding and Judging Movies*. Harmondsworth, UK: Penguin Books, 1972.

Persson, Per. *Understanding Cinema: A Psychological Theory of Moving Imagery*. Cambridge: Cambridge University Press, 2003.

Pinker, Steven. *How the Mind Works*. New York: W. W. Norton and Company, 1997.

Pittam, Jeffrey, and Klaus R. Scherer. "Vocal Expression and Communication of Emotion." In *Handbook of Emotions*, edited by Michael Lewis and Jeannette M. Haviland, 185–98. New York and London: Guilford Press, 1993.

Plantinga, Carl. "Roger and History and Irony and Me." *Michigan Academician* 24 (1992): 511–20.

———. "Notes on Spectator Emotion and Ideological Film Criticism." In *Film Theory and Philosophy*, edited by Richard Allen and Murray Smith, 372–93. Oxford, UK: Clarendon Press, 1997.

———. *Rhetoric and Representation in Nonfiction Film*. Cambridge: Cambridge University Press, 1997.

———. "Spectacles of Death: Clint Eastwood and Violence in *Unforgiven*." *Cinema Journal* 37, no. 2 (Winter 1998): 65–83.

———. "The Scene of Empathy and the Human Face on Film." In *Passionate Views: Film, Cognition, and Emotion*, edited by Carl Plantinga and Greg M. Smith, 239–55. Baltimore: Johns Hopkins University Press, 1999.

———. "Cognitive Theory in Film Studies: Three Recent Books." *College Literature* 33, no. 1 (Winter 2006): 215–24.

Plantinga, Carl, and Greg M. Smith, eds. *Passionate Views: Film, Cognition, and Emotion*. Baltimore: Johns Hopkins University Press, 1999.

Plantinga, Carl, and Ed Tan, "Interest and Unity in the Emotional Response to Film." *Journal of Moving Image Studies* 4, no. 1 (2007). www.avila.edu/journal/vol4/Plantinga_Tan_JMIS_def.pdf

Plutchik, Robert. "Emotions: A General Psychoevolutionary Theory." In *Approaches to Emotion*, edited by Klaus R. Sherer and Paul Keman, 197–219. Hillsdale, NJ: Lawrence Erlbaum, 1984.

Prince, Stephen. "The Discourse of Pictures: Iconicity and Film Studies." *Film Quarterly* 47, no. 1 (Fall 1993): 16–28.

———. "Psychoanalytic Film Theory and the Case of the Missing Spectator." In *Post-Theory: Reconstructing Film Studies*, edited by David Bordwell and Noël Carroll, 71–86. Madison: University of Wisconsin Press, 1996.

———. "True Lies: Perceptual Realism, Digital Images and Film Theory." *Film Quarterly* 49, no. 3 (Spring 1996): 27–37.

———. *Classical Film Violence: Designing and Regulating Brutality in Hollywood Cinema, 1930–1938*. New Brunswick, NJ: Rutgers University Press, 2003.

Radford, Colin. "How Can We Be Moved by the Fate of Anna Karenina?" *Proceedings of the Aristotelian Society*, supp. vol. 49 (1975): 67–80.

Riis, Johannes. "Naturalist and Classical Styles in Early Sound Film Acting." *Cinema Journal* 43, no. 3 (Spring 2004): 3–17.

Rizzolatti, Giacomo, and Laila Craighero. "The Mirror-Neuron System." *Annual Review of Neuroscience* 27 (2004): 169–82.

Roberts, Robert C. *Emotions: An Essay in Aid of Moral Psychology*. Cambridge: Cambridge University Press, 2003.

Robinson, Jenefer. "Startle." *Journal of Philosophy* 92, no. 2 (February 1995): 53–74.

———. "L'éducation sentimentale." *Australasian Journal of Philosophy* 73, no. 2 (June 1995): 212–27.

———. *Deeper Than Reason: Emotion and Its Role in Literature, Music, and Art.* Oxford, UK: Clarendon Press, 2005.

Rodowick, David. *The Difficulty of Difference.* New York: Routledge, 1991.

Romao, Tico. "Spectatorship and Social Cognition." *New Review of Film and Television Studies* 4, no. 1 (April 2006): 53–61.

Rorty, Amelie Oksenberg, ed. *Essays on Aristotle's Poetics.* Princeton, NJ: Princeton University Press, 1992.

Rozin, Paul, Jonathan Haidt, and Clark R. McCanley. "Disgust." In *Handbook of Emotions,* edited by Michael Lewis and Jeanette Haviland, 575–94. New York: Guilford, 1993.

Sacks, Oliver. "In the River of Consciousness." *New York Review of Books* LI, no. 1 (January 15, 2004): 41–44.

Schachter, S., and J. Singer, "Cognitive, Social and Physiological Determinants of Emotional State." *Psychological Review* 69 (1962): 379–99.

Scheff, Thomas J. *Catharsis in Healing, Ritual and Drama.* Berkeley: University of California Press, 1979.

Scheman, Naomi. "Anger and the Politics of Naming." In *Women and Language in Literature and Society,* edited by Sally McConnell-Ginet, Ruth Borker, and Nelly Furman, 174–87. New York: Praeger, 1980.

Sharrett, Christopher. "End of Story: The Collapse of Myth in Postmodern Narrative Film." In *The End of Cinema as We Know It: American Film in the '90s,* edited by Jon Lewis, 319–31. New York: New York University Press, 2001.

Singer, Ben. *Melodrama and Modernity.* New York: Columbia University Press, 2001.

Smith, Adam. *The Theory of Moral Sentiments.* London: Dover Publications, 2006.

Smith, Greg M. *Film Structure and the Emotion System.* Cambridge: Cambridge University Press, 2003.

Smith, Jeff. "Movie Music as Moving Music: Emotion, Cognition, and the Film Score." In *Passionate Views: Film, Cognition, and Emotion,* edited by Carl Plantinga and Greg M. Smith, 146–67. Baltimore: Johns Hopkins University Press, 1999.

Smith, Murray. "Altered States: Character and Emotional Response in the Cinema." *Cinema Journal* 33, no. 4 (Summer 1994): 34–56.

———. *Engaging Characters: Fiction, Emotion, and the Cinema.* Oxford, UK: Clarendon Press, 1995.

———. "Film Spectatorship and the Institution of Fiction." *Journal of Aesthetics and Art Criticism* 53 (1995): 113–27.

———. "Gangsters, Cannibals, Aesthetes, or Apparently Perverse Allegiances." In *Passionate Views: Film, Cognition, and Emotion,* edited by Carl Plantinga and Greg M. Smith, 217–38. Baltimore: Johns Hopkins University Press, 1999.

Sobchack, Vivian. *The Address of the Eye: A Phenomenology of Film Experience.* Princeton, NJ: Princeton University Press, 1992.

————. *Carnal Thoughts: Embodiment and Moving Image Culture.* Berkeley: University of California Press, 2004.

Spackman, John. "Expression Theory of Art." In *Encyclopedia of Aesthetics.* Vol. 2, edited by Michael Kelly. New York and Oxford, UK: Oxford University Press, 1998.

Staiger, Janet. *Interpreting Films: Studies in the Historical Reception of American Cinema.* Princeton, NJ: Princeton University Press, 1992.

————. *Blockbuster TV: Must-See Sitcoms in the Network Era.* New York: New York University Press, 2000.

————. *Perverse Spectators: The Practices of Film Reception.* New York: New York University Press, 2000.

————. *Media Reception Studies.* New York: New York University Press, 2005.

Stam, Robert. *Film Theory: An Introduction.* London: Blackwell Publishers, 2000.

Stam, Robert, Robert Burgoyne, and Sandy Flitterman-Lewis. *New Vocabularies in Film Semiotics: Structuralism, Post-Structuralism and Beyond.* London and New York: Routledge, 1992.

Stein, Nancy L., Tom Trabasso, and Maria Liwag. "The Representation and Organization of Emotional Experience: Unfolding the Emotion Episode." In *Handbook of Emotions,* edited by Michael Lewis and Jeannette M. Haviland, 279–300. New York: Guilford Press, 1993.

Stempel, Tom. *American Audiences on Movies and Moviegoing.* Lexington: University of Kentucky Press, 2001.

Stern, Daniel. *The First Relationship: Infant and Mother.* Cambridge, MA: Harvard University Press, 2002.

Stern, R. M., R. W. Botto, and C. D. Herrick. "Behavioral and Physiological Effects of False Heart-Rate Feedback: A Replication and Extension." *Psychophysiology* 9 (1972): 21–29.

Studlar, Gaylyn. "Masochism and the Perverse Pleasures of the Cinema." In *Movies and Methods.* Vol. 2, edited by Bill Nichols. Berkeley: University of California Press, 1985.

Studlar, Gaylyn, and Kevin S. Sandler, eds. *Titanic: Anatomy of a Blockbuster.* New Brunswick, NJ: Rutgers University Press, 1999.

Tan, Ed S. *Emotion and the Structure of Narrative Film.* Mahwah, NJ: Lawrence Erlbaum, 1996.

Tan, Ed S. H., and Nico H. Frijda. "Sentiment in Film Viewing." In *Passionate Views: Film, Cognition, and Emotion,* edited by Carl Plantinga and Greg M. Smith, 48–64. Baltimore: Johns Hopkins University Press, 1999.

Thompson, Kristin. *Storytelling in the New Hollywood: Understanding Classical Narrative Technique.* Cambridge, MA: Harvard University Press, 1999.

Tinkcom, Matthew. *Working Like a Homosexual: Camp, Capital, Cinema.* Durham, NC: Duke University Press, 2002.

Tomkins, Silvan. *Exploring Affect: The Selected Writings of Silvan S. Tom-

kins. Edited by E. Virginia Damos. Cambridge: Cambridge University Press, 1995.

Truffaut, Francois. *Hitchcock/Truffaut.* Rev. ed. New York: Simon and Schuster, 1983.

Vickers, Earl. "Music and Consciousness." www.sfxmachine.com/docs/music andconsciousness.html (accessed November 5, 2004).

Vince, Gaia. "Disgust Is Good for You, Shows Study." www.newscientist.com/ news/print.jsp?id=ns99994563 (accessed June 23, 2004).

Walton, Kendall. *Mimesis as Make-Believe: On the Foundations of the Representational Arts.* Cambridge, MA: Harvard University Press, 1990.

White, Hayden. *Metahistory.* Baltimore: Johns Hopkins University Press, 1973.

Williams, Linda. "Melodrama Revisited." In *Refiguring American Film Genres,* edited by Nick Brown, 42–87. Berkeley: University of California Press, 1998.

———. "Film Bodies: Gender, Genre, and Excess." In *Film Theory and Criticism: Introductory Readings,* 5th ed., edited by Leo Braudy and Marshall Cohen, 701–15. New York and Oxford, UK: Oxford University Press, 1999.

Wilson, Robert Rawdon. *The Hydra's Tale: Imagining Disgust.* Edmonton, Canada: University of Alberta Press, 2002.

Wimsatt, W. K., and Monroe Beardsley. "The Affective Fallacy." In *Critical Theory since Plato,* edited by Hazard Adams, 1022–31. New York: Harcourt Brace Jovanovich, 1971.

Wirth, Werner, and Holger Schramm. "Media and Emotions." *Communication and Research Trends* 24, no. 3 (2005): 3–39.

Wispé, Lauren. *The Psychology of Sympathy.* New York: Plenum Publishing, 1991.

Wittgenstein, Ludwig. *Philosophical Investigations.* 3rd ed. New York: Prentice Hall, 1999.

Wood, Robin. *Hitchcock's Films Revisited.* Rev. ed. New York: Columbia University Press, 2002.

Wyatt, Justin. *High Concept: Movies and Marketing in Hollywood.* Austin: University of Texas Press, 1994.

Yanal, Robert. *Paradoxes of Emotion and Fiction.* University Park: Pennsylvania State University Press, 1999.

Young, Paul Thomas. "Feeling and Emotion." In *Handbook of General Psychology,* edited by B. Wolman, 749–71. Englewood Cliffs, NJ: Prentice-Hall, 1973.

Zillman, Dolf. "Excitation Transfer in Communication-Mediated Aggressive Behavior." *Journal of Experimental Social Psychology* 7 (1971): 419–34.

———. "Transfer of Excitation in Emotional Behavior." In *Social Psychology: A Sourcebook,* edited by J. T. Capacioppo and R. E. Petty. New York: Guilford Press, 1983.

―――. "Empathy: Affect from Bearing Witness to the Emotions of Others." In *Responding to the Screen: Reception and Reaction Processes*, edited by Jennings Bryant and Dolf Zillman, 135–67. Hillsdale, NJ: Erlbaum, 1991.

Zillman, Dolf, and J. B. Weaver II. "Gender-socialization Theory of Reactions to Horror." In *Horror Films: Current Research on Audience Preferences and Reactions*, edited by J. B. Weaver II and R. Tamborini. Mahwah, NJ: Lawrence Erlbaum Associates, 1996.

Index

Text & Display: Aldus
Compositor: BookMatters, Berkeley
Indexer: John Muether

9 780520 256965